FOUNDATIONS OF MORAL OBLIGATION

FOUNDATIONS
OF MORAL
OBLIGATION
THE STOCKDALE COURSE

JOSEPH GERARD BRENNAN

PRESIDIO

Acknowledgment is made for permission to reprint:
Extract from the poem "Carrousel Tune," taken from *In the Winter of Cities: Poems
by Tennessee Williams*. Copyright © 1956. Reprinted by permission of New
Directions Publishing Corporation, New York.

Extracts from "Lepanto." taken from *Poems* by G. K. Chesterton.
Copyright © 1915. Reprinted by permission of Burns & Oates Ltd., London.

Acknowledgment is also made:
For permission to draw upon, for the preface of this book, "The Stockdale
Course" by Joseph Gerard Brennan in *Teaching Values and Ethics in College,*
M. J. Collins, ed. Copyright © 1983. New Directions for Teaching and Learning
(no. 13), San Francisco: Jossey-Bass.

Originally published by Naval War College Press
Newport, Rhode Island 02841

This edition published 1994 by Presidio Press
505 B San Marin Drive, Suite 300
Novato, CA 94945-1340 .

Library of Congress Cataloging-in-Publication Data

Brennan, Joseph Gerard, 1910-
    Foundations of moral obligation: the Stockdale course / Joseph Gerard
Brennan: [foreword by James B. Stockdale].
        p.   cm.
    Based on the course taught at the Naval War College.
    Includes bibliographical references and index.
    ISBN: 0-89141-528-9
    1. Ethics. I. Title.
BJ1012.B674 1992
170–dc20   92-5134
                                                   CIP

Printed in the United States of America

For All Those Who Took the Course

There are three roads by which a human being can reach that transcendental realm which only those of authentic greatness enter and which is the home of truth: desire for the truth, ceaseless effort to achieve it, and obedience to one's calling.

Simone Weil

Contents

Foreword by Vice Admiral James B. Stockdale, U.S. Navy (Ret.)

Preface   xv

1. Prison and the Hermetic   1
2. Job and the Problem of Evil   20
3. Love: From Eros to Agapē   37
4. Aristotle: The Ethics of Happiness   57
5. Kant and the Metaphysics of Morals   74
6. Utilitarianism: John Stuart Mill   96
7. Existentialism: Sartre and Camus   120
8. Lenin and Soviet Philosophy   141
9. Evolution and Ethics   160
10. Wittgenstein and the Ethic of Silence   182

Epilogue   201

Appendix   211

Notes   213

Bibliography   241

Index   249

Foreword

This book is a rather unusual survey of moral philosophy. It is based on the lectures delivered by Joseph Gerard Brennan for the Naval War College course titled "Foundations of Moral Obligation"—a course which had its roots in my experience as a prisoner of war in Vietnam from September 1965 to February 1973. The course was established in 1978, during the first year of my presidency of the Naval War College. Joe Brennan and I designed the course and co-taught it during the academic year 1978-79. I retired from the navy in 1979, and since that time Joe has continued to teach the course on his own.

I first closed ranks with philosophy in 1961, during a two-year navy-sponsored master's degree program at Stanford University. My teacher was Dr. Philip Rhinelander, who remained my friend until he died in 1987; and his two-term course was titled "The Problems of Good and Evil." The course consisted of readings philosophical and literary (Plato, Aristotle, Spinoza, Hume, Kant, and Mill on the one hand; Job, Aeschylus, Dante, Shakespeare, Dostoyevsky, and Camus on the other); and it focused on man's need to believe that virtue is rewarded and evil is punished, when the evidence is overwhelming that no such moral economy exists.

From these intimate textbook visits with some of the best minds that have ever graced our planet, I gained a new appreciation for how many ways there are to skin a cat, and a rather large helping of self-confidence in realizing how much all human minds—even those of these heavyweights—work very much the same, in terms of intuitions, fears, guilts, and occasional flashes of reasoned insight. The course was not taught in a way that suggested any direct military applications, but during my last tutorial session Rhinelander made a very important nod in that direction by giving me as a gift a copy of *The Enchiridion*, by the Stoic philosopher Epictetus. "I think this little manual should be of particular interest to you," he said. "This is the philosophy for the man who sees the world before him as a buzzsaw."

So I went back to my fighter squadron well provisioned for what was to come. Throughout the two-and-a-half combat cruises before I was shot down, I kept that copy of *The Enchiridion* on my bedside table, committing many of its passages to memory. I knew·that life is not fair, that there is no moral economy in the universe. I knew that for centuries there had existed a working philosophy based on the assumption that the world is a buzzsaw, and that this philosophy was specifically geared to deal with man's inherent inhumanity to man.

And how lucky I was to know even that much about the way of the world! I observed that the average American, when thrown into a political prison with torture and leg irons, is shocked at this positive evidence of human debasement, which sharply contradicts our popular myth of human progress; and as a result, he sees himself as a victim of outrage. Stoicism, on the other hand, taught that the right-thinking man can become a victim of no one but himself—that treachery is to be expected, but that the inner self can be vanquished only by such seeds of destruction as it allows *itself* to carry. My education had built a hedge against frustration and disappointment, and had driven into me an acute sense of the perils of allowing yourself to be manipulated by others. It had taught me the importance of emancipation from entanglements, enhanced willpower, and a conditioned habit of maintaining the *moral* leverage throughout all struggles. The feeling of well-being, objectivity, and freedom that grew from my immersion in philosophy served me well as a group and squadron commander in combat and as the leader of the underground in prison; and it was too good to hide under a bushel when I became president of the Naval War College.

Before coming to Newport, my happiest tour in the navy had been as a classroom instructor at the test pilot school. I was determined to get back in front of a class at the war college; but in the case of philosophy, I knew that I needed an "old pro" in my corner. That "old pro" turned out to be the man who had been my pen pal since 1975, when he had written me as the result of a newspaper article mentioning how Epictetus had influenced my life in prison. Almost as if by Providence, he had just assumed emeritus status at Barnard College of Columbia University by the time I got him on the phone. We met at Newport, and though he had a State Department lectureship in the offing, he agreed to help me put together a course at the war college that *just might* be a crowning achievement for each of us. And my learning curve arched upward as we set about designing our course. If Philip Rhinelander was the sparkplug of my philosophic interest, Joe Brennan became the locomotive that drove it home.

And now it's fourteen years later, just over twelve since I left the navy, and Joe has taught our course twice each year to enrollments that had to be limited to allow him to give that personal attention to each class member that is in keeping with his style. In addition, he has taught his course "Philosophy in American Values" and has been cultural advisor to the Naval Command College, resident lecturer on intellectual subjects that only he could handle, and "court musician" throughout a wonderfully productive second career as teacher and mentor.

Between these covers are the ten lectures that Joe has given for our course, each lecture honed to satisfy the intellectual hungers of men brought up to fight. We are interested not only in the major *ideas* that underpin our civilization, but in the *lives* of those who came up with them. We live our own lives against the backdrop of their thought, and we bank the fires of our smoldering willpower in preparation for the time when we must lay our personal honor, that "enigmatic mixture of conscience and egoism," on the line.

After a hard life of slavery and risk and danger, Epictetus spent his most productive years in exile in Greece, teaching a course in moral philosophy to the well-educated sons of the elite. He called a spade a spade and thereby sent his students away feeling good about themselves, ready to take on responsibility with poise. "Let others practice law suits, logical puzzles, and syllogisms," he preached. "Let your study be how to suffer death, bondage, the rack, exile. . . . Difficulties are what show men's character; therefore when a difficult situation meets you, remember that you are as the raw youth with whom God the trainer is wrestling."

Nowhere does education of this sort give one more comfort than when called into the lair of one's interrogator—or into the corridors of power. Thus Epictetus:

> When you come into the presence of some prominent man, remember that Another looks from above on what is taking place, and that you must please Him rather than this man.
> He, then, who is above asks of you,
> - In your school what did you call exile and imprisonment and bonds and death and disrepute?
> - I called them "things indifferent."
> - What do you call them now? Have they changed at all?
> - No.
> - Tell me, then, what are things "indifferent"?
> - Those that are independent of moral purpose.
> - Tell me also what follows.
> - Things independent of moral purpose are nothing to me.
> - Then enter in, full of confidence and mindful of all this, and you shall see what it means to be a man who has studied what he ought, when he is in the presence of men who have not studied.
> As for me, by the gods, I fancy that you will feel somewhat like this: "Why do we make such great and so many preparations for nothing? Is this the thing which is named power? All this is nothing."

The moral challenges of life come to us every day, in many different forms and in many different circumstances. To meet these challenges successfully, to emerge from them with our integrity intact, we need to prepare ourselves, we need to "see what it means to be a man who has studied what he ought." The course "Foundations of Moral Obligation" was designed to fill this need.

James B. Stockdale
Vice Admiral, U.S. Navy (Ret.)

Preface

It all began this way. In the autumn of 1975 I noticed a short news story in the *New York Times* about a Rear Admiral James B. Stockdale receiving eight medals for, among other things, "resisting all attempts by the North Vietnamese to use him." The piece mentioned that "Stockdale credits the Stoic philosopher Epictetus for helping him endure this ordeal." Curious as to what this man had found in the old Stoic sage to sustain him in his long captivity, I obtained his address from navy sources and wrote to him. Almost by return of post I received a seven-page letter in reply. I give it here in full because it affords necessary insight into the character of Jim Stockdale and reveals his motive for establishing at the Naval War College the course that was to bear the title "Foundations of Moral Obligation":

Dear Professor Brennan,

I was honored to receive your inquiry about the comfort and strength philosophical readings gave me throughout my seven and one-half years in prison. Perhaps I can best explain how this came to be with a rather rambling chronology.

I came into the Navy as a Naval Academy Midshipman in 1943 at the age of 19. For the next twenty years or so I was a rather technically oriented person. I was a seagoing destroyer officer, an aviator, a landing signal officer, a test pilot and academic instructor at the test pilot school, a many-times-deployed fighter pilot and ultimately a squadron commander of a supersonic F-8 Crusader outfit.

In 1960 I was sent to Stanford University for two full years' study in politics/history/economics, etc. in preparation for later assignments in politico-military policy making. I loved the subject matter, but noticed that in many courses my interest would peak at about the time the professor would say, "We're getting into philosophy— let's get back to the subject." I had more than adequate time to get the expected master's degree, and suggested to my advisor in my second year that I sign up for some courses over in the philosophy corner of the quadrangle. He was dead set against it—thought it would be a waste of my time. He said, "That's a very technical

subject—it would take two terms to learn their peculiar vocabulary."
Finally, after I persisted, he said, "It's up to you."

It was my good fortune on that first morning that I wandered
through the halls of the philosophy department, grey haired and in
civilian clothes (of course), to come by an open office whose
occupant looked me in the eye and asked if he could be of help.
When I told him that I was a graduate student in the humanities
with no formal philosophy background he could scarcely believe it.
When I told him I was a naval officer he asked me to have a seat.
He had been in the Navy in WWII. His name was Philip
Rhinelander. To jump ahead, his background was as follows: As a
Harvard lawyer he had practiced in Boston for 15 or 20 years before
Pearl Harbor, volunteered for war service at sea, and thereafter took
his PhD at Harvard under Whitehead. After tours as a dean at
Harvard and Stanford, he was back in the classroom at his own
request. He was in the midst of his two term "personal" course: The
Problems of Good and Evil. This he had built upon the lessons of
the Book of Job ("Life is not fair"). He offered to let me enter the
course, and to overcome my shortcomings of background, to give
me an hour of private tutoring each week. What a departure from
the other departments! (In some, PhD candidates sat outside their
advisor's office for hours on end awaiting a ten minute conversation.) I loved Rhinelander's class, and particularly our hour together
each week. I remember how patient he was in trying to get me to
realize the full implications of Hume's "Dialogues on Natural
Religion" (I still have page after page of notes on that).

To jump ahead again, I completed the course in fair fashion, and
went on to others from a visiting professor from Michigan named
Moravcsik, but Epictetus had already come into play during my last
tutorial session with Rhinelander.

As we parted after our last session, he reached up to his bookshelf
and said something like, "As I remember it, you are a military
man—take this booklet as a memento of our hours together. It
provides moral philosophy applicable to your profession." It was
The Enchiridion.

That night I started to peruse my gift. I recognized nothing that
applied to the career I had known. I was a fighter pilot, an organizer,
a motivator of young aviators, a martini drinker, a golf player, a
technologist—and this ancient rag talked about not concerning

oneself with matters over which he had no control, etc. I thought to myself, "Poor old Rhinelander—he's just too far gone." Nevertheless, I read and remembered almost all of it—if for no other reason than that it was given to me by the man I had come to worship as the most complete human being I had ever met: a sensitive scholar, a man who devoted himself to teaching quality kids quality concepts after a full career of legal and academic administrative success, a music composer, a kingpin of all major phases of university life, and a sophisticated gentleman of kindness and generosity.

About three years after I had said good-bye to "poor old Rhinelander," while in the midst of my second combat tour against North Vietnam as a Wing Commander, I pulled off a target one September morning in the midst of heavy flak when all the lights came on (fire warning, hydraulic failure, electrical failure, etc.). As I sped over the treetops it became immediately apparent that I had lost my flight controls—by reflex action I pulled the curtain and ejected—and was almost immediately suspended in air 200 feet above a village street, in total silence except for rifle shots and the whir of bullets past my ear. So help me in those fleeting seconds before I landed among the waiting crowd I had two vivid thoughts. (1) Five years to wait (I had studied enough modern Far East history and talked to enough Forward Air Controllers in the south to fully appreciate the dilemma of Vietnam—I turned out to be an optimist by two and one-half years). (2) I am leaving that technological world and entering the world of Epictetus.

The world view of the Stoics, Professor Rhinelander had joked, was that their environment was a buzz saw in which human *will* was the only salvation. I was to spend over four years combatting a veritable buzz saw (until the torture and extortion machine was set in idle in the late autumn of 1969) and over three more years of simple deprived detention of the sort one would expect in a primitive, hostile country. Over four years were to be spent in solitary confinement, nearly half of it in leg irons. Throughout, until 1970, every effort was to be made to break my will, to make me a cat's paw in tinhorn propaganda schemes. Real or fabricated "violations of the established regulations for criminal's detention" (e.g., tapping on the walls to another prisoner) would result in torture, with the end aim of sequential (1) confession of guilt, (2) begging for forgiveness, (3) apology, and (4) atonement (signing an anti-war statement). A similar sequence would be set up with *particular* gusto if I were found to be exercising leadership of others via the tap code ("inciting other criminals to oppose the camp authority").

The situation was thus framed in the above context. I was crippled (knee broken, eventually to become rigidly fused by nature; shoulder broken, partial use of arm); alone; sick (weight down 50 pounds); depressed (not so much from anticipating the next pain as from the prospect of my eventually losing my honor and self-respect); and helpless except for will. What conditions could be more appropriate for Epictetus' admonitions? As a soldier, I had bound myself to a military ethic:

(Chapter XVII of The Enchiridion)

"Remember that you are an actor in a drama of such sort as the author chooses—if short, then in a short one; if long, then in a long one. If it be his pleasure that you should enact a poor man, see that you act it well; or a cripple, or a ruler, or a private citizen. For this is your business—to act well the given part; but to choose it belongs to another."

I was crippled:

(Chapter IX of The Enchiridion)

"Sickness is an impediment to the body, but not to the will unless itself pleases. Lameness is an impediment to the leg, but not to the will; and say this to yourself with regard to everything that happens. For you will find it to be an impediment to something else, but not truly to yourself."

I was dependent on my extortionists for life support, and soon learned to ask for nothing to avoid demands for "reciprocity":

(Chapter XIV of The Enchiridion (last sentence))

"Whoever then would be free, let him wish nothing, let him decline nothing, which depends on others; else he must necessarily be a slave."

I could stop my misery at any time by becoming a puppet; was it worth the shame?

(Chapter XXVIII of The Enchiridion)

"If a person had delivered up your body to some passer-by, you would certainly be angry. And do you feel no shame in delivering up your own mind to any reviler, to be disconcerted and confounded?"

Relief from boils, heat, cold, broken bones was "available" for the asking—for a price. What should I say?

(Chapter XXIV of The Enchiridion (selected sentence))

"If I can get them with the preservation of my own honor and fidelity and self-respect, show me the way and I will get them; but if you require me to lose my own proper good, that you may gain what is no good, consider how unreasonable and foolish you are."

Epictetus was not the only valuable philosophic memory in my predicament: Job (Why me? . . . Why *not* me?), Descartes' bifurcation of mind and body, and many other readings were invaluable.

It is important to note that I am speaking *only* for myself. Some of my prison mates had more doctrinaire religious concepts which served them well, some drew resolve from their concepts of political virtue, and so on in a broad spectrum of varying levels of sophistication. Thoughts of God and country helped me, too—but my "secret weapon" was the security I felt in anchoring my resolve to those selected portions of philosophic thought that emphasized human dignity and self-respect. Epictetus certainly taught that.

This has been a much longer explanation than I planned, but I am enthusiastic about the wonders a man in your profession and discipline can bring about in the lives of people in need. I wish I had the qualification to be in your shoes, teaching in a good school. From firsthand experience I am committed to the position that the study of moral philosophy is a particularly relevant part of education. And though education, as one of my favorite quotations reads, may be but an ornament in prosperity, it is a refuge in adversity.

I wish you well and appreciate your dedication to the teaching of such an important discipline.

Sincerely yours,

J.B. Stockdale
Rear Admiral, U.S. Navy

More correspondence followed. In late 1977, two months after Stockdale became president of the Naval War College, he asked me to come up to visit him at the college. In a sunlit office overlooking Narragansett Bay, I found myself stared at by a man who looked a little like James Cagney in his prime, but more handsome. Piercing blue eyes bored into me from under a shock of thick, prematurely white hair. Intense, feisty, and impatient with anything but directness, Stockdale moved about restlessly, stumping back and forth on the leg that had been broken by the fall from his shot-down plane and rebroken by beatings from his North Vietnamese captors. And on his uniform he wore another reminder of his Vietnam experience: the blue and white-starred ribbon of the Congressional Medal of Honor. He asked me if I would help him put together a course in moral philosophy and teach it with him. I had just retired as professor emeritus of philosophy, Barnard College, Columbia University, and was considering accepting a State Department offer of a Fulbright lectureship in India. Stockdale said, "There's a phone on that desk. Phone those characters in Washington and tell them to go to hell." I did so in polite language, and we set to work at once on organizing the course.

The Naval War College, I found, offered a three-trimester graduate course of study to military officers in midcareer. The curriculum centered on three core courses: strategy and policy, defense economics and management, and naval operations. Stockdale had increased the number of elective courses, most of which were related in some way to the three core courses. At that time the student body consisted of about three hundred midgrade officers ranging in age from about thirty-two to forty-two, and in rank from lieutenant commander to commander, or from major to lieutenant colonel. There were a few Navy and Coast Guard captains, as well as a sprinkling of colonels from the Marines, the Army, and the Air Force. About half the student body was navy, with the rest split among the other services. A few civilian officers from various government agencies were also enrolled. Two groups of foreign officers formed autonomous colleges that were integrated within the larger whole—the Naval Command College (senior) and the Naval Staff College (junior). All the officers wore civilian clothes to class, as did the military faculty, except on days when august personages made official visits.

How were we to organize the Stockdale course for this formidable student audience? The first question was the title. Stockdale did not like the word *ethics*. He thought the contemporary "ethics explosion" had eroded the older, nobler sense of the word. He knew that ethics courses were spreading rapidly, not only in military institutions but also in business, industry, and the professions. Harvard Business School was becoming the Vatican of business ethics. IBM and Electronic Data Systems were taking advice from "ethicists," and a prominent engine company had hired a professor of ethics from a major university at a salary for which the sophists of ancient Greece would have sold out Athens. Stockdale preferred the term *moral philosophy*, which seemed to suggest the tradition of the humanities. He believed that without some background in the humanities, without some familiarity with ancient and modern philosophical classics, it would be hard to teach ethics without being superficial and preachy. Stockdale was convinced that many people tended to reduce ethics to a branch of psychology, but education in the humanities would show that much of what goes by the name "social science" serves up ideas expressed earlier and better in classical philosophy and modern literature.

"Foundations of Moral Obligation" was the title we finally agreed on. We had only a ten-week trimester to get through the readings, lectures, seminar discussions, papers, and examinations. The course opened with the idea of the hermetic—the alchemical transformation that may occur when a human being is subject to intense pressure within a crucible of suffering or confinement. Stockdale's own *Atlantic Monthly* article "The World of Epictetus" (April 1978) led easily to discussion of the prison experiences and reflections of Socrates, Boethius, Cervantes, Sartre, and Solzhenitsyn. We went on to readings and discussions of the Book of Job, the Socratic dialogues of Plato, Aristotle's *Nichomachean Ethics*, Kant's *Foundations of the Metaphysics of Morals*, and Mill's *On Liberty* and *Utilitarianism*. These readings were supplemented by selections from the works of Emerson, Sartre, Camus, Conrad, Koestler, Dostoyevsky, and Solzhenitsyn. The course drew to a close with Epictetus' *Enchiridion* and Wittgenstein's ethic of silence.

Among Stockdale's favorite pages of Aristotle's *Nichomachean Ethics* were those in which the philosopher distinguishes between

voluntary and involuntary actions, analyzes the role of choice
and intention in human acts, and describes the way free choice
and compulsion can coexist. Stockdale denied the existence of
brainwashing; one was always to some degree responsible. If one
broke under torture—and at some point everybody did—one
could always make the torturers start all over again the next day.
"They don't like that," said Stockdale; it made things much easier
for both sides if the victim "cooperated." When his comrades,
racked by twisted ropes, had "spilled their guts" and were
thrown back into their cells weeping with shame, Stockdale, as
the senior POW, would comfort them via tap code on the wall:
"We've all done it. Just make them work for it. Don't give
anything away free." And so to our Naval War College class
Stockdale read from the *Nichomachean Ethics*, "There are some
instances in which actions elicit forgiveness rather than praise,
for example, when a man acts improperly under a strain greater
than human nature can bear, and which no one could endure.
Yet there are, perhaps, also acts which no man can possibly be
compelled to do, but rather than do them he should accept the
most terrible sufferings and death." Stockdale himself risked
death when he beat himself into bleeding insensibility with a
wooden stool to prevent himself from being filmed by the North
Vietnamese for propaganda purposes.

Team-teaching the course with Admiral Stockdale during that
memorable academic year of 1978-79 proved a unique experience. Word got around that a Vietnam war hero with the
Medal of Honor was teaching a course in moral philosophy at
the Naval War College, and the media moved in with tape
recorders, television cameras, and fast-writing reporters.
Celebrities ranging from senators to nationally known football
coaches (Woody Hayes, for one) listened with knitted brow as
Stockdale and his teammate held forth on everything from
Epictetus to Sartre. The first examination was formidable; the
admiral and I were determined to throw everything in. (That
was a mistake, and we did not repeat it.) Senator John Glenn
was visiting that first examination day, and Stockdale brought
his old test-pilot classmate to my office. Clutching the copy of
the exam that Stockdale had proudly thrust upon him, John

Glenn stood shaking his head in bewilderment, saying "Pretty heavy test, Professor!" Meanwhile, screams of anguish were painfully audible from the officers taking the test down the hall.

The Naval War College has a detailed course evaluation system, and the student officers are frank in their comments. How did they react to the Stockdale course? Most of them admired Stockdale just short of idolatry and gave the course very high ratings. All applauded the opportunity to read the works that were discussed. For the greater part of their military careers, these officers had concentrated on technological subjects. Studying the actual texts of men such as Plato, Mill, Aristotle, and Kant came as a new experience for most of them, but, having quick intelligence, they soon made themselves at home with the material. To the discussion of moral problems they brought a wealth of experience of ethical choice, of character formed by a mature response to life. The same holds true down to the present.

Admiral Stockdale retired from the navy in the summer of 1979 in order to assume the presidency of The Citadel, the military college of South Carolina, a post he held for little more than a year before becoming a senior research fellow at the Hoover Institution, Stanford. He has held that fellowship to the present day, writing and lecturing copiously. To his teaching teammate fell the task of carrying on the Stockdale course through the thirteen years that followed—years that reached from the depressing aftermath of the Vietnam conflict to the dissolution of the Soviet Union, the unification of Germany, and the end of the Cold War. In February 1991 television monitors in our classroom brought us General Schwarzkopf live from the battle area, describing the three-day action that put an end to the Gulf crisis and Iraq's invasion of Kuwait.

In the autumn of 1989 microphones were installed in the classroom and the course lectures were taped and stored. Spring 1991 brought welcome news that the Naval War College Press had obtained funds to make a book based on the tapes, and for the first time the "sermons" were written down, amended, updated, and edited. The present volume constitutes the result.

Now, in my eighty-second year, the moment has come for me, a lesser Prospero on another island, to break my staff and drown my book. Not this one, though, for it was put together with constant thought of all those military men and women who enrolled in the course—men and women who proved once more by their academic and personal deportment that there is no such thing as "the military mind," only intelligence, character, and a sense of calling. Thinking of them all, I remember the words of Alyosha in Dostoyevsky's *The Brothers Karamazov*:

> Even if we are occupied with more important things, if we attain to honor or fall into great misfortune, still let us remember how good it once was here when we were all together united by a good and kind feeling that made us perhaps better than we are.

*

By way of grateful acknowledgement, my thanks are due to James Bond Stockdale, *condicio sine qua non* of the course. To Rich Megargee for his guardianship of the course, and to his able assistant Louise Miller, for whom Verdi wrote an opera. To Marvin Rice and the staff and students of the Naval Command College, whose presence has meant so much to me.

To Stuart Smith, former managing editor of the Naval War College Press, who was the first to see a book in the lectures and who, as my editor and demiurge, transformed the lectures into readable prose, bringing form and order out of cosmic muddle. To Phyllis Winkler, who, while busy taking the course herself, taped the lectures without missing so much as an instructor's headscratch. To Robert S. Wood for supporting the project with insight and humor. To the Naval War College Foundation, with the generous help of the Earhart Foundation, for providing the funds for the printing of the book, and to all those at the Naval

War College who had a hand in it, particularly reference librarian Alice Juda, finder of the unfindable. To Carole Boiani, Gina Vieira, Diane Cote, Allison Sylvia, Justina Victorino, and Victoria Florendo for their typographical expertise. To Pat Sweeney for her editorial assistance in the final stages of its preparation for publication. To the Emma S. Clark Library, Setauket, New York, for helpful assistance and resources.

To Loren Graham for all those copies of *Voprosy filosofii,* and for much else besides. And to my wife Mary for that courage Plato's General Laches calls "endurance of soul."

To Frank Uhlig, editor of the Naval War College Press, for making publication's possibility into a welcome actuality.

1

Prison and the Hermetic

Hermetics—what a lovely word, Herr Naphta! I've always liked the word *hermetic*. It sounds like magicking, and has all sorts of vague and extended associations.

Hans Castorp in Thomas Mann's
The Magic Mountain

He [Sergeant Reynal] had spent eight years in the Marines cloistered in the hermetic world of the military, rising in the ranks. "I thought I was one of God's chosen few," he said.

Chris Hughes, *The New York Times*,
30 May 1991, on U. S. Marines
returning from the Persian Gulf

The theme of the day is prison and the closed space, and it starts with the Stockdale experience, which you can read about in his essay "The World of Epictetus." The Egyptian leader Anwar Sadat said in his autobiography that there are only two places in this world where a man cannot escape from himself—a battlefield and the prison cell. Prison is a dire form of the closed-space experience, and its major effect is usually dehumanizing, depressing, degrading. It is like a disease that makes us twice-over body, that pulls us down from spirit to matter. So for most, indeed for all, prison has a negative effect, both moral and physical. But for some few, in addition to the initial depressing and degrading effect, prison can be a trans- forming and uplifting experience, a place of self-discovery, a locus of finding within themselves something that they did not know was there and that helps them transcend the dehumaniza- tion of captivity.

Back in the 1950s Jack Kerouac, king of the beats, said, "Prison is where you promise yourself the right to live." And Pat Benatar, a rock star of the eighties, used to sing a number claiming,

"When they close you in, you open out!" Jim Stockdale says, "It was in prison that I discovered a happiness I had not known before." Talking to an association of navy carrier pilots in the fall of 1988, the admiral quoted Alexander Solzhenitsyn recalling his prison experiences in the U.S.S.R.: "As I lay there on the rotting straw, I felt goodness stirring within me. Thank you, prison, for being part of my life." And in 1989, looking back on his own prison days, Czech president Vaclav Havel said, "Jail gave me an extremely good preparation for the office [the presidency]. In the first place it taught me not to be surprised at anything." He had learned by experience the meaning of the Stoic motto, "Nil admirari!" ("Be astonished at nothing!").

Now prison, although it is the most dire form of what we may call the closed-space experience, is not the only way of it. You may not yourself have been in prison as a POW or for some other reason, but I would bet that in your personal or professional life, at one time or other, in one form or other, you have made acquaintance with the closed-space effect. Although you may not have known it under the arcane label of the *hermetic*, you have experienced it nonetheless. The military profession knows it well.

Consider this word *hermetic* for a moment, a rather lovely word as Mann's young hero says. We may take two meanings from it, one quite familiar: sealed off, *hermetically* sealed. When you want to put up fruit or vegetables in jars you must seal them in very tightly, and if the seal is successful then the corrupting effects of time are stopped, for a year anyway, and when you open the jar the fruit or vegetable is as fresh as the day you *hermetically* sealed it into that container. The other meaning, less familiar perhaps, belongs to a tradition that ran parallel with the history of science, philosophy, and of religion as well. Some say the hermetic culture had its beginnings in ancient Egypt, for the Greek divinity Hermes was originally the Egyptian god Toth, and that deity's name was associated with magic. Thus the second meaning of *hermetic*: magic; and, by extension, magical transformation.

The hermetists of the late Middle Ages and the early Renaissance numbered among them certain people we know as alchemists. In popular understanding, even then, the aim of the alchemist was thought to be the power to change base metal by magical means into one of the precious metals, gold for example. But an ancient tradition tells us that the true alchemists, those who stood in the inner circle of the secret art, knew that vulgar metal-changing was not really their business, that the hermetic change referred to in alchemy of the highest sort was a moral and spiritual transformation. These alchemists used the sealed crystal retort as a symbol of what might be experienced by simple and complicated souls alike. Put some material, outwardly ordinary, in the retort; irradiate it by powerful magical forces, making sure that the seal is tight; and then light under it (still metaphorically speaking) a fire. Now this fire may be dangerous; it may even have some congress with fire from the Inferno, hellfire. This is a risky business and it is not for everyone; one must undergo an ordeal. Now if the material irradiated is not only outwardly ordinary but ordinary all the way through, nothing will happen. But if there is something a little unusual in it, you may witness or experience a phenomenon which some call *Steigerung*, that is to say, an upward movement, a metamorphosis, a transformation from a lower to a higher state. This is what can happen to a human under hermetic influences: a transformation of the soul from an inferior to a superior state, but in surroundings that are strictly sealed off, and in an environment which is dangerous.

Those of you who are familiar with the arcanum of Freemasonry will recognize this process, because the initiation into the brotherhood has a hermetic property. The initiation takes the form of an ordeal—dangerous, requiring a stout heart to undergo it. Mozart makes enchanting music and fun too in his Masonic opera, *The Magic Flute*. The first act is full of delightful foolery, but in the second act things get rather grim. The two young lovers of the piece must undergo a rigorous ordeal, and every symbol of the hermetic, the Freemasonry of Mozart's time, is present.

Now you may say this is all very interesting, but what has it to do with ordinary experience? In answer, let us look for a moment at some of the closed-space experiences in which this kind of transformation takes place, perhaps not with the elaborate trappings of the mystical tradition, but hermetic all the same.

Take religion. Consider the ark, which figures so prominently in Judaic religion. The Latin word *arca* means simply a box, but there are older words—*aron* (a chest) in Hebrew and *tebah* in Egyptian. Remember the charming story of Moses when he was a little baby. Fearing he would be killed, his poor mother could not keep him, so she put him in a basket and sealed it with pitch and sent it out on the water of the great river. There it was discovered among the reeds by an Egyptian princess coming down with her handmaidens to bathe. She released the baby from his confinement in the little pitch-sealed boat, and he grew up to lead the children of Israel out of the house of bondage. And they kept well guarded the Ark of the Covenant.

Or think of the temple. The temple was a sacred place with strict boundaries within and without. The outer area, the temple court, was given over to many affairs, including vendors of birds and animals for sacrifice. If you were a poor person and you and your spouse came and could only afford a small sacrifice, then you bought a little pigeon or two; but if you had more money you could buy a lamb. Merchants had their stalls in the temple court, and one of the puzzling things about the Gospel according to Saint Mark is that Jesus is represented as getting very angry and driving out not only the money changers but "them that sold doves." Perhaps there had been some encroachment on the inner space, the sanctuary, which was itself divided in two. The Levites, or candidates for the priesthood, and the priests themselves had free admission to the outer sanctuary, but not to the "holy of holies." Only the high priest, he who carried the fire of God, was permitted to enter the most strictly sealed-off sanctuary, and then only on certain high holy days of the year.

Or consider the tabernacle. Originally the tabernacle was a portable sanctuary, but it acquired through the ages a more restricted dimension, a place where the sacrament is kept. In the Roman Catholic rite or that of the Greek Orthodox church, there is an enclosed space for the Eucharist, the sacrament commemorating the sacred meal at the Passover time before the Crucifixion. If you attend a Greek Orthodox mass you will see that at intervals the priest disappears into this closed space; you don't see him. The idea of the Eucharist, the divine presence within the species of bread and wine, represents an extraordinary religious use of the closed space. If one could speak without irreverence, one might say that the Eucharist is the "coercion of God," that its consecration "compels" the transformation of the bread and wine into the body and blood of Christ. (Of course, theologians would not put it that way.)

Finally, the central element of the Christian revelation, the Resurrection. If you read the New Testament you sense that the writers are bedazzled by the Easter experience, the appearance of the risen Christ. Matthew tells us that the disciples took the body from the place of crucifixion and deposited it in a sepulchre, made out of a cave perhaps and donated through the kindness of a rich man. Pilate ordered them to seal the sepulchre: "So they went, and made the sepulchre sure, sealing the stone. . . ." There follows the radiant story: the ancient mystery of the breaking of the seal, the resurrection, the glad tidings, the wonder that out of death comes life.

Leaving religion for science, physical science, we know that it is only in this century, and close to our own time, that the enormous power and energy sealed in the atom has been released through the work of the men and women of science. Not until the 1930s was it discovered how to release, for good or ill, the tremendous force locked in the miniscule prison of the atom, an entity so small that space as we know it does not exist in the hermetic fastness of the subatomic world. Early in the century physicists had shown that if the ordinary element carbon is placed in a casing of metal, heated to a very high temperature, then suddenly plunged into deep cold, the pressure thus created is so great that a transformation, almost magical, occurs; and ordinary carbon, so plentiful on our planet, is transformed into diamond, immortal diamond. Granted that

the result was a very tiny diamond, for the concepts and tech-
niques that were later applied to release the stupendous energy
hermetically locked in the atom were not yet available for
anything beyond this comparatively modest pressure-cooker
experiment.

In biology the basic unit corresponding to the atom is the cell.
Notice the multiple meanings of the word *cell*. It is the place of
prison confinement as well as the little room in the monastery
where the monk lives, praying, fasting, planning good works.
The secrets of the cell were revealed, and then only partially, by
the experiments of the 1950s that allowed us to understand the
structure of the DNA molecule, which allows organic life to
replicate itself almost magically, to pass on its stable structure,
genetically securing the perpetuation of its kind. Take, from the
incredible richness of living forms, that of a human baby: two
tiny cells interlock and the developing embryo is sealed in,
floating in a protective fluid, until the magical moment comes
when what had been just a juncture of almost invisible ovum and
spermatozoa now enters the world as a human being, body and
soul. Who was the French molecular biologist—François Jacob,
perhaps—who said, "The dream of every cell is to become two
cells"?

If you want to think of the related science of medicine, you
can start with the capsule that seals in the medication, and go
on from there to the hospital, the hospital bed, the sanatorium
balcony. Maybe you have had the experience of being ill or
injured at some time and have sensed the peculiar effects of
confinement, though nobody is strapping you down. History is
full of examples of those who, confined to bed by illness, have
had time to take stock, to reflect on their lives, and then have
risen in restored health to a new life, a second biography, with
a debt owed to hermetic transformation. Such recoveries and
new beginnings are not confined to the chronicles of the lives
of the saints. It can happen to us ordinary folk as well.

Suppose we give a moment's reflection to sports and the
sports ethic. Nowhere in ordinary life is more strict attention
paid to boundaries, to closed space, than in sports and games.
The Dutch scholar Johan Huizinga titled his great book *Homo*

Ludens (Man the Player), defining humans not as rational animals as did Aristotle but as animals that play games—games with rules and boundaries. Consider the forms from the hermetic tradition employed in common sports and games: the circle for the circus, the square for chess, the diamond for baseball, the rectangle for soccer, rugby, football, tennis. In the 1983 Newport yacht race, when the Australians took the great cup away from the U.S. Americans, the course was laid out in the form of an upended isosceles triangle.

In sports, the boundaries that seal in the playing area are very strict, and so too are the corresponding rules of play. It's human weakness to make excuses, but in sports excuses do not count. What would you think, for example, of a baseball player who, having had his three strikes, were to turn to the umpire and say, "I had a real rough night last night. My friend was ill and I got no sleep at all. Couldn't I have a fourth strike?"

The boundaries of sport are strict. If in football you catch a pass and go just a little out of bounds, the play is over. If it's out, it's out, no matter how angrily John MacEnroe jumps up and down on the tennis court. (Did you happen to see that wonderful wire service photo of Ivan Lendl agonizingly unbelieving that the shot should be called in when it was out?)

Sport's strict boundaries have moral implications. There is such a thing as a sports ethic, and experience in sports can be an effective moral teacher. In August 1986, at the Manufacturer's Hanover Trust golf tournament in Harrison, New York, golfer Ray Floyd, addressing the ball, saw it move by itself a few inches. He penalized himself one stroke, though no one else saw the ball move, and he lost the match by that one stroke. Interviewed by reporters, Floyd said that's the way you do it in sports, and if you run your life by the rules of your sport, you can't go far wrong. Writing about that match for the *New York Times*, Wayne Tryhuk observed, "That's why it's so heartening to see the sports ethic kept fresh. . . . Ray Floyd was not victorious in the Westchester Classic. But who could honestly call him anything but a winner?"

In the military the role of strict rules, the hermetic, sealed-off experience itself, is not confined to war games. Consider the

ship, so often used by writers of imaginative literature to portray
a world set off from the world. In an informal discussion of how
people can always remember where they were when certain
significant events happened, such as the assassination of President Kennedy, talk turned to where we were at the time of the
first landing of humans on the moon. A navy commander
present said, "I cannot remember where I was because I was on
a destroyer off the coast of Vietnam. We were deployed without
relief for sixty days, and I had no idea of what was going on in
the world. We were so sealed off, concerned only with our duty,
that there was a sense of confinement in a little world where you
got news from the outside by radio only days or weeks after it
happened."

That was a destroyer. Think now of a submarine, where one
must take special psychological tests to join the crew, hermetically sealed off from the outside world, sometimes for months
at a time. Think too of armor; the tank; the combat information
center, complete with its spooky red and green lights, the
shrouding darkness. Think of the closed space of the airplane,
whether an F-14 fighter or a P-3 with a crew of twelve. No wonder
so many fliers have been inspired to write a bit of verse about
flying. Most of it is not great poetry, but the compulsion to write
about that particular sealed-in, pressure-cooker experience is
rather great. The French flier Saint-Exupéry wrote well about
flying. And William Yeats, no flier he, has left us his lovely poem,
"An Irish Airman Foresees His Death." Read it sometime.

We should not forget that the military profession itself is in
its special way hermetically sealed off from the large, inchoate
civilian society; and in this resides at once its difference, its
obligation, its sense of isolation, and its honor.

One could go on to cite further examples of transformation
within closed space, but there is time for just a couple more
mentions. A garden is a special marked-off place, and if you
bring proper influences to bear on the seeds and the soil, you
will get something beautiful or good to eat. And there is the
alchemy of the still. Nicholas Freeling writes, "Perhaps when a
painter took his brush and made the first strokes on canvas it

was alchemy, the heating of the still to the 148 degrees Fahrenheit at which alcohol takes leave of sugar and water."

Oftentimes closed space does not have the positive effect of transformation toward the good: the prison, of course, but then too there is the library, heavy with antique learning which even scholars sometimes find stifling. In his novel *The Name of the Rose*, Umberto Eco describes the oppressive effect of the library of a Benedictine monastery of the fourteenth century. This library is the seedbed of crime and the crucible of a great fire, a conflagration that not only destroys the library but brings the whole monastery crashing in flames to the ground. Consider the bell jar as a symbol of hermetic isolation. Have you ever seen an unfeeling science teacher extinguish the life of a mouse by putting it under a bell jar and extracting the air by a pump? If so, you can understand why Sylvia Plath, the poet and novelist who fell upon evil days and in the end killed herself, titled her well-known novel *The Bell Jar*. Compressed into a single frightening sentence, the whole story reads, "To the person in the bell jar, blank and stopped as a dead baby, life itself is the bad dream."

*

What is left to say about the hermetic transformation experience? Four tales that may interest you, some of which you already know. There is Plato's dialogue the *Phaedo*, perhaps the most influential of the so-called Socratic dialogues. It was written twelve years, scholars say, after the death of Socrates; and while the setting is probably described with some accuracy, the doctrine, particularly in its developed form, is Plato's adaptation of an old Orphic tradition.

Plato recreates the scene. Socrates is in prison in Athens, having been found guilty by a judge-jury of his peers on a capital charge of impiety and corrupting the youth. In one hour he will be executed by drinking poison (hemlock or aconite). He has said farewell to his family, and we see him surrounded by his favorite students. His final discourse to his students centers on the question of why a philosopher should not be afraid to die: death is not an evil to a wise man.

Why? Because death will separate the soul from the body, releasing the soul to return to its proper place, the high invisible world of the divine Forms. These Forms (the "Platonic Ideas") are the eternal models of all visible things. Unchanging and deathless, they are the archetypes, of which all mortal things are transient copies, feeble images. While they are one, things of this world are many; while they are true being, the visible world is only becoming, composed of things that come into being, pass out of being, and never really *are*. The soul belongs to this higher world beyond sense perception, while the body's origin is in the realm of matter. And to most philosophers of ancient Greece, matter is the principle of heaviness, sluggishness, inertia. It is that which drags us down, obscuring the clear light of reason, through which alone we can enjoy partial glimpses of the world of the really real. At birth—by which time we have forgotten our prenatal acquaintance with the bright world of the Forms—the soul is tied only lightly to the body. As we grow and give in to desire, to the passions (which represent the cry of the body for satisfaction), the soul becomes more and more closely united to the body, thus making it harder for the soul to distinguish reality from illusion, truth from falsehood. If as a philosopher or scientist one lives the life of the mind, free from the drag of the material body, one can welcome death as the final liberation of the soul from matter. Now the soul is free to return to the world from which it came, to the fair and deathless realm of the Forms, the unities to which the pluralities of the visible world owe their brief and flickering existence.

The ancients, you know, adorned their sarcophagi with obscene symbols, in this way striving to convey their belief that out of death, life is generated. Opposites generate opposites, and out of death comes life. This doctrine Plato puts into the mouth of the Socrates of the *Phaedo* as he comforts his students who will attend his execution: ("There now, Apollodorus, don't cry!") And Socrates quotes the old Orphic saying "sōma sēma"— the body is the tomb of the soul, the prison-house of the spirit. Perhaps he pointed to himself and to the walls of the prison, which was probably no more than a cave dug out of the side of the Acropolis, with iron gratings sealing the mouth of it.

Notice how often a cave comes into these stories. One tradition has it that Jesus was born in a stable ("and they laid him in a manger because there was no room for them in the inn"). It was not uncommon to use a cave as a stable; there the animals could be kept, and food and water brought in to provide for them. The Holy Koran tells us that it was in a cave, on the side of Mount Hera, three miles north of the holy city of Mecca, that the Prophet used to spend parts of the year in meditation. It was in that cave that he had the great vision, in which he felt everything that had impeded him fall away, and he heard a great voice crying, "*Read!*"

So we can imagine Socrates saying to his pupils, "Look, you see I am in prison and in a few moments I shall die. I await my death in this cave. And isn't it right that I should compare the soul's relation to body to that of a captive held within a cave, a prisoner within a prison-house? I welcome death. It is the release of my immortal part." And the weeping jailer administers the poison to the old man.

*

A second story. Between the fifth and sixth centuries of our era there lived a philosopher named Boethius, who before the end of his life served as consul and chief officer to the barbarian Theodoric, an Ostrogoth who proclaimed himself emperor of Rome. Theodoric was an Aryanized Christian and a very suspicious man. In due course his suspicions fell upon his first officer, who was falsely accused of inciting the Roman senate to disaffection as well as secretly communicating with the Byzantine emperor to the east. Boethius was stripped of his office; his house, his library, and all his property were confiscated; and he was executed after torture. (Today his ashes lie in the little church of San Pietro del Cielo d'Auro, not far from Milan, close by the relics of Saint Augustine.)

Boethius has a place in the history of Western philosophy, in part because he was one of the very few Christian scholars who could translate the Greek classics in philosophy into Latin. Boethius' translation of Aristotle's treatises on logic served for nearly a thousand years as a standard text in philosophy. And his best loved book endures under the title *The Consolation of Philosophy*. It was written in confinement, while he was awaiting execution. He tells us that he is bowed down, weeping, because he has lost everything—his office, his house, his library, the loyalty of his sons. All has been taken away from him.

This situation of the ancient philosopher fascinated Admiral Jim Stockdale, for he knew what it was to be stripped of everything. In his writings he comes back again and again to the theme of loss. Here is the American fighter, loaded with the most sophisticated weaponry that science and technology can devise, weapons that can pour out a Niagara of fire. Strip that fighter of his weapons, strip him of everything, even, quite literally, as in Stockdale's case, strip the shirt from his back. The question then is, What does the American warrior have to rely on? The answer is, Only what is in the self.

Boethius makes this point: "I am condemned. I have lost it all—honors, riches, my library with its shelves of ivory and crystal. Why did this happen to me, a just man? What am I to do?" Suddenly he sees a light at the end of the room in which he is held. He looks more closely and sees a beautiful lady dressed in white. He knows who she is because of her stole, embroidered with the letters *Alpha* and *Omega* on either end. She is Lady Philosophy. She asks him why he is crying, and he tells her that he has lost everything and that he is unjustly condemned. And he weeps afresh.

"I am surprised at you," she says, "you a philosopher, mourning and weeping like this. Don't you realize that Dame Fortune is a very fickle lady, that what she gives with one hand she takes away with the other? Did you come into this world with your riches, honors, fine house, library, high office? No, you came into the world with none of these things. They came to you from the outside, and now it is time for you to return them, to give them back. Riches and honors were not given to you, they were just lent to you, and now the debt must be paid. You say you are deeply unhappy. But true happiness does not come from what is external to us. It comes from within. And the origin of happiness is the good, the good itself. That absolute good is God, who measures things not in terms of time but of eternity, the simultaneous whole and perfect possession of eternal life."

"But if God is all good," Boethius responds, "why does he permit evil to be done to me? I am a just man. I have been unjustly accused." She answers, reminding him that he is a philosopher, "Don't you remember Socrates saying to his judges after his condemnation, 'No evil can befall a good man. It is better to suffer evil than to do it.'?"

"But those who have betrayed me prosper," Boethius complains, "while I, a just man, have lost everything, and must die because of false witness." She replies that those people are not really happy, though they think they are. They dwell in a fool's paradise. Unaware, they appear to flourish, but they are excluded from the proper order of things.

Then, like the old Stoic philosophers who urged the faint-hearted to live like a soldier ("Vivere militare!"), she uses a military metaphor: "You are a philosopher. Dry your tears. Would a brave soldier stop in the middle of battle to bewail how unhappy he is? No more should the wise man lament the strokes of fortune than the soldier weep at the alarums and noises of battle." Then she disappears, and the bright light fades.

*

Another story. This time about a Spanish soldier in the great sea battle of Lepanto in 1571. You remember that the Turks had moved into Cyprus with the aim of using it as a springboard to extend their power to the central and western Mediterranean. Venice and the pope appealed to Spain for help, but King Philip was distracted by his own political concerns and the need to examine his conscience. At last his half-brother, John of Austria, assumed the leadership of the Christian states, took command of an allied fleet, and sailed to meet the Turkish armada off Lepanto. The ensuing battle was the last great sea-fight with vessels powered by oars. The fighting was fierce—eight thousand wounded on either side, including our Spanish soldier, whose left hand was shattered, leaving him crippled for life. But the Turk was defeated, his fleet destroyed. Perhaps you remember Chesterton's spirited ballad "Lepanto," which recalls the sea-fight with this refrain:

> Vivat Hispania!
> Domino Gloria!
> (*Don John of Austria is going to the war.*)

Later, on his way back from the East, our soldier was captured by Algerian corsairs and brought with some of his men to the court of the Bey of Algiers, where they were thrown into a dungeon in chains and later farmed out as slaves. Their captivity would last five years. At first our imprisoned soldier found himself so depressed he could hardly move. But gradually he felt a sense of strength, of leadership, arising within him. He helped his men recover their spirit by organizing them and providing them with elaborate escape plans, all of which failed. By his example he persuaded his men not to abjure their Christian religion in return for fuller rations and better treatment. In the end the Bey of Algiers embarked the captives to take them to Constantinople, but at the last moment before sailing released them at half-price ransom to representatives of one of the religious orders of Spain. The five years' captivity was over.

When this Spanish soldier returned to the court of Spain, expecting with humility to be rewarded in some way for his services, he received nothing at all. Later he petitioned for a post in the Indies, perhaps the governorship in Guatemala. His petition came back with one line scrawled on it: "Let him look for something nearer home." So he returned to his writing, for he was of a literary turn of mind, and he eked out a living checking government grain commissaries. Twice he served time in jail, had trouble with both civic and ecclesiastical authorities, received no children from an unhappy marriage—in a word, for most of his life a failure.

At last he sat down to write a story that he thought would be entertaining enough to sell many copies. It was a story about an old gentleman whose mind was obsessed by tales of chivalry, romances that told of brave knights rescuing beautiful damsels from fearful giants and slaying dragons in the process. So the old gentleman rode forth from his home on an ancient hack he thought a handsome steed, attended by his "squire," an earthy peasant loyal to his deluded master. The two had all kinds of adventures, most of which saw the old gentleman knocked flat on his face, an object of ridicule as he tried to defeat what he thought were enemy armies, wicked magicians, or detractors of his noble liege lady at home (who was really just a kitchen wench). At the end the old gentleman, worn out by his chivalrous labors, prepares himself for death, confessing that his knightly visions were but *sombras* (illusions).

Of course you know the name of this soldier of Lepanto, Miguel de Cervantes, and his work, *Don Quixote*, more widely translated than any book in the world save the Bible. Chesterton closes his ballad with these words:

> Cervantes on his galley sets the sword back in the sheath.
> (*Don John of Austria rides homeward with a wreath.*)
> And he sees across a weary land a straggling road in Spain,
> Up which a lean and foolish knight forever rides in vain,
> And he smiles, but not as Sultans smile, and settles back the blade.
> (*But Don John of Austria rides home from the Crusade.*)

*

One last story. It brings us back to Plato, to his famous Myth of the Cave. We find this the story of a prisoner who frees himself, finding his way out of the darkness of illusion to the light of true knowledge. The story is in Plato's great dialogue *The Republic*. You remember that Plato never forgave the Athenian democracy, for it was under the democracy, and not the tyrannous oligarchy that preceded it, that Socrates was indicted, tried, condemned, and executed. Plato put to himself this question: If we say that democracy is undesirable because it means the rule of the average, the mediocre, the man in the street untutored in the art and science of government, can we propose a better alternative? In answer to the question Plato wrote *The Republic*, in which, using the metaphor of the ideal city-state, he endeavors to illumine, to throw light on human nature itself and on that nature's various parts, functions, ideals, hopes, triumphs. And it is in *The Republic* that the story of the cave is told.

But before telling the story, Plato diagrams the tale in a rather abstract way. He invites us to look at the Divided Line. It can be drawn this way:

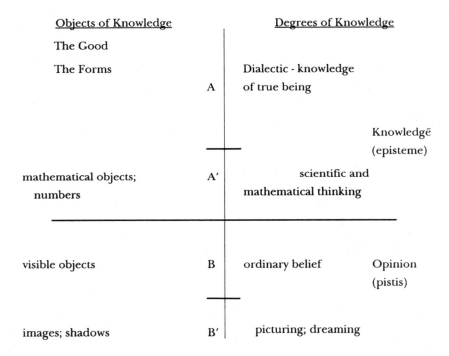

Objects of Knowledge		Degrees of Knowledge	
The Good			
The Forms	A	Dialectic - knowledge of true being	
			Knowledgē (episteme)
mathematical objects; numbers	A′	scientific and mathematical thinking	
visible objects	B	ordinary belief	Opinion (pistis)
images; shadows	B′	picturing; dreaming	

Consider the vertical line. Let's divide it into two unequal segments, A and B. Then, in the same proportion in which we divided the long line, divide A and B to make the segments A′ and B′. Now Plato suggests that this will represent the degrees of knowledge (or that which pretends to be knowledge). Above the long horizontal line lies the realm of true knowledge; below it is opinion or apparent knowledge, ordinary belief. Note the sub-divisions. Pictures and fables represent the lowest degree of (apparent) knowledge. We introduce children to the way of knowledge by giving them books of pictures and telling them fairy stories. These, with their undeveloped minds, they can understand. As we go up the line we deal with what grown-up people consider knowledge. Most of it is just opinion, ordinary belief, not true knowledge.

Take an example from our own time. It is common for social scientists to do "empirical" studies. They ask people what should be done about the war, what their feelings are about family planning, what they think of the president, et cetera. The investigator takes all the various answers and, correcting to allow for this and that, reaches some conclusions, and these are put into a book or paper.

Plato would have little use for this kind of exercise: collecting opinions is not knowledge; true knowledge begins when we start to leave off what can be observed by the senses. Physics has little use for ordinary sense perception, mathematics none at all. Mathematics is our model for true knowledge, says Plato, but it is only a model. You can take a concept and you can fit that concept into the total coherent structure we call a mathematical system—geometry, for example. And the aim of *dialectic*, the highest form of knowledge, is to take some kind of thing and put it into the structure of being, being itself.

At the very top of the line we have knowledge of the Forms, the originals of all things, after which everything visible and material is but a reflection, a shadowy copy. The Forms, the archetypes of things, are eternal and unchanging. In contrast to the objects of the world of sense perception, the Forms do not change, and they are not multiple, but unitary. They belong to the realm of being, not the realm of becoming, and they, including the very highest model, the Form of Good, are the really real. With knowledge of them, however fragmentary and imperfect our vision, we leave the world of sense perception, of ordinary opinion, of shadows and illusion far behind.

Now all that about the Divided Line is a rather abstract way of preparing us for the Myth of the Cave, to make it easier for us to understand, considering the limitations of even the most active human mind. Here then is the story of the cave. Imagine a deep, dark cave in which prisoners are bound sitting to a bench. They are bound in such a way that they can only look straight ahead at a blank wall facing them, on which dance flickering images. (Think of yourself strapped into a narrow seat on a commercial airliner watching a movie.) The images are caused by a fire kindled in back of the prisoners and close to a sort of runway, along which some men, slaves perhaps, are carrying various objects—figures of men and animals in wood or stone. The prisoners believe that the moving shadows they are watching are what is really real; they know nothing of the fire, and they are chained with their backs to the cave's opening.

Now suppose one of the prisoners is set free (or frees himself), stands upright, turns around, and is dazzled for a moment by the bright light of the fire. When his eyes become accustomed to the light, he sees that the images on the cave wall are not the real thing but shadows cast by the servants carrying objects across the runway.

Suppose further that this prisoner is hauled (or hauls himself) up the steep ascent to the mouth of the cave and out into the sunlight of the upper world. He is almost blinded at first, but when his vision adjusts itself he can see the beautiful world with its growing things, lighted and warmed by something in the sky far brighter than the stars (which he can only dimly make out), something which he takes, perhaps, to be the source of all growth, a light so bright that he cannot bear to look directly at it. He does not know it but this is the sun, the emblem of the Form of Good, perhaps another way of speaking of God himself.

So enthusiastic is our prisoner about all this beauty of the upper world, his first experience with reality itself, that it occurs to him that he has a duty: he must go back down into the cave. The old hermetists used to say, "For every upgoing there is a downgoing," or, in the words of Saint Bonaventure, "Let us die, therefore, and enter into darkness." So, reluctantly, the prisoner leaves this beautiful upper world and crawls back awkwardly into the gloom of the cavern, past the slaves still carrying the objects across the runway, past the fire that casts the shadows on the wall his fellow prisoners face. We can imagine him saying, "Come on, a little effort and you can get out of here! There's a bright fire over there and there are slaves, real men, carrying figures of men. It is shadows you see there on the wall. If you give yourself a little pain, you can see a wonderful world illumined by an incomparable radiance which causes growth and lights up and nourishes everything, the beautiful blue river, the green grass and trees."

But they don't believe him. They think he's crazy, his eyes damaged. Some argue that such a man is dangerous. As a later poet would say, they murmur, "Get him up and begone as one shaped awry—he disturbs the order here!" And Plato himself says, "If they could lay their hands on the man who was trying to set them free and lead them up, they would kill him."

Plato never forgot what the democracy did to his teacher. . . .

Now, to make an end of this, isn't it just possible that the man who had the dream of this course, and much more beyond that—lying in prison in Hanoi, in a little, narrow, four-by-ten prison cell in solitary, in leg-irons—is it not just barely possible that he today is putting his hand gently but urgently on our shoulders to shake us awake to an awareness of a clearer light, a brighter fire?

2

Job and the Problem of Evil

I form the light and create darkness. I make Peace and create
Evil. I the Lord do all these things.

Isaiah 45:7

So God cannot be the cause of all things, but only of good
things; of evil things he is not the cause.

Plato, *Republic*

Boethius asks Lady Philosophy why it is that the just suffer
evil while the wicked go unpunished, even prosper. Her
answer reflects a paradox of Socrates: "It is better to suffer evil
than to do it." Dame Philosophy tells Boethius that we can only
be truly happy if we possess the good, the ultimate source of
which is God. Those who do evil cannot really be happy because
they do not possess the good.

While this answer may not have satisfied Job, Boethius'
question is identical to that of the man from Uz. Job was a good
man who had many possessions. To test his faith God allowed
Satan to take away his possessions, his children, and his health.
Job is a faithful servant of God but a reasonable man as well. He
wants to know, "Why me? I am a just man; I have done no evil.
Why do the wicked prosper and the innocent suffer if God is
all-mighty and all-good?" That poignant cry we still hear today,
particularly from those who without fault have experienced or
witnessed unbearable suffering, irremediable loss.

In September 1983 a Korean airliner carrying hundreds of
passengers strayed into Soviet territory and was shot down,
killing all aboard. The day after, when I came home from the
Naval War College to Little Compton, I met an old religious man
who approached me and said, "You're an educated man. Tell

me, where was God when they shot down that plane and all those innocent people died?"

I could not answer, but remembered an accident in France about a year before. On the night of July 31, 1982, all of France was driving out on the roads bound for the August vacation. As the rain beat down hard in the darkness, five autos and two great buses smashed into one another on the main highway at Chalons-sur-Saone. Fifty-five people died in this terrible crash, including forty-four small children who were off to camp. In the early morning hours, on the still rainswept road, an elderly woman wandered up and down, distraught. She was the grandmother of four of the children who had been burned to death, and she asked over and over again, "Where was God during the night?"

The absence of God. . . . Job himself wonders about that. "Oh, that I might find Him. . . . Behold, I go forward, but He is not there; backward, but I cannot perceive Him. On the left hand, where He doth work, I cannot behold Him. He hideth Himself on the right hand, that I cannot see Him."

Come forward a thousand years or more. In the middle of the sixteenth century of our era there was a learned monk, Fray Luis de Leon, a noted teacher at the University of Salamanca in Spain. He had many brilliant students who testified to his wisdom, among them Saint John of the Cross. But he got into trouble with the Inquisition because he was writing a *commentario* on the Book of Job, and his research material included a number of books in Hebrew, including the Bible. Rumor had it that one of his grandparents was Jewish, though a *converso*, one who had converted to the Catholic faith. (You remember that in 1492, the year that Columbus landed in the New World, the laws of Ferdinand and Isabella ordered the Jews out of Spain. Some Jews converted only nominally to Christianity in order to stay in Spain and keep their families intact. The Spanish authorities worried about those *conversos* who did not really change their faith but secretly practiced their old religious rites.) Under suspicion of "Judaizing," Fray Luis was put in prison and remained there for five years. Apparently he was allowed reading and writing material, and his meditations on Job, like Stockdale centuries later remembering Epictetus, helped him to endure his long imprisonment. Finally Fray Luis was released.

Was Fray Luis Jewish? Was *Job* Jewish? Scholars tell us that it is unlikely that Job was a Jew. But Elie Wiesel says, "Read the book. If Job wasn't Jewish to begin with, he became Jewish as the book goes along!"

Elie Wiesel was one of many who have experienced "the absence of God." In 1944, when he was twelve years old, he and his family—father, mother, two sisters—were deported to Auschwitz from their native Transylvania. The boy and his father were sent to one of the satellite camps of Auschwitz, while the mother and sisters went directly to the gas chambers. Later the boy saw his father die, worn out by weakness and malnutrition. The boy remembers hearing the older Jews talking at night; he remembers them debating about the apparent absence of God in Auschwitz. In Wiesel's little book *Night*, he describes his own sense of the absence of God and tells us that in Auschwitz he lost his faith: God, creator of the universe, all-good and all-mighty, did not exist.

Years later, having survived Auschwitz, he wrote a play called *The Trial of God*. It was produced in the little town of San Minato in Italy, where every year a religious play of some kind is staged. (Pope John Paul II contributed a play of his own one year, a religious drama written when he was a seminarian.) Wiesel's play is based on a historical event, a seventeenth-century pogrom in which almost the entire Jewish population of the little town of Shamgorod was killed by the townspeople. One of the survivors is an innkeeper who has lost his family, and with them his belief in the goodness of God. To his inn there comes a troupe of strolling Jewish players who stage a Purim play, the subject suggested by the innkeeper himself: a trial of God. The innkeeper plays the part of the prosecutor, who presents the terrible evidence of the absence of God: the innocent who died at the hands of murderers. God is defended by a dubious local character named Sam, who, for all his disquieting strangeness, makes a brilliant defense, proving by apparently irrefutable arguments that there is a God who is both all-good and all-powerful. But as the last of the inn's candles is extinguished (in keeping with the feast of Purim), Sam, God's advocate, makes a signal to a mob waiting outside the door of the inn. The brilliant defender of God is none other than Satan himself, and the massacre, the pogrom, is now complete.

The idea of a trial of God is not Wiesel's invention. Jewish lore from the shtetls of Poland and western Russia tells us of earlier trials of God. In Leo Rosten's charming book *The Joys of Yiddish* he tells the story of a *zayda*, the "saint of Shpolle," a devout Jew in a little congregation who despairs because of the suffering of the poor innocent people in his village. So he summons nine Jewish men to make ten, a *minyan* (that makes it legal), and God is put on trial. For three days and three nights they consult the Torah, the law, and a number of learned commentaries. At the end they reach a verdict. God is found guilty on two counts of the indictment: he has let loose the spirit of evil in the world, and he has failed to provide for widows and orphans.

There are many of these traditional stories in Jewish lore that combine a sense of intimacy with God and the awe before the creator of the universe. God is petitioned in simple family language yet his very name is never used except on high holy days, and then only by the high priest. The sacred name is written by using only the consonants, never the vowels, because the vowels are passed on orally from high priest to high priest. To refer to the Almighty other names are used—Adonai, Shaddai, Elohim, Eli—but never the real name, the sacred name, which we pronounce Yahweh. There is a story in the tradition of a man who questions God as Job does, and God rebukes him: "One does not ask questions of the creator of the universe." To which the reply is humbly offered, "How can one be a Jew, O Lord, and not ask questions?"

Job is a questioner. He asks for an answer that will explain the reason for the infliction of suffering upon him, a just man who serves God. Why has he lost his possessions, his cattle, his family, his health, when he is innocent of sin? If God can give him some sort of reason for this, maybe he can put up with it. But God offers only a *retorquendo*: in effect, "You complain of my absence. But where were *you* when I created the splendid war-horse, the great Leviathan, the starry universe itself?"

The German philosopher Nietzsche says, "He who has a *why* to live by can put up with almost any *how*." In Arthur Koestler's novel *Darkness at Noon*, based on the great Stalinist purge of the late 1930s, we find the sophisticated old Bolshevik Rubashov awaiting execution. He is walking up and down in his cell in the Lubyanka, knowing that he is soon to die, and he is thinking about suffering—the suffering which makes sense, and the suffering which is senseless. It is the senselessness of so much suffering that bothers him. And that is what puzzles Job, that is the cause of his lamentations: the absence of a reason *why*.

Zophar, one of Job's friends who comes to give him cold comfort as Job sits on his ash-heap scraping his flesh with potsherds, will have it that Job has no right to question God about reasons: "Canst thou by searching find out God?" This is but one manner of saying that God's ways are not our ways. In theology this answer is put forth by Søren Kierkegaard, who says that the difficulty lies in the *incommensurability* between the Infinite (God) and the finite (that which God has created). We must not apply to God a yardstick, even an elongated one, made out of human ethical standards. The ways of God may be inconsistent with human ethics. Sometimes they seem unrelated to human moral standards, and sometimes they may seem positively anti-ethical, as in the story of Job. (Kierkegaard makes much of God's command to Abraham to sacrifice his son Isaac, which Abraham, heavy of heart, prepares to do until God stays his hand.)

In prison and after, Jim Stockdale's attitude toward the vicissitudes of life, an attitude derived in part from his reading of the Stoic Epictetus and in larger part from his reflections on his own life, quickly reached an answer to the eternal question "Why me?" Anticipating his classmate Jimmy Carter's "Life is not fair," Stockdale replied, "Why not me?"

*

To take a closer look at the so-called problem of evil, we must first identify the assumptions that philosophers, theologians, and ordinary folk make when they set out to deal with the question. If we take the problem of evil as it appears in the context of traditional religious belief, we find that there are certain assumptions that don't always fit easily together:

First, there is a God, in some sense the creator of the world, the foundation of all reality.

Second, God is both all-good and all-powerful, and of infinite perfection.

Third, there is evil in the world—physical evil (like floods, earthquakes, volcanic eruptions, disease, even death itself) and moral evil (the bad things humans do to each other).

Fourth, there are innocent people, children and adults, who suffer evil in one or many of its various forms.

Now, if you move within one of the Western religious traditions (*Western* may be a misleading term since Judaism, Christianity, and Islam have their roots in the simple pastoral lands of the Middle East), you find that you must deal with certain real or apparent contradictions if you hold all four of these theses simultaneously true.

The third proposition—that there is evil in the world and it is real—was denied by the ancient Stoic philosophers and a few moderns (including two or three right-wing Hegelians who interpreted the German master's "Whatever is, is right" to mean that what *seems* to be evil really isn't, that we lack the comprehensive overall view of the Absolute).

How about those who deny the first proposition, the existence of God? Is there a problem of evil for them? The answer is yes. The French philosopher Jean-Paul Sartre and his sometime friend and associate Albert Camus recognized the ineluctable nature of evil but denied the existence of a reality that transcends this world. For them God did not exist, but both men agreed with Dostoyevsky that whoever denies the existence of God must face some embarrassing questions. Sartre and Camus faced them, though their answers to these questions may not satisfy us. But that is a matter for later discussion.

Now, let us at least for the sake of argument assume the truth of the four propositions we associate with our traditional religious beliefs: that there is evil in the world, moral and physical, and it is real; that there is a God whose being transcends this world (though this should not be taken to deny his immanence or indwelling in the cosmos); that God is all-mighty and all-good; and that there are innocent people who suffer through no fault of their own. Statement of the problem? One phrasing of it is classical: Either God *could* do something to abolish or at least mitigate the evil in the world, or God *cannot*. Now if God *could* do something about evil but chooses not to, he is not all-good; and if he *cannot* do anything about it, he is not all-powerful. Therefore, he is either not all-good or not all-powerful. But traditional religious teaching holds that God is both. How can the dilemma be resolved? Let us look at some of the attempts made in the past to deal with it.

*

The poets and playwrights of ancient Greece were fascinated by undeserved misfortune. Terrible things happen to a man like Oedipus, who had no intention of doing wrong yet found that he had unwittingly murdered his father and married his mother. These poets and tragedians believed that there is something in the cosmos above the gods, and that something is what they called Necessity (*Anagkē*), which is woven into the very fabric of what is real. It is a crimp in the nature of things to which even the gods are subject.

There was a strong tendency in Greek philosophy to believe that *matter* lies at the root of all irrationality, all disorder in the world. In the case of ourselves, the body is the representative of matter, while soul, spirit, or mind belongs to a higher order, its clarity of vision impeded by the physical aspect of our nature, particularly by the downward drag of the passions. This doctrine is presented in an extreme form in Plato's *Phaedo*, in which matter, like the poets' "Necessity," exists outside of God, and the Divine Power itself is unable to fully overcome the limitations of matter. For this reason the Divine cannot be held to be all-mighty; its power is limited by the independent and negative effect of matter.

This dualism of matter and creative spirit is set forth in the form of a beautiful creation myth in Plato's dialogue *Timaeus*, named for a Pythagorean cosmologist whose ideas interested Plato in his later life. For nearly ten centuries the *Timaeus*, in the form of commentaries upon it, stood as a standard cosmological work for the Christian Middle Ages. The *Timaeus* asks us to accept that God, who is one, resembles a supremely skillful artist or sculptor, all-good but not all-powerful, since he must work with what lies to his hand, which, roughly speaking, is matter (or, more specifically, a matrix that Plato calls the Receptacle, aspects of which are matter, space, and motion).

Now the Divine Sculptor draws form out of this matrix insofar as he is able. The beauty and order of the visible world we owe to the goodness and skill of the Divine Artificer, whom Plato names the Demiurge, and to the beauty of the Forms, unchanging and deathless, upon which the Artist looks as a fair and lovely model. But insofar as the world is faulty, cracked, full of disorder, this comes from the imperfect material with which the Divine Author must work. It is as if a handsome statue is acknowledged to owe its perfection of form to the skill of the sculptor and the beauty of the model upon which he gazes as he does his creative work. This concept of the Demiurge as the creator of the world was destined to have a profound and rather unhealthy effect on early Christian theology. Destructive heresies sprang from it.

*

In the first centuries of the Christian era, there were times when orthodox Christianity nearly choked to death on the problem of evil because of certain Christian sects which believed themselves to be purifiers of doctrine. Some Christian philosophers and theologians held that the teachings of the early church were too simple and unsophisticated, that in their naiveté they failed to make use of the wisdom of the Greek philosophers. Greek philosophy was a help to early Christian teachers, but it could turn out, if pushed to the extreme, to lead the church into heresy.

Consider the Gnostics, a Christian sect who believed that they had the true insight, knowledge, *gnosis*, where Christian doctrine, teaching, and practice were concerned. Their message contained a powerful element: dualism, twoness, a theological ingredient that was to have a long and perilous career right down through the close of the High Middle Ages. The Gnostics held that "the few" had the *gnosis*, true knowledge, while "the many" had only opinion. So you have the Christian congregation divided in two—those who know and those who simply hear, the *electi* and the *auditores*. This intellectually fashionable dualism extended to the books of sacred revelation. The New Testament was accepted nearly at face value. God is the loving Jesus of the New Testament. But the God of the Old Testament, Jehovah, is none other than Plato's Demiurge, the world-creator who fashioned matter into imperfect form. The Old Testament itself should be regarded by true believers with great caution, if not put aside altogether. The evils in the world, the suffering of the innocent, should not be blamed on the Jesus-God of the New Testament; they should be attributed to the work of the Demiurge, the Jehovah-God.

To the Gnostics and their allies who shared their dualist perspective, the human body became something irretrievably bad and was linked, Greek-fashion, to matter. We mortals are unstable compounds of light-seeking spirit and of matter, which obscures the clear luminosity of vision.

Of late in the scholarly world there has been a revival of interest in the Gnostics, particularly in light of the feminist and pacifist elements in their teaching and practice. In the Gnostic churches it appears that women could exercise some form of the priestly office (though that office was not fully developed at the time). It is probable that the Gnostic Christians taught that no true Christian should serve in the military because the military kills. But this was not a doctrine peculiar to the Gnostics. Some of the greatest fathers of the early church—Tertullian, Origen, Lactantius, for example—taught that when Christ struck the sword from the apostle Peter's hand at Gethsemane, he disarmed all Christians. But not all of the early fathers held this, for did not Jesus say, "Render to Caesar the things that are

Caesar's"? In any case, the question of Christians serving in the military in the second and third centuries was in a way an academic question, since Christians were not subject to the Roman military draft. Christians were considered by the Romans to be a peculiar Jewish sect, and Jews were exempt from the draft into the Roman armed forces.

But when the Emperor Constantine became a Christian and urged his followers to do the same, the question of Christians serving in the military took on a new light, for now Christians were forced to take responsibility not only for spiritual good but for the secular order as well. Constantine died in 337 A.D., and only seventeen years later Augustine was born. It was he who first laid down the conditions of a just war. The conditions were strict: "War should be waged only as a necessity, and carried out only that God may by this just war deliver men from necessity and preserve them in peace."

Another powerful dualist tradition came out of the East and in one form or another threatened orthodox Christianity for a thousand years. It had a dualist solution to the problem of evil. The medievals called this dualist heresy Manichaeism after Mani, a Christianized Persian teacher. His teaching had its origin in ancient Iran, where the prophet Zoroaster (or Zarathustra) preached that there were two Gods—Ormuzd or Ahura Mazda, the God of Light, and Ahriman, the God of Darkness. From the first of these coequal deities comes all good, and from the second, evil. The symbol of the God of Light was fire (hence the erroneous belief of orthodox Christians that the Zoroastrians were fire-worshippers). There is a tradition that the three wise men who came to Bethlehem to see the infant Jesus were Zoroastrians from Persia, and had made the long trip from the Iranian plateau. Zoroastrianism survives today in the Parsee sect of India. Zubin Mehta, director emeritus of the New York Philharmonic orchestra, is a Parsee; and it was his custom, before conducting a performance of Richard Strauss' tone poem *Also Sprach Zarathustra* (Thus Spake Zarathustra), to tell his audience that his personal religion was founded by Nietzsche's favorite seer of ancient times.

Now Mani taught a dualism akin to Zoroastrianism, but containing certain Christian elements. The dualist current set by Mani and the Gnostics flowed on down through the early Christian era as far as the late Middle Ages, causing at least three crises in which it was touch and go whether Christianity in the form we know it today would survive the break over the problem of evil. Through the centuries these dualisms moved slowly but inexorably from East to West. There were the Paulicians in Armenia, the Bogomils in Bulgaria, the Patarenes in Bosnia, and the Cathars in northern Italy and southern France. These last, the Cathars (the "pure ones"), were the greatest and most attractive of all the medieval dualists, the richest in tradition and in poetry, song, and art, as well as graciously lived lives. They listened to troubadours as well as to saintly preachers of their dualist Christianity.

The medieval Manichees were ruthlessly persecuted and were accused of all sorts of abominations. The vulgar word *bugger* comes from the medieval French word *bougre*, which in turn derives from Bulgaria, where the Bogomils, a dualist sect, were alleged to have engaged in sodomy to avoid cooperation with the Demiurge in the work of generation, to avoid committing themselves to the world of matter instead of the pure world of the spirit.

In the thirteenth century, the age of Thomas Aquinas, the northern knights and the Burgundian dukes, hungering after the riches of southern France, were struck by an attack of holy orthodoxy and begged Pope Innocent III to bless a crusade against the Cathars. Were they not wicked heretics, holding fast to the belief that Christ never had a human body, that that which hung up there on Calvary was but a phantom, an illusion, thus denying the human nature of Jesus as an insult to his divinity? Did not these rich princesses and lute-playing lordlings refuse to say the Lord's Prayer, hold the cross in horror, and engage in sexual practices not to be thought of? At last the pope, troubled by the aggressive movements of the king of France, reluctantly gave his consent, and bands of knights under the leadership of Simon de Montfort invaded the south, burning, raping, pillaging. Finally the last two hundred of "the pure" took refuge in the castle of Montsegur, carrying their sacred texts with them. They administered the Catharist sacrament, the *consolamentum*, to each other, and then surrendered to be laid down in a field of brush and burned to death. Their tragedy, says the historian Steven Runciman, was the tragedy of the dualist tradition: "Confident of the truth of their cause, but in no expectation of their own salvation, its children went uncomplaining to the stake, and their hopeless faith was burnt with them." But their ashes did not smother the enduring question: Why, if God is good, does he permit the suffering of the innocent?

*

What did the orthodox, those who believed that God is infinite, all-mighty, all-good, have to say in answer? Early and very influential pronouncements on this question came from Saint Augustine, who died in 430 A.D. as the Vandals were hammering at the gates of the North African city of Hippo, seat of his bishopric. Augustine had been a Manichaean for a while, though never one of the inner circle of the sect. Leaving his teacher, Faustus, he took up Neo-Platonism and studied the metaphysics of Plotinus of Alexandria. Plotinus taught that all reality is one, and that is God, who *is* the One. Creative energy radiates from God, becoming in successive stages mind (*logos*), the soul of the world, individual souls, and finally at the end of this process of divine emanation matter sets in, as a kind of congealing of the divine energy. Plotinus used this kind of analogy in his teaching: Suppose you are standing at night by a bright, warm fire reading a book. As you move away from the fire the light lessens and the air cools. When you have reached a certain distance, far away from the fire, it is cold and dark; you can no longer read your book. Now, do you blame the darkness and the cold on the fire? No. It is the *distance* from the fire that accounts for the cold and the dark; it is not the fault of the fire. So matter, the last stage of emanation, is the source of all the imperfections in the world, including what we call moral and physical evil. The disorder in the nature of things is the result of

the metaphysical distance of the visible world from the source
of the divine energy.

Dissatisfied with the Neo-Platonists' sophisticated variations
on the theme of matter as the original cause of evil, Augustine
was converted to Christianity, baptized by Ambrose, bishop of
Milan, and became the most gifted and influential of the church
fathers. Still fascinated by the apparent incongruity between
God's power and goodness on the one hand and the presence
of evil in the world, including the sufferings of the innocent,
Augustine set down some answers to the problem.

First of all, said Augustine, evil is not a positive thing, but
rather an *absence* of an order which should be there. Take
blindness, for example—a physical evil, and a serious one. Blindness is the lack of an order of vision which under normal
circumstances would be there. We can discern the same situation in moral evil, the bad things people do to each other. Moral
evil, sin itself, is an absence of that order we know as the moral
good. So we cannot say that evil has its origin in a defect of God's
goodness or power, because God is being itself, while evil is
nonbeing. You can see here the reflection of Augustine's learning from the Neo-Platonists: God is being itself; evil is not light
and warmth but a result of cold and dark, the distance from the
divine source; evil is not being, but nonbeing.

Augustine inclined as well to an argument associated with his
predecessor and fellow African convert, Lactantius. What we call
evil is the result of our *finitude*. We are creatures, finite and
limited; both physical and moral evil are entailed by our finitude,
our creatureliness. As Lactantius said, "He who would have
himself perfectly without harm wants to be not a created being,
but a god." Although we have a spiritual part, we must not forget
that we are natural beings, not spirits, not angels; hence we are
subject to the limitations of nature, the realm of the created
order of being.

Nor should we forget, said Augustine, that evil often serves
the good; in some cases we see how this is so, in others our
limitations prevent us from perceiving it. In his *Confessions* (the
first great autobiography of the West), Augustine says that
having to renounce the woman he loved, though terribly painful,

nonetheless served the ultimate good, his own salvation. Even at the very highest level we can see how evil may serve the good. His famous cry "O felix culpa!" ("Oh happy fault!") refers to the primordial offense of Adam, who stands as the representative of all humankind. Because, says Augustine, had it not been for the Fall there would have been no redemption, no Incarnation; Christ would not have come to take upon his shoulders the burden of human guilt, offering himself as a victim to atone for it.

*

We ourselves know from our ordinary experience that illness, failure, disappointments, deprivations, losses, real enough as they were, causing depression, even tears, sometimes did enable us to choose or experience a higher good. Think of the sickness that interrupted our career, the appointment denied, the college admission rejected, the manuscript returned, the longed-for tour canceled, the lovely girl we let slip through our hands. To how many of these do we now say, "I'm glad it happened that way. Had I been successful in securing that desired object back then, I would have missed that later better opportunity. Had I not been ill and missed out on that which I wanted so badly, I would not now enjoy this much superior good." (Even though we may still feel a pang when we think of the lovely girl we let slip away.)

The trouble with this kind of argument—the claim that evil serves the good—lies in the fact that it will do for some but not for all situations. Suffering purifies, says Solzhenitsyn, and the sports physician Dr. George Sheehan says that fellow-suffering is the ultimate human communication. True, perhaps, but cold comfort to the mother who has lost her child devoured by hopeless disease and agonizing death. One day on my way to the Naval War College, a little boy getting off the school bus dropped his lunch box and it slid under the vehicle. Reaching for it, he was crushed to death under the wheels of the bus as it moved on. Strange how the mortal sufferings of a single innocent can move us more than the news that twenty-five thousand died in a volcanic mud-slide in Colombia, or a hundred thousand in a fatal flood in Bangladesh. One or many, the innocent suffer, and Job, on his ash-heap, still asks, "Why?"

To that question we can imagine a humble father of the ancient church raising his hands in a gesture that is at the same time one of despair and hope. The only answer he can give is to urge us to return to the simple faith of a child, to believe that a key to the enigma exists, that each tear counts, each drop of blood.

Imagine then the old Jews, when one of their number was led out to the place of execution, gathering round in prayerful attention. And as the last breath of life was choked out of the hanged man, they shouted the last thing the dying man heard, the great public prayer of the Jews: "Schma Isroel! Adonoi eluhenu. Adonoi echod!" ("Hear, O Israel! The Lord thy God is one God!").

The holy men of ancient India were convinced that the only possible answer to the sufferings of the innocent must lie in reincarnation—that each of us has had a life before our present one, that each will have a life to follow, and that the deeds one does in a previous existence bear upon one's lot in this life. Even, they said, the good deeds we do in this life may help us too in the hour of need. Thus Bahtrahari:

> In the forest, in battle, amid javelins, arrows, fire; out on the great sea, on the precipice edge of the mountains; in sleep, in fever, in delirium, in deep trouble, the good deeds a man has done before defend him.

To extirpate suffering, taught Siddartha Gautama, later known as the Buddha, the Enlightened One, we must rid ourselves of the conviction ingrained in all of us that the *self* is the most important thing in the world, like a citadel around which the whole of reality revolves. We are told that when Prince Siddhartha was very young, he was led for the first time out of the great park, the estate of his rich father. His tutor accompanied him, for it was time that the boy learned the sacred truth about our existence. The tutor stopped the boy three times on their walk. First they paused meeting an old man, gaunt, toothless, trembling upon his stick. The boy had never seen an old man in that state, and he pulled back in distaste. But his tutor held up his hand, saying, "Tat twam asi" ("This thou art"). Next they stopped at a sick man, whose leprous sores oozed pus. Again the boy pulled back and again his tutor shook his head, saying, "Tat twam asi" ("This thou art"). The third time they stopped at the rotting corpse of a dead man. Again the boy recoiled, but again his tutor forced him to look, saying "Tat twam asi" ("This thou art").

In this way the boy who was to become the Enlightened One, the Buddha, began to learn that all "selves" are interconnected parts of that one great whole, being itself, which alone is real. He began to understand that the belief in our own self, separate from all others, is *maya* (illusion). To extract the arrow of suffering, one must first cleanse oneself of the error of believing in the reality of the separate, sovereign self.

Our own Yankee poet Walt Whitman took note of these old religious traditions of India. In many wonderful poems, like "Song of Myself," he celebrates the imperial glory of the self, himself, Walt Whitman. But at the same time, through the mediating idea of democracy plus a little Indian metaphysics, he insists on the interconnectedness of all souls, all selves. In "Crossing Brooklyn Ferry" he says to the passengers, "I've been here two hundred years before now, and I'll be here two hundred years from now, so you'll recognize me, won't you?"

> I am with you, you men and women of a generation, or ever
> so many generations hence,
>
> Just as you feel when you look on the river and sky, so I felt,
>
> Just as any of you is one of a living crowd, I was one of a
> crowd,
>
> Just as you are refresh'd by the gladness of the river and the
> bright flow, I was refresh'd,
>
> Just as you stand and lean on the rail, yet hurry with the swift
> current, I stood yet was hurried,
>
> Just as you look on the numberless masts of ships . . .
> I looked.

In "Song of Myself" he takes us on a tour of the suffering-places of the world—the hospital, where people are sick and dying, the torture chambers, the crowded and rudderless wreck of a sinking ship—and he says,

> Whoever degrades another degrades me.

And, pointing to the man led out to the place of execution amid howls of execration from the mob,

> I am the man. I suffered. I was there.

3

Love: From Eros to Agapē

Love is neither mortal nor immortal, but a mean between the two. . . . It is a great spirit mediating between the divine and the mortal.

Plato, *Symposium*

Love seeketh not her own. . . . Though I give all my goods to feed the poor . . . and have not love, it profiteth me nothing.

Paul, 1 Corinthians 13

In our first discussion we met great men in prison under duress, and in the second a just man sitting on his ash-heap scraping his flesh with potsherds and asking, "Why me?" We could continue to develop the same dark themes by considering those dialogues of Plato that describe the indictment of Socrates, his trial, his defense, his subsequent imprisonment before execution, and the last hours of his life. But wouldn't it be better to cheer ourselves up by looking at another dialogue of Plato that is just sheer fun? This dialogue tells the story of a banquet which features Socrates as the star speaker on the theme of eros. It is Plato's *Symposium*.

You in the military profession should be particularly interested in the topic of eros (love) for at least two reasons. First, according to ancient Greek cosmogony—we have it from the poet Hesiod—the first in order of creation was chaos, then broad-bosomed earth, and then eros, or love. Second, we know that the archetype of all wars is that between the Greeks (Achaeans) and the Trojans, and it was started by eros, the love for a beautiful woman that struck a man so violently that he had her kidnapped. The lady was Helen of Troy, and the conflict generated by her is celebrated by Homer in his great epic, the *Iliad*. That long chronicle of war includes another intervention of eros. The Greeks were ready to withdraw because their best fighter, Achilles, was sulking in his tent (King Agammenon, leader of the Achaean expedition, having taken Achilles' beautiful slave-girl, Briseis, for himself). Only when his best friend and comrade is killed by the Trojans does Achilles get over his sulk, and the result is victory for the Achaeans and terrible defeat for the Trojans, their best warrior slain by Achilles and dragged around the fallen city in the dust.

In Love and War is the title of Sybil and Jim Stockdale's book about their Vietnam experience—Sybil at home fighting for her man and his POW comrades, Jim sitting in solitary in leg irons awaiting the next day's interrogation as a "war criminal." A year or two after his return from Vietnam, Stockdale spent an afternoon with J. Glenn Gray, professor of philosophy at Colorado College, where all four of the Stockdale sons did their undergraduate work. Gray wrote a book called *The Warriors*, which was first published in 1959 and later brought out with an introduction by Hannah Arendt, who shared with Gray an interest in the German philosopher Martin Heidegger. *The Warriors* tells of Gray's reflections on his experience in the Second World War in Europe, where he served first as an enlisted man interrogating German prisoners and then as a lieutenant commissioned in the field. In his book Gray reminds the reader that ancient Greek poets and philosophers held that the love of the sexes is just one manifestation of the working of a cosmic force called *eros*.

Empedocles, a philosopher-physicist who lived before Socrates, taught that there are four basic kinds of material substances (familiar to us as earth, air, fire, and water), and that the universe constantly undergoes a cyclic transformation, the first stage of which is the combining of these elements by the cosmic force of eros. In this first stage the universe is in complete order and harmony. In the second stage of the cycle, strife (*neikos*) enters, with eros' presence diminishing. In the third stage strife is supreme, while the fourth sees eros coming back in, partial harmony restored, and order once more revived.

In *The Warriors* Gray recalls Empedocles' doctrine and notes how well some of the categories and distinctions fit what he observed in his own wartime experience. He mentions that eros is just one kind of *philia*, the generic term the Greeks used for any kind of fondness or liking. (We see it as the root of *philosophy*, the love of wisdom.) *Philia* would include love of comrades, friendship, love of family. Gray's observations of men at war convinced him that Empedocles made a good point when he cited the love of the sexes as one showing of the great pulse of eros that drives through the world. Gray noted that war heightens the erotic in every degree. He observed the coarseness, the brutality, the loveless search for quick satisfaction in the brothels sought out by soldiers. He also marked the kind of man who, though selfish in his pursuit of pleasure, has some sophistication, some refinement, and heightens his own pleasure by providing for that of his partner as well. Higher still, he finds that kind of love which begins with the physical attraction of the sexes but contains much more than that, even an element of the spiritual. He sees the enormous power of eros in the way that it leaps over national boundaries, over the conflicts of warring powers. His own book *The Warriors* he dedicates to Ursula, his wife, "formerly one of the enemy" (for Gray married a German girl whom he met as the Allied armies moved with massive force into her shattered country).

In *The Warriors* Gray tells how he was struck by the power of *comradeship*, noting the fierce ties that bind men together in combat. In the pressure cooker of combat, under conditions of shared mortal danger, "we become drunk with the power that union with our fellows brings":

> In moments like these many have a vague awareness of how isolated and separate their lives have hitherto been, and how much they have missed by living in the narrow circle of family or a few friends. With the boundaries of the self expanded, they sense a kinship never known before. Their "I" passes insensibly into the "we," "my" becomes "our," and the individual fate loses its central significance.

Gray distinguishes between comradeship and friendship—friendship in the highest sense, that which Aristotle calls true friendship, making the point that he who has many friends has no friends. True friendships are rare. The difference between true friendship and comradeship, says Gray, is that comradeship requires a "we," while in the highest kind of friendship the sense of "I" is retained by both parties. The same distinction had already been made by a different voice, that of Simone Weil, a teacher of philosophy who, in her own strange way, died of heartbreak for her country, France, and for justice: "In a perfect friendship, the two friends have consented to become two, not one."

There is a kind of love that grows out of comradeship. When he talks of his prison experience, Stockdale will often speak of the POWs in solitary confinement tapping on the cell wall to the man who has just been beaten up, put in the ropes, and thrown back into his cell; and the tap from his comrades would be, "I LOVE YOU PETE." A film, *84 Charlie Mopic* (1989), written and directed by Patrick Duncan, looks at men in combat in Vietnam through the lenses of a combat film photographer. These men not only consider themselves brothers but often, and without embarrassment, use the word *love* with regard to their fierce loyalty to one another.

*

It is interesting that two great moral teachers of the West, Jesus and Socrates (Plato's Socrates, at least), both teach a doctrine of love. With the philosopher it is eros, and the method of teaching is reason—until that moment in *Symposium* when reason, as we shall see, is overtaken by vision. In the case of Jesus it is *agapē*, the Greek word used by the chroniclers of his teaching. As for method, we are told that Jesus taught by the way of faith.

How do we know about Jesus and Socrates? Did they write anything? Were they perhaps illiterate? Does the New Testament mention Jesus writing at any time? There is one instance in which he is described as writing something. It is in the Gospel of Saint John, where we read that some men are preparing to stone a woman to death. Jesus asks what wrong she has done and is told that she has committed adultery, for which, they say, the penalty is death, according to the law of Moses. They ask Jesus if he has anything to say about it. Acting as if he did not hear them, he stoops down and writes with his finger on the ground. What he wrote we do not know. They continue to press him until he suggests that "he who is without sin among you, let him first cast a stone at her." Then he writes on the ground once again, and again we do not know what he wrote. Shamed, the would-be executioners slink away one by one, leaving Jesus alone with the woman. He asks her if there is anyone left to condemn her, and she answers, "None." His reply: "Neither do I condemn thee: go and sin no more."

Could Socrates write? He speaks disparagingly of teaching by writing rather than by talking to students. In the dialogue *Phaedrus*, he says that you can ask a teacher a question and receive a reply, but you cannot ask a book a question and get a response. There is only one mention of him writing, and that is in the dialogue *Meno*. Here Socrates is trying to prove a favorite thesis, that we have knowledge ingrained within us: we come into the world with it, and it is the job of a teacher to bring out this knowledge by asking the right sort of questions. "I'll show you," he says, and calls over a boy servant, asking him if he knows any geometry. "No, not a bit," says the boy. So Socrates says, "Watch me," and with a little stick he draws in the dust. What he draws is a geometrical figure in the form of a triangle and, in stage after stage, by asking the boy "the right sort of questions," he gets the boy in the end to "demonstrate" a rather complicated geometrical theorem involving one or more of the Pythagorean properties. (At the time he wrote *Meno*, Plato was up to his ears in mathematics.) So, if this figure-drawing counts for writing, Socrates could write.

If neither Jesus nor Socrates left us any writing of their own, how do we know of them? In the case of Jesus we have the four Gospels, the Acts of the Apostles, and the letters of Paul. They are all in Greek, so they could not have been written by Jesus' immediate disciples, who are described as relatively unlettered men who would not have known Greek (though Judea at that time was subject to a strong Hellenistic influence). We have no writing of anyone who knew Jesus and was present as he taught.

Scholars say that the Gospels and Paul's letters were collected in stages directly or indirectly by others and copied down by them, the earliest in 50 A.D.

It is different with Socrates, for we have three sources written by people who actually knew the philosopher. Plato is by far the richest source of what we know about Socrates, though we must always remember that Plato often writes of what Socrates would most likely have said, and in the later dialogues it is clear that Plato is putting his metaphysical theories into the mouth of his beloved teacher. Plato was with Socrates when he (Plato) was a young man and Socrates was in the last years of his life. Plato was of the social class that Socrates seemed to attract and preferred to teach—the young blue-blooded elite of the city-state of Athens.

Xenophon, another of Socrates' students, wrote a book of reminiscences of the philosopher known as *Memorabilia*. It is just one small volume compared to the shelfful that Plato left us, and without any of the creative imagination of grand scope possessed by Plato. Xenophon's talents lay in the military direction. He became a general, enlisted ten thousand Greek mercenaries to serve a Persian king, and found himself dangerously stranded when the king died. By a brilliant exercise of generalship he managed to get the ten thousand safely out of Anatolia and back to Greece, virtually without losses. Xenophon wrote it up afterwards in *Anabasis*, which students of my generation were required to translate in their elementary Greek class.

Mention of Xenophon's generalship suggests a useful book that might be written. I could not write it, but you could. I might offer the title—*Masters of Retreat*—with a suggestion that the first chapter tell the story of Xenophon and the ten thousand's cry, "Thalata! Thalata!" ("The sea! The sea!"), as they caught sight of the Euxine (Black) Sea that would bear them back to Greece. You might like to include a chapter on General Washington, of his retreat from Long Island across the water to Manhattan, then to the north of the island, then crossing the Hudson to New Jersey—all in the face of superior British forces, and at all times keeping his own in being. You might want to include a chapter on German Field Marshal Erich von Manstein's masterly retreat from the Sevastopol area, leading his army group intact and out of danger, thus avoiding the disaster that befell Paulus at Stalingrad. Anticipating the possible encirclement of the French forces at Dienbienphu, General de Castries had ready an operational plan to pull out those forces unharmed. The plan was named Xenophon, but the Viet Minh came down on the besieged French too fast to allow the plan to be put into operation.

The third source of information about Socrates comes from a man present at the banquet described by Plato in *Symposium*—the comic playwright Aristophanes. His play *The Clouds* represents Socrates as a mad scientist who runs a school which promises to teach any man, whether by the old logic or the new logic, all he needs to know to get on, including how to cheat on his tax returns. In the play, a father and his ne'er-do-well son visit this "Thinkery," for the father is looking for someone to teach his son to mend his ways. The Thinkery is a riot. Socrates sits high up in a basket hoisted aloft by a windlass so that he reaches Cloud Cuckoo-land, where he may study the heavens.

This mad comedy, coarse in language and jokes, might just be a take-off on Socrates' earlier studies, when he may have been somewhat involved with the philosopher-scientists of the Greek Enlightenment, their aim being the study of physical nature to identify natural rather than supernatural causes of things and events. In *Phaedo* Socrates does mention a time when he began to read a book by Anaxagoras, one of the physics-minded philosophers who aimed to account for things in material rather than other-worldly terms. Socrates tells us that he became disillusioned with such explanations. The cause of his quarrel with those who indicted him for impiety and corrupting the youth was moral, not physical: "It was not my old bones, sinews, muscles that brought me to this prison, but rather my accepting the Athenians' right to condemn me according to law." Socrates makes clear that he is not a cosmologist searching for mechanical causes; he is a moral philosopher, whose job is to examine his life and to get those who will listen to him to examine theirs.

Socrates' method was dialectical. You take an idea you are inquiring into—say, the meaning of knowledge, or of justice, or of respect for religious belief—and then you ask someone to tell you what he thinks knowledge or justice or impiety really is. To that end we need a satisfactory definition of that into which we are inquiring; this will help, because the function of a definition is to set out clearly what a thing is. If Socrates asks one of his students for a definition of knowledge, the fellow may answer, "I believe, Socrates, that knowledge is sense perception." Socrates will then try to show him that defending this definition will lead him into contradictions. Starting out by holding "P," the student will soon find himself, under Socrates' relentless questioning, defending "Not-P." The result: one must start back at square one and begin the search for a satisfactory definition all over again.

Socrates' dialectical method could be taken as a form of badgering, and this may have been one of the causes of the irritation of the leaders of the Athenian democracy that led to their indictment of the philosopher. True, there were political reasons why Socrates was under suspicion: though he himself had no connection with the tyrannical oligarchy that the democracy had overthrown, he did have some students whose relations supported the infamous Thirty; perhaps there was fear that Socrates might be used as a symbol by the surviving forces of reaction. In any case, the Athenian leaders did not like to be made to look like fools by Socrates' incisive questioning (we are given a sample of this in *Apology*, Socrates' defense at his trial).

Michael Levin has written a novel called *The Socratic Method* (1987), a thinly disguised account of the author's experiences as a student at Columbia University's law school. The dialectical method of questioning, resembling Socrates' method of inquiry, leads at least one of the professors to intellectual bullying and outright browbeating of his law students. Admiral Stockdale tells of his experience at a seminar on philosophy set up for business executives and other professional people at Aspen, Colorado. The seminar was under the leadership of philosopher Mortimer Adler, who had his own version of the Socratic method. Said Stockdale afterwards, "He ran that seminar like a correctional institution."

Jesus' method of teaching was quite different from that of the Athenian philosopher—a method some scholars call *gnomic*, common in Eastern countries, where the master teaches by using

stories and parables. Jesus speaks of the need to love one's
neighbor as oneself. When asked, "Who is my neighbor?" he
does not enter upon various definitions of the term *neighbor* but
tells a story: "A certain man went down from Jericho and fell
among thieves. . . ." The gnomic method survives, indeed,
flourishes in the Talmud and in the wealth of commentaries
written upon it. To teach by telling stories aids understanding,
said Jesus: "Therefore I speak to them in parables: because they
seeing, see not; and hearing, they hear not; neither do they
understand."

As for the social status of the two great teachers, Jesus was
poor, a carpenter's son, and came from a family not well known
(though later chroniclers of his life supplied him with a genealogy that claimed descent from the house of David). Apparently
Socrates too was poor, his mother a midwife he says, yet his
ancestry was respectable enough to rank him as a citizen of
Athens, and he could afford, or somebody afforded for him, the
heavy armor that a hoplite would wear. Socrates insists that he
does not take money for his teaching, like those "sophists" or
"wise men" (he uses the term ironically). Socrates says that he
ekes out his slender means of existence by accepting the dinner
invitations that his students offer him. He dined out two-thirds
of all the nights of the year, leaving his wife and sons at home.

As for their domestic life, Jesus was not married; Socrates was.
Nietzsche found something funny about that: "A married
philosopher; a subject for comedy." We catch a glimpse of
Socrates' wife, Xanthippe, in Plato's *Phaedo*. There she is
described coming into the prison with the three children to bid
a weeping farewell to her husband. In antiquity, Xanthippe was
reputed to be a shrew and Socrates a henpecked husband. Plato
says nothing about this, nor does Xenophon, though in
Memorabilia he includes a short dialogue between Socrates and
one of his sons who complains of his mother's "vile temper." To
this the philosopher replies soothingly, reminding the boy of all
he owes his mother, including his very life.

Xanthippe's reputation as a scold comes from a school of
ancient writers known as doxographers, Diogenes Laertes
most prominent among them. (Nietzsche wrote his doctoral

dissertation on the sources of Diogenes Laertes.) In those days little books about the lives of great men and women were much sought after, and in a number of biographies of Socrates, Xanthippe is represented as a scold and Socrates her put-upon mate. There are many stories, completely without foundation, of Xanthippe's ill-treatment of her philosopher-husband. In one anecdote she gets so angry at the failure of Socrates to bring home any money that she gets a stick and chases him around the marketplace, with citizens cheering one side or the other: "Go for it, Xanthippe!" or "Hang in there, Socrates!" Or there is the tale in which Xanthippe, away from her house, hears that a pretty lady of doubtful virtue is visiting Socrates at home to get some pointers in philosophy. Whereupon Socrates' wife comes tearing back home like a . . . like a wife!

Jesus was not married, nor did he show much interest in what today might be called "family values." Neither Socrates nor Jesus seems to have come into this world to make people feel comfortable. Jesus said, "Think not that I am come to send peace on earth: I came not to send peace, but a sword." To this he adds, "For I am come to set a man against his father, and the daughter against her mother. . . . And a man's foes shall be they of his own household." In more than one of the Gospels we find the story of the man who asked if he might follow Jesus, but first he had to see to the burial of his father, who had just died. To which Jesus responds, "Let the dead bury the dead." On the other hand, it is recorded that Jesus simultaneously blessed marriage and wine. Jesus' action at the marriage feast at Cana was his first public miracle, the changing of the water into wine. (There is a story about an old Irish temperance priest, Father Theobald Matthew, who condemned drink bitterly. One day one of his auditors asked, "But Father, did not our divine Lord bless wine by changing the water into it?" The old priest grumbled in reply, "Well, that wasn't one of his good days.")

*

The subject of wine takes us directly to Plato's *Symposium*, with Socrates enjoying a modest draught of it. A symposium (*sun-posion*) was a wine-drinking party. The format was this: first you had dinner—all male, of course, no women present save a dancer or a flute girl—and after dinner the table was cleared to make way for the wine, and the object was to get drunk. The Athenians drank their wine out of shallow bowls (*kraters*) and they always mixed the wine with water. Macedonians, who drank their wine straight, were considered semi-barbarians. And it is said that Alexander the Great died of acute alcoholism at the age of thirty-three, when he still had many more worlds to conquer.

There is an extraordinary book dating from third-century Alexandria written by Atheneus of that city and titled *Dneipnosophistae* (Banquet of the Wise). You will find there a recipe for serving wine to your guests in such a way as to keep the evening from getting out of hand. A contemporary scholar translates this recipe as follows:

> Three kraters only do I mix for the temperate.
> The first is toasted to health,
> The second to love, the third to sleep.
> After this the wise guest goes home.
> The fourth krater belongs to us no longer,
> but to hubris, or overweening pride.
> The fifth belongs to drunken revelry,
> the sixth to uproar,
> the seventh to black eyes,
> the eighth to the policeman,
> the ninth to biliousness,
> and the tenth to madness and hurling the furniture.

The provenance of Plato's symposium, starring Socrates topped and tailed by the wits of Athens, is this. Agathon, the host, has just won a prize for the best tragedy in a public competition. There has been a banquet the evening before at which everybody got drunk. Agathon lays on a second dinner the next night, and the general feeling is that one ought not to get drunk this time around because many of the guests are still somewhat hung over from the evening before. Phaedrus, a former pupil of Socrates, suggests that instead of indulging in much wine tonight, there should be a discussion of some interesting topic worthy of celebration by the distinguished guests, of whom Socrates will be one. Young Phaedrus suggests eros, or love, as a stimulating theme for elegant discourse.

All agree to let wit and wisdom flow instead of wine; they will drink only a little. But where is Socrates? The guests have gone ahead with their dinner, and still the philosopher has not appeared. Someone says he is coming, that he is standing outside having one of his spells; he'll get over it in a minute or two. It seems to be historically true that Socrates sometimes experienced moments of altered consciousness in which he would stand quite still in a fit of abstraction, listening to some sort of inner voice. He tells his judges in *Apology* that this voice or "sign" never tells him what to do, only what not to do. Perhaps it represents momentary contact with the divine, even though today some spoil-sports in mental science claim that it was no more than Socrates' left brain talking to his right brain. Or the other way around.

Anyway, Socrates does snap out of it and enters the banquet hall. For once he is dressed up. Usually he appeared in a well-worn robe of the same weight winter and summer, and was barefooted. But tonight he wears sandals and a clean white robe. So he comes in and sits down, smiling in the best of humor. The philosopher seems to have been no beauty—bald with a pushed-in face and bulging eyes, a bit like Silenus, the satyr. The guests tell him what the plan is—to talk about love, to tell what love is. All agree that love, like war to the generals, is too important to be left to the lovers. Since young Phaedrus suggested the theme, it is agreed that he should speak first.

Love is divine, says Phaedrus, and the oldest of the gods. For Hesiod tells us that in the order of creation first came chaos, then broad-bosomed earth, then eros. Love is a great power; the very animals will give their lives to protect their young. Among humans it is the same and more. Alcestis died for the love of her husband (and Phaedrus might have added that Antigone gave her life to ensure her dead brother a decent burial). Which is closer to the divine, the lover or the beloved? The lover, answers Phaedrus, for eros is in him. Thomas Mann paraphrases this in *Death in Venice*:

Then, sly arch-lover that he was, he said that subtlest thing of all, that the lover was nearer the divine than the beloved, for the god was in the one, but not in the other — perhaps the tenderest, most mocking thought that was ever thought and source of all the guilt and secret bliss the lover knows.

The next speaker is Pausanius, grandson of the Spartan general Pausanius. He makes a distinction between good and bad love, or at least between love which is superior and that which is inferior. Aphrodite Pandemos represents the rough connubialities of peasants, while Aphrodite Ouranos denotes love of high refinement, with which, of course, all guests present have acquaintance. The better love seeks the good of the beloved and never does anything to harm the other. Good love is educative rather than exploitive if it is to pass the bar of high moral virtue. Nor should we forget, says Pausanius, that true love should be open: if your love is a good love, why hide it? No sense in concealing high and refined love, for it is the power of the divine working for the good of both lover and beloved.

Aristophanes, the playwright, should be next, but he is having a severe attack of hiccups. What should he do? Eryximachus, a physician, suggests informal remedies, some of which survive to this day: drink a little water and gargle it; hold your breath; get someone to tickle your nose to induce sneezing. That should do it. Aristophanes is left for a moment to deal with his hiccups while Eryximachus volunteers to take his place.

The physician deals with love from the medical aspect. Just as one should be moderate in eating and drinking as well as in exercise and sport, one should be moderate in lovemaking. Nothing too much. Eryximachus offers a holistic theory of medicine and applies it to love. We must think of spirit and mind as well as body, he says, for so many ailments come from the disorder of our spiritual and emotional part. We must be careful to have body and mind, heart and spirit, in harmony. Lovers should listen to music as much as they can because music is the science of harmony, and lovers should seek harmony in love: "If music be the food of love, play on!" (but, as singer Joni Mitchell would say, that's a steal from Willie the Shake).

By this time Aristophanes has recovered from his hiccups and takes his turn. He will explain the cosmic origin of love between the sexes. Originally there were three sexes, but to simplify we can confine our attention to two. Primordial humans came in the form of spherical beings with two of everything of which we have one, and four of which we have two. These grotesque beings became bored and restless and moved toward Olympus to destroy heaven. To deal with the threat, Zeus himself cut these globular beings in half, and that put an end to their violent revolution. Forever after, to this day, they run around each seeking its proper other half, wanting only to be merged into utter oneness with its true beloved. (Should we then conclude with Aristophanes that true happiness in love comes when we have found our authentic other half? Not all people have such luck. Perhaps tonight at home we should steal a covert look at our spouse to confirm that we have indeed found and joined our very own "better half.")

Host Agathon speaks next. He gently disagrees with his young friend Phaedrus, who said that Eros is the oldest of the gods. On the contrary, says Agathon, love is the youngest of the gods. Doesn't love have for its proper sphere the realm of softness, suppleness, flexibility—the attributes of youth? Love has everything to do with youth and little or nothing to do with old age. When people get old they get arthritis and become stiff in the joints, moving creakily in jerks. With old age, moral and spiritual arthritis sets in; older people get set in their ways, fixed in their opinions, immovable by persuasion, however gentle. They listen to nobody. We respect, we honor old age, but we do not love it (or at least not in the way the young god Eros would have us love). So love is not the oldest of the gods, but the youngest. Agathon ends with a rhapsodic hymn to Love the Navigator:

> In toil or in terror,
> In drink or dialectic,
> Our helmsman and helper,
> Our pilot and preserver,
> Chief ornament of heaven and earth alike.

With this, Agathon hands over gracefully to Socrates, the star of the occasion, the philosophical life of the party.

With his customary ironic modesty, Socrates confesses that he could not possibly compete with the wisdom and eloquence of the preceding speakers. But he might manage one or two words of comment. While I admired all the speeches, he says, I noticed that they all agree in the belief that love is a god, that eros is a divine being. For my part, I do not think that love is a god. My reason is this: The divine wants for nothing; it is complete in itself, like the heavenly Forms, of which this world is but a feeble copy. Love, on the other hand, is not self-sufficient. Love cannot be beauty itself, for love wants beauty, desires it, pursues it. Nor is love the good itself. Love wants the good and looks to the beautiful to bring it. Love is not divine because the divine is changeless, deathless, immortal. We humans seek immortality, we don't possess it. Most of us ordinary folk look for a bit of immortality through our children. Generals and statesmen seek immortality through honor and fame. Artists and poets strive for immortality through their works. The love the young have for these works is a beautiful and comforting sign, a sign that our art will outlast us, at least for a little while.

Now let me tell you, says Socrates, what I was taught about love from a wise woman with whom I talked when I was a young man. She was Diotima of Mantinea, the prophetess. (Diotima is said to have prophesied the great plague that struck Athens, postponing the great war with Sparta for ten years.) Socrates, she said, let me tell you what love is. Love is not a god. Nor is it mortal. It is something in between. Eros is a spirit, a daimon acting as a mediator between the divine and the mortal. Eros shuttles back and forth, like a messenger, Hermes-fashion, between the realm of the gods and that of our earth. Love's mission is to keep the divine and the mortal in touch with one another; otherwise our mortal world and ourselves with it would fall away to nonbeing.

Let's interrupt Diotima's message for a moment to observe how interesting it is to see the analogue of this concept of eros in the Christian doctrine of the Holy Spirit, the third person of the Trinity, after Father and Son. Those who told the gospel story to those who wrote it down were men dazzled by the Easter experience. To them Jesus is first of all the Risen Christ. You may remember—we read it in Saint John's gospel—that just before the Crucifixion, Jesus tells his disciples that the Paraclete, the Holy Spirit, will come to them and remain with them unto the consummation of the world. In Plato, the cosmic function of eros anticipates in a way (but only in a way) the Christian doctrine of the role of the Comforter, the Holy Spirit. The Christian doctrine, of course, is not simply an idea borrowed from Plato but a concept independently arrived at, and operating within a very different theological context. With Plato, even in his highest metaphysical flights—as in the quasi-mystical doctrine of cosmic love he puts into the mouth of Socrates—we are reading Greek philosophy, not Christian theology. Nonetheless, the parallel between the "keeping in touch" mission of the Platonic eros and the Christian teaching of creation as the continuous contact of the Uncreated with the created order, mediated by the Holy Spirit, is rather striking.

Now to return to Diotima, who tells Socrates about the Ladder of Love. We begin our ascent, she says, by way of mortal, visible, transient beauty. We start with the beautiful rather than with the true or the good because beauty is the only one of the divine Forms that can be perceived by way of the senses. Even then, in the visible world we see only a radiant reflection, a shadowy loveliness concealed by matter. We begin our ascent aided by the love of perceptible things, fair bodies, embodiments of loveliness that we can see and touch. From beauty reachable by the senses we move up to fair and beautiful things of the mind, to shining souls, to the sciences in order of their independence from the senses (especially mathematics, which leaves sense perception completely behind). As we mount the Ladder of Love, passing by all earthly beauties and noble institutions, we arrive at the highest point of our ascent, an incandescent burst of luminous certitude where dialectic gives way to vision, where we no longer know but see—face to face with the Form of beauty itself (*tó kalón autón*), visible for one unforgettable moment. That radiant experience comes to only a few of us, and then very rarely.

Such is the true meaning of Platonic love. We must try, says Diotima, to cultivate this doctrine and practice, to teach others that while love begins in the senses, indeed, cannot begin without them, it must not remain there. Love must mount up as far as it can toward the source of all light, of all beauty and its divine Form. Those who remain rooted in sense become twice-over body, weighted down by matter, the principle of heaviness, sluggishness, inertia. For them love easily turns into its opposite, hate, or what is worse, indifference and disgust. But there is no love, however spiritual, that does not have its root in the senses. Nor is there any love, however coarse and brutal, that does not have some spark of the spiritual buried in it, as in a dark mine. The good lover fans that spark; the bad lover snuffs it out. May it be granted to the good lover the reward of seeing that which is the source of the beloved's beauty, the eternal radiance of the divine.

This, then, is Socrates' answer to the question, What is love? As he sits down amid a burst of applause, there is heard a crashing at the door and Alcibiades enters, leading a band of drunken revellers. This handsome man, brilliant and devious, had been a pupil and war comrade of Socrates. In later life he was one of the three generals elected to lead the Athenian expedition against Syracuse, ruined in part, it was said, by his sacrilege and by his treachery and double-dealing with Athenians and Persians alike. But in this scene of *Symposium* Alcibiades is just a charming rascal, quite drunk, and anxious to gate-crash Agathon's party to join the wits. To his delighted surprise he finds Socrates there, and he demands the privilege of publicly expounding on his old teacher's virtues.

Two of these virtues he selects for mention to the company: Socrates' courage and his self-control. Telling his audience that Socrates is indeed ugly but it's a beautiful ugliness, Alcibiades recalls the time when on the field of battle at Potidaea Socrates carried his pupil out of danger at the risk of his own life, thus qualifying for the medal of valor, which he passed over in favor of Alcibiades. As for self-control, Alcibiades says that Socrates is rich in that virtue; he can vouch for it out of personal experience. It seems that one night long ago, when Alcibiades fancied himself in the bloom of youth and irresistible to either sex, he proposed that Socrates sleep over at his house and, in exchange for a bit of sex, Socrates might give him a lesson in wisdom—an offer which Socrates politely declined to accept.

By this time Alcibiades's drunkenness has ruined Agathon's party. With the exception of Socrates, everyone is drunk, lying on the floor or passed out under the table. The last man standing, the narrator of *Symposium*, tells us that he is held upright by Socrates, who is trying to convince him that the genius of tragedy is the same as that of comedy; whereupon the helpless guest slides gently to the floor. Dawn is breaking as Socrates walks out the door. He goes to the public bath to wash up, and then he proceeds to the marketplace to see if he can collect some young people for a little seminar on the foundations of moral obligation. Such is the story of Socrates and eros.

*

In the Greek text of the New Testament, the word *eros* does not appear. Instead we have the word *agapē*, which has a different shade of meaning. Usually rendered in English as *charity* or *love*, neither of these is quite satisfactory: *charity* suggests public donations, while *love* is too broad and may lead to sentimental interpretation. Many prefer to settle for the Latin word *caritas*, without trying to force *agapē* into English. Paul's exaltation of *agapē* in his thirteenth letter to the Corinthians is well known. In the compressed excerpt below, from the King James translation, we can see that charity (*agapē*) does not mean "giving to feed the poor":

> Though I speak with the tongues of men and of angels and have not charity, I am become as sounding brass, or tinkling cymbal. . . . And though I bestow all my goods to feed the poor . . . and have not charity, I am nothing. . . . Charity suffereth long and is kind . . . is not puffed up . . . seeketh not her own. . . . And now abideth faith, hope, charity, these three; but the greatest of these is charity [*agapē*].

Yet Augustine, greatest of the early church fathers, is perplexed by the notion of love not wanting anything for itself. Do we not search for good things we do not have—money, pleasure, health, possessions, children, honor? Is not God the highest good, and do we not seek God? How then can love be completely selfless if it wants that which it does not yet possess? Deeply read in Plato, Augustine finds no contradiction in love arising from incompleteness, wanting something other than itself to fill our mortal emptiness, seeking the love of God or the image of God in earthly things. Indeed, metaphors of erotic love may be found throughout the writings of the Christian mystics. The erotic imagery of the mystical writings of the Spanish saint, John of the Cross, seems startling even today. And writers in the tradition of Christian piety have often looked back to the Old Testament's great love poem, The Song of Solomon.

In the post-Christian tradition, the German philosopher Arthur Schopenhauer said that Plato was right, that there *is* a great pulse of cosmic desire throbbing through the universe. But, said the author of *The World as Will and Idea*, the cosmic thrust (the World Will) is not God, though it is the First Cause. It is not good; it has neither love nor mercy; it is a blind, irrational force that manifests itself in the human in the form of the sexual impulse. For the most powerful instinct we have, that of sexual desire, is the least rational. The only aim of the World Will is to perpetuate itself, to bring more creatures into the world— willing, striving, needing, desiring, without hope of ever quenching their thirst. Schopenhauer is the metaphysician of pessimism, believing that the source of human misery lies in the fact that our desires, the product of the World Will, are created all out of proportion to the possibility of their being satisfied.

Preparing his great music-drama *Tristan and Isolde*, Richard Wagner happened to read Schopenhauer's book, and he cried that it made everything clear to him, and that his *Tristan* would convey the effect of the World Will inflaming the souls and bodies of the two death-doomed lovers. The leading musical theme of *Tristan* is the *Sehnsuchtmotif*, the theme of world-longing; you hear it first in the four notes the cellos intone as the orchestra begins the prelude. The tragedy of Tristan and Isolde is the tragedy of all earthly love: never to be satisfied, to reach fulfill-ment only by giving oneself over to death. Such is the Schopen-hauerian metaphysics of Wagner's opera. But the music is beautiful all the same. Only through art, says Schopenhauer, can we experience a moment of surcease from the eternal pain of longing. In such moments we keep the Sabbath of eternal longing; the wheel of Ixion stands still.

Freud is Schopenhauer's metaphysics changed to psychology. The Id corresponds to Schopenhauer's Will. Mind, reason, logic is helpless, or nearly so, in its battle with the blind, amoral drive of the will, instinct, Id. In its frail helplessness against the power of the instinctive, which manifests itself in the erotic character of the libido, the ego seems hardly more than a thin veneer over the subconscious and irrational drives that move us. But Freud is not quite the pessimist that Schopenhauer was. Civilization, wrested with pain from the power of the irrational drives within us, is a partial victory, but a victory nonetheless. We must go on with courage to hold back the irrational, as the Dutch dikes hold back the sea.

In his ethical writings, Aristotle—to whom we will turn in our next chapter—has little to say about eros (though in his discus-sion of moral weakness he makes passing mention of the power of Aphrodite, "Cyprus-born, weaver of wiles," whose girdle, Homer says, carries "the whisper of wooing"). But in Aristotle's metaphysical treatises he speaks of the creative power in the cosmos as something akin to desire, of the world moving toward God as to an object of appetition. This notion was picked up by the philosophers of the High Middle Ages. Aquinas agrees that the world moves toward God as toward an object of love. And the poet Dante, up to his ears in Thomistic cosmology, works this idea into his *Paradiso* when he says,

Ce l'Amor che muove il sole e l'altri stelle,

which, translated, is something we all know perfectly well:

It's love that makes the world go 'round.

4

Aristotle: The Ethics of Happiness

> If happiness is activity in accordance with virtue or excellence,
> it is reasonable to suppose that it is in accordance with the highest
> virtue, and this will be the virtue of the best part in us.

> Aristotle, *Nichomachean Ethics*

Did Fate have her wits about her when she arranged that a certain boy and a man of forty should come together for a few years in the ancient world? The boy was Alexander, the son of a king and destined to become one of the world's greatest military leaders. The man was Aristotle, whose thought would rule the learned world for two thousand years. Not content with that, did Fate see to it that the philosopher-scientist should study for twenty years under Plato, leader of the Academy of Athens?

At the age of seventeen, Aristotle came down to Athens from Stagira in Chalcidice, a northern region under Macedonian influence. He entered Plato's academy and stayed there twenty years, first as a student and then as a teacher. The personal relations between the two were cordial but never very close. On Plato's death in 347 B.C. Aristotle expected to gain the headship of the academy, but he was not selected. The Athenians feared Macedon, and the academicians knew that Aristotle's father had been court physician to the Macedonian king.

Aristotle then left Athens, staying on certain Greek islands to the east and continuing his scientific work, particularly his study of marine biology. While residing in Mitylene he was called to the Macedonian court by the ruler Philip, father of the lad Alexander. For three years Aristotle served as tutor to the boy, but of the relation between them we know little or nothing. A plausible story has it that years later, when Alexander was leading his expeditionary force to the East, he sent back to Athens specimens of fish packed in salt so that Aristotle might add them to his marine-life collection. We do know that after his return to Athens from his tutorship, Aristotle founded a school of his own called the Lyceum. The title lasted: Emerson and Thoreau lectured at the Concord Lyceum, and many old U.S. movie-houses bore the honored name.

When Alexander died in 323 B.C. there was a wave of anti-Macedonian feeling in Athens, whose citizens feared Philip's expansionist policies. Hurriedly quitting the city, Aristotle is said to have stated that he was leaving because he did not want Athens to sin against philosophy twice.

*

Though he did remarkable work in several branches of biology, Aristotle did not hit on the idea of organic evolution. His name came up, however, in an evolution case that came before the U.S. Supreme Court in 1986. The state of Louisiana had decreed that "creationism" (one version of which is found in the Old Testament book of Genesis) be given equal time in the public schools with the evolutionist (Darwinian) theory of the origin of plant and animal forms. Against Louisiana's position, a lawyer argued that "creationism" was a religious doctrine and, according to the rule of separation between church and state, should not be taught in public schools. Justice Antonin Scalia asked the lawyer if Aristotle's doctrine of the "Prime Mover" should be barred from the classroom as a "creationist" and therefore a religious doctrine.

The account of creation given in the Judaic tradition (taken up and somewhat modified in traditional Christian teaching) claims that the world was created *ex nihilo*, that is, from nothing. The Greek philosophers had no idea of creation from nothing. To them creation was always a transformation of something that was already there, usually taken to be unformed matter. In his cosmological dialogue *Timaeus* Plato taught that God (who is all-good), wishing to share being with others, fashioned the world out of an unformed matrix which had the characteristics of space, time, and motion. Time, we read in *Timaeus*, came into being with God's forming of the universe. And if you read popular science books like Stephen Hawking's *A Brief History of*

Time, you will find that many of today's cosmologists hold that time began with the big bang; before that primordial explosion, there was no time.

Plato's theory of the origin of the cosmos was not quite that of the big-bang theorists. The universe and ourselves with it are the work of a caring God, to whom Plato applies the names Father and Shepherd. Plato's God is the author of good things only; the imperfections of creation come from matter, the basic material eternally existing outside of God with which he had to work. Insofar as the world is fair and orderly, it owes this to the skill and goodness of the Maker and to the divine Forms, upon which the Maker looked as a bright and noble model. Insofar as the world is disorderly, irrational, even the seedbed of evil, this comes from the recalcitrant nature of the matter with which the Creator had to deal.

Aristotle will have none of these Pythagorean rhapsodies in his theory of creation, though his teaching, like Plato's, remains one of the transformation of resistant matter rather than creation from nothing. Aristotle's theory is more like a steady-state cosmology than a big-bang affair. Aristotle says that the world is eternal; it has always been. Reason: God is eternal, matter is eternal; and from all eternity the world has been forming itself under the influence of God's presence. This doctrine of the world's eternity was so well argued in Aristotle's *Physics* and his *Metaphysics* that medieval theologians like Maimonides and Aquinas held that if we did not know from divine revelation that the world was created from nothing, we would not know that Aristotle was wrong in his account of creation.

Aristotle says that God, as Pure Form and Pure Act, has from all eternity induced form and act out of the matter that stands outside him. What does it mean to say that God is the principle of Pure Form and Pure Act? To answer this question we must turn for a moment to Aristotle's metaphysics (or "First Philosophy," as he called it). First Philosophy is the study of being itself, not some particular kind of being like metals or birds or stars. While we cannot define *being* (since we would have to use the concept in any definition of it), we can understand it a bit by dividing it into its kinds. Aristotle divides being into *mutable* and *immutable* being. Mutable being is the kind which is subject to change, like the things in the visible world that we see about us; while immutable being is changeless, a perfection consistent with its divine character. (Only in times very close to our own has the superiority of changelessness been challenged, though Aristotle himself, in studying the processes of organic life, was struck by the marvels of the kind of change we find in the growth and development of living things. Organic growth is a positive change, not negative, not a falling away to nonbeing.)

We can divide mutable being—the things we see in the world around us—into *substances* (independently existing things) or *accidents* (the qualities that substances possess, like color, which cannot stand by themselves). Here is a mouse or a sailing ship; each can stand alone, in contrast to its color or shape.

And we can look at substances *statically* (with reference to their structure) or *dynamically* (directing our attention to their change, development, becoming). If we take the first viewpoint, we can distinguish between two aspects in every substance: *matter* and *form*.

Every substance is made out of something—the table of wood, the dress of silk or wool, the mountain of stone. This "something" Aristotle calls matter. And in every substance this matter is disposed in a certain way; it is organized according to a particular structure which enables us to recognize the substance for what it is—lamp, stone, star, wood, mouse, and so on. This is form.

Matter and form are relative to one another. Wood is matter organized in a certain way. But while wood is form compared to those elements which go to make it up, wood is matter relative to the finished substance or thing we call "table."

Suppose we choose to consider substances from a dynamic rather than a static viewpoint, that is, from the aspect of their change, becoming, development. In this case we can distinguish between *potentiality* and *actuality*. Potentiality refers to what a thing can become, that which it is on the way to becoming. Potentiality is not mere possibility; it is more definite, more positive than that. An acorn is a potential oak, a kitten a potential cat, a good piece of flat maple a potential tabletop. A boy or girl with certain firm qualities of personality represents a potential leader.

Potentiality refers to a thing having "what it takes" to reach *actuality*, which is potentiality realized. The oak is the actuality of the acorn, the horse the actuality of the foal. The mature man or woman represents the actuality of the boy or girl.

Like matter and form, potentiality and actuality are relative concepts. The kitten is potentiality compared to the mature cat, but actuality compared to the cat embryo. The sapling is potentiality with respect to the oak, but actuality with respect to the acorn. To Aristotle, all substances retain an element of potentiality, despite the relatively full degree of maturity (actuality) they may attain. Only God is Pure Act, Pure Form.

Having considered Aristotle's analysis of mutable being, we should now turn to that kind of being he classifies as immutable. Here, Aristotle says, we can make another two-part distinction: there is immutable being which is visible, and immutable being which is invisible. Visible immutable being is represented by the heavenly bodies. We can see the fixed stars; they are immutable and therefore the visible aspect of the divine. To us today this seems a naive belief coming from so sophisticated a mind as Aristotle's. But we must remember that brilliant as Aristotle was, he had no instruments as we have. (It was not until the seventeenth century that the telescope turned up as a Dutch toy, and Galileo quickly saw that it was much more than a toy in potentiality.) Belief in the divinity of the stars, the glorious heavens, was so ingrained in the Greek mind that even such a dispassionate scientist as Aristotle could not get it out of his head.

The invisible part of immutable being is God. What is the nature of Aristotle's God? Unlike Plato's Divine Artificer, who cares for the world, wanting to share his own being with it as much as possible, Aristotle's God is completely unaware of the world. Why is that? God, says Aristotle, is the complete actualization of mind; his activity is thought. Now when one thinks, there must be an object of thought; one thinks about something, not about nothing. What does God think about? Not the world, Aristotle says, for its degree of being makes it an unworthy object of God's thought. What, then, does God think about? What is the object of his thought? Answer: He thinks about the only thing that's worth thinking about, namely, himself. God's eternal activity is self-thinking thought.

This may seem no more than ancient metaphysical reasoning until one realizes that Aristotle's idea of self-thinking thought has had a distinguished philosophical career. Hegel's Absolute Spirit may be represented as becoming, eternally striving for greater, more complete consciousness, in the process thereof throwing off the history of art, nations, religion, philosophy. Marx took that notion and made it into a philosophy of history that is only lately being discredited. (Stockdale got lectures on the subject from his interrogators in Hanoi.) Hegel himself said that his task was to make the abstract universal of Aristotle the concrete universal of his own philosophy—a concrete universal which, he believed, exhibits itself in world historical figures like Alexander the Great, Napoleon, and, well, Hegel himself. (Excessive modesty was not one of Hegel's faults.)

If God is unaware of the world, how then was the world created? As we noted earlier, Aristotle holds that the world is eternal, matter having always existed. Since God is eternal as well, matter has from all eternity been influenced by his creative presence. Self-thinking thought, without being aware of that being which is below it, exercises a formative, creative influence.

Perhaps we could illustrate by two examples which Aristotle would not like—the first because it is too mechanical, and the second because it is too sentimental. As to the first, suppose we postulate an eternal magnet and a coexistent bar of iron. Let us imagine them placed in a position where the influence of the magnet can be felt by the bar. Now the magnet is unaware of its effect on the iron bar and yet, since the magnet has been there from all eternity, so too from all eternity the bar of iron has had magnetism induced in it. That's the mechanical example; the sentimental metaphor is a little more human.

Imagine a man who is so deeply depressed that he is thinking of suicide. He lives in a large apartment house by himself, and he is very unhappy. His life no longer has meaning; it is not worth living. But one day he notices a woman who lives in another apartment in the house. She is very beautiful, and the man finds himself beginning discreetly to observe her without going anywhere near her, avoiding the slightest appearance of wishing to approach her. Day after day he sees this lovely woman going about her affairs, to business or whatever engages her attention, and he falls in love with her. It is love at a distance, for he never takes occasion to speak to her, but that love gives him a renewed sense of confidence, a reawakened desire to live. He regains hope, picks up the work which he had abandoned, and does better at it than he ever did before. You see the somewhat exaggerated analogy here: the beautiful woman is unaware of this man—he's careful not to allow his interest in her to be seen—and yet her influence has induced in him something good, an order, a transformation. So to Aristotle, God, while unaware of the world, is the cause of all order and perfection in it.

How do we know that such a being as God exists? Did not the Greeks believe in many gods? Certainly Socrates seems to have shown sincere and devout respect for the gods of the city-state. To the Greeks, the gods of the city protected it, and that is one reason why "impiety," "atheism," and "teaching strange things about the gods" constituted a charge that might lead even an eminent citizen to judgment, exile, even death. With all due respect to whatever divinities protect the city, Aristotle teaches that there is but one God, who, as Pure Form, Pure Act, has created and ever creates the world. Aristotle sets forth a formal argument for the existence of this Prime Mover; we can read it in his *Physics* and his *Metaphysics*. The world is a series of things moved and things moving. We must postulate a First Mover because otherwise we are going to have an infinite regress, an unending series of movers who are moved by other movers. Such a conclusion would violate Aristotle's principle of parsimony: of two explanations, equally good, choose the simpler.

This "proof from motion" was based on a physical model of the universe which was quite wrong. Aristotle believed that our world stands at the center of an array of concentric circular tracks or shells, each of which provides for the circular movements of the bodies in that track or shell. Beyond the orbit of the stars lies the unseen realm of the First Mover. Not that God moves the world by a push or shove. Rather, his eternal self-thinking thought induces and has always induced movement in the world toward that origin of motion. God, as it were, is the object of the world's desire. Aristotle says that the world moves toward God as toward an object of appetition.

Aristotle's argument for the existence of God from the idea of a First Mover had a long career in natural theology. Aquinas offered three versions of the proof for God's existence, one of them in the language of First Cause. The world is a series of events, each of which has a cause or causes. It cannot be denied then that the world itself must have a cause. This cause is what we humans call God. If the question is asked, But who made God?, Aquinas replies that this question enmeshes you in an infinite regress, an endless series of causes which are caused by other causes; but this is absurd, since an infinite series of zeros will not help if you are looking for a One.

The argument for the existence of God as First Cause persisted well into the eighteenth century, with Leibniz substituting the principle of "sufficient reason" for "cause." In the twentieth century Alfred North Whitehead argued for the existence of God in order to explain why the world is this way rather than some other; to shrug off the need for such a cosmological factor, he said, is no more than reason refusing to assert its rights.

In our day these arguments for the existence of God have had a very bad press. Few academic philosophers find them convincing. At most some will concede that, while the various versions of the argument are invalid, there may be a hidden question, hard to answer, which lies back of each of them. It is this: *Why should there be something rather than nothing? Why should there be anything at all?* Even Ludwig Wittgenstein, who says that talk about such things is meaningless, observes in his *Tractatus* that "not *how* the world is, but *that* it is, is the mystical."

*

What has all this to do with Aristotle's ethics? The answer lies in the idea of "good." Aristotle does not begin his inquiry into ethics by asking what is "right" and what is "wrong." Instead, he starts by assuming that we all desire what is good or seems so to us—money, pleasure, health, honor, fame, family, or whatever. And he asks, What is the highest good? Answering his own question, he says that happiness (*eudaimonia*) is the highest good, for we desire happiness for itself and not because it is a means to some other good:

> . . . for we always choose happiness as an end in itself and never for the sake of something else. Honor, pleasure, intelligence and all virtue (excellence) we choose partly for themselves, but partly for the sake of happiness, because we assume it is through them that we will be happy. On the other hand no one chooses happiness for the sake of pleasure, and the like, not as a means to anything at all.

By *happiness* Aristotle does not mean just a subjective sense of good feeling. Happiness is to live in an objectively good way, and there are many things that contribute to it. Some of these are quite easy for us to understand—having a family; seeing your children flourish; having enough money to do a little more than just get by; enjoying a deserved place in your city-state and friendships with other citizens. But when he talks about the higher end of the spectrum of happiness, Aristotle is less worldly. (After all, he didn't spend twenty years in Plato's academy for nothing.) Reminding us that in the study of ethics as well as politics we must not expect that degree of precision we find in mathematics, Aristotle offers a succinct definition of happiness (one that President John Kennedy liked to quote in his public speeches):

> The good of the human is activity in conformity with excellence or virtue, and if there be several virtues, in conformity with the best and most complete.

Aristotle's ethics, then, is an ethics of *character* rather than an ethics of *rules*. He talks about the virtues or excellences possessed by a person of high character. (Kant, as we shall see in our next chapter, gives us a rule with which to determine an act of moral worth.)

In introducing his examination of character, Aristotle distinguishes between the intellectual and the moral virtues. The good man has both. The intellectual virtues include wisdom and knowledge, and the moral virtues represent a mean or balance between excess and defect in certain important traits of character. We are not born with these virtues, says Aristotle, but we are fitted by nature to receive them. We acquire them by habit, training, and education.

Of the moral virtues, Aristotle gives first place to courage (*andreia*), particularly military courage. This virtue, as do all the moral excellences, represents a mean or balance between too much and too little. The excess of that which makes a man courageous we call rashness; the defect, cowardice. Military courage is the highest kind of courage because on the battlefield the fear of death is ever present, and death is the most terrible of evils (though there are circumstances in which death is preferable to dishonor). The courage shown by one who is mortally ill or by sailors in a deadly storm is admirable, but somewhat less so than courage on the battlefield. Reason: the fighting man has the choice of retreating or running away, while the sick man cannot run away from his illness nor sailors from their foundering ship.

Self-control (*sophrosune*) is that virtue which distinguishes the man who rules his passions from the man who is ruled by them. Generosity or liberality is another virtue, the excess of which is prodigality and the defect, miserliness. (Aristotle adds that it is better to be extravagant than stingy, though each is a vice rather than a virtue.)

Aristotle's treatment of pride is particularly interesting. Pride: to the Greeks a virtue, to the Christians a vice. But *pride* in Aristotle's usage does not mean that which Jesus condemned in the Pharisees. *Magnanimity* is a better word for what Aristotle had in mind, but even that will not quite do for us since we tend to think of magnanimity as the virtue of the conqueror toward the conquered (as in Churchill's phrase, "in victory, magnanimity"). Aristotle's model of this virtue is the magnanimous or great-souled man. Aristotle draws a remarkable portrait of the magnanimous man in the fourth book of his *Nichomachean*

Ethics. Such a man has a just estimation of his own worth; he seeks honors before pleasure or wealth, but these honors must be conferred on him by those worthy to give them.

This leads Aristotle to comment on ambition, which he would like to include as a quality of the magnanimous man. But the Greek word for ambition (*philotimía*) had a pejorative sense even as it does today, and as it did in Shakespeare's time:

> The noble Brutus
>
> Hath told you Caesar was ambitious:
>
> If it were so, it was a grievous fault,
>
> And grievously hath Caesar answered it.

(In *On War*, Clausewitz expresses regret that seeking honor and renown, a powerful stimulus to men in battle, is associated with ignoble meanings, as in "greed for honor" (*Ehregeiz*) and "hankering after glory" (*Ruhmsucht*), adding that "so far as the commander-in-chief is concerned, we may well ask whether history has ever known a great general who was not ambitious.") Aristotle solves the problem by calling ambition in the honorable sense "the Nameless virtue," noting that its excess is the seeking of honors of which we are not worthy, and its defect we find in the poor-spirited or small-minded man. The seeking and attaining of deserved honor is the mean between the excess and the defect.

How do we determine the mean in matters of moral virtue? Aristotle answers that the mean (*meson*) is not fixed; it is not a geometrically equal distance from excess and defect. The location of the mean must be determined by reason:

> Virtue or excellence is a characteristic involving choice. . . .
> It consists in observing the mean relative to us, a mean which
> is defined by a rational principle such as a man of practical
> wisdom would use to determine it.

To illustrate the mean, a circle is a better figure than a line; moral excellence lies in hitting the center of a target—or as near to the center as possible—rather than finding the midpoint of a line.

Having described virtue as a characteristic involving choice, Aristotle transfers this principle without change from the good *character* of a human to the *act* of moral worth. An ethically right act must be free, not compelled; voluntary, not forced. Sometimes a person may be in a situation in which he feels forced to do something he does not want to do, yet an element of choice remains. Aristotle cites the example of a ship captain caught in a storm who is "forced" to throw part of his valuable cargo over the side. But he could have chosen otherwise by electing to keep the cargo and ride out the tempest.

Does torture deprive us of choice? Does it turn a confession from a voluntary into an involuntary act? Given a certain degree of torture, may we say that it is no longer within our power to resist? This is a hard question. Aristotle says that everyone is responsible for his or her choice. But can I be held responsible if I yield under the terrible pain inflicted on me by my interrogators? Is my confession then a true *act*, or is it just something that happens to me, like my being pushed down stairs? Aristotle speaks of a man breaking under torture as something forgivable ("for example, when a man acts improperly under a strain greater than human nature can bear and which no one could endure"). But then he says that "there are perhaps also acts which no man can possibly be compelled to do, but rather than do them he should accept the most terrible sufferings and death." Speaking of the torture inflicted on him and his comrades by their interrogators in Hanoi, Jim Stockdale says, "Everybody breaks at some point or other. The important thing is to make them do it all over again the next day. And they don't like that."

Aristotle's analysis of the moral virtues seems to be good common sense, and indeed it is. But we must not forget that he begins and ends his ethical inquiry with the assertion that the highest good is happiness and that happiness, in its highest degree, is enjoyment of a very exalted kind. Consider his remark in the tenth book of the *Nichomachean Ethics*:

> If happiness is activity in accordance with virtue or excellence, then it is reasonable that it is in accord with the highest excellence and this will be the best thing in us. Whether this

element in us is reason or something else, whether it is itself divine or only the most nearly divine thing in us, contemplation of that will be perfect happiness.

We find the same combination of common sense with a touch of the other-worldly in Aristotle's psychology treatise, known by its Latin title as *De Anima*. This treatise deals with the nature and capabilities of organic life, particularly that of the human. As a scientific observer, Aristotle was struck by the differing degrees of life represented respectively by plants, animals, and humans. He believed that *soul* is a name we can give to that complex organization of matter that we call life. Each degree of life has its characteristic capabilities. Plants have the capacity to nourish themselves, grow, and reproduce. Animals have these capacities too, plus consciousness and the ability to move about. Humans in turn possess the capacities of plants and animals but exhibit what they do not, that is, rationality. This generic quality, reason, manifests itself in many ways: the ability to talk, read, laugh, cook food, to carry on abstract reasoning, practical or theoretical.

To Aristotle the psychologist, soul stands to body as form to matter, as actuality to potentiality. The good at which living things aim is their actuality, to "become what they are," to reach and exhibit the perfections of maturity. This process Aristotle calls *entelechy*, a moving toward a *telos*, an end, that which is aimed at. The "end" (*telos*) of the sapling, we remember, is to become a full-blown oak; the "end" (*telos*) of a kitten is to reach the perfections of the mature cat. That is the "good" at which these aim, through growth and development.

We owe to Aristotle the first careful construction of the idea of potentiality, particularly with regard to living things. The idea of actualization also began its long career with the Greek philosopher's analysis in *De Anima*. In our time, certain schools of psychotherapy (Maslow, Erikson, Horney, for example) have made much of the concept of actualization, though some critics find that their emphasis on *self*-actualization leans toward sentimentality, another way of making people "feel good about themselves." Aristotle believed that the good of a human is indeed actualization, but not *self*-actualization, not the bringing out of perfections peculiar to individuals like Nichomachus or Pythia, but developing the excellences of a *human*.

Are soul and body separable? No more, says Aristotle, than the form of a table is separable from the table. Yet in three places in *De Anima* he refers to a part of the human that *may* be separable, even immortal. This he calls the active intellect (*nous energeaia*), a concept difficult to understand. His brief account of the active intellect seems to invoke the distinction between matter and form, between potentiality and actuality. If the rational soul with its characteristic activity of thought may be considered the form of the body, can we not apply the same distinction to thought itself, dividing it into the capacity for thought and the activity of thought? The latter would then be seen as the "form of a form," the "actuality of an actuality," and this aspect of our rational self may be separable. He says in *De Anima*,

> With the mind it is different. It seems to be an independent substance lodged within the soul and incapable of destruction. . . . Thinking, loving, and hating are affections, not of mind but of that which has it. Mind is no doubt something more divine and impassible.

And again:

> We have no evidence as yet about mind or the power of the soul to think; it seems to be a widely different kind of soul, differing as what is eternal from what is perishable; it alone is capable of existence in isolation from all the other psychic powers.

Aristotle's puzzling doctrine of the active intellect stimulated centuries of controversy over its interpretation. Does it mean that each of us has, as it were, a divine spark in the soul which is related to the eternal fire that is God? Alexander of Aphrodisias and the Cappadocian fathers took it that way. Aquinas understood the active intellect to mean the separable soul, which is (because of the grace of God) immortal and which persists in being after the death of the body.

Closely connected with the concept of the active intellect is Aristotle's teaching that contemplation is the highest kind of knowledge. Practical knowledge is concerned with doing, while contemplative knowledge is concerned only with knowing. It is possible to study the same subject, mathematics for example, for a practical as well as a contemplative purpose. But Aristotle makes it clear that he considers the study of mathematics for its own sake to be prior to and superior to the study of mathematics for navigational or business calculations. The highest form of knowledge is contemplative rather than practical.

Though Aristotle does not speak directly of contemplation in *De Anima*, many of the qualities attributed to the active intellect seem compatible with the exercise of contemplative knowledge. In the *Ethics* he says, "Perfect happiness is a contemplative activity . . . such is the activity of God." And again: "This activity alone would seem to be loved for its own sake; for nothing arises from it apart from contemplating, while from practical activities we gain more or less apart from the action."

Aristotle's moral philosophy, then, is what we might call an ethic of earthly happiness with an other-worldly resonance in its highest grades. The good life aims at happiness—activity in accord with the excellences, intellectual and moral, that we can develop within ourselves by education and habit. This together with good things external to us—a decent living, family, friends, a society with just laws—enables us to practice in harmony the virtues proper to the life of reason. Such fulfillment will encourage us to aim higher still, to search for that kind of being which is immutable and deathless, and for that moment of supreme satisfaction, that instant of incandescent apperception, when it seems we are at one with the unchangeable, the really real, as a spark would merge with the flame that is its source. This to Aristotle is the highest satisfaction open to us in the ethical dimension of our lives.

*

The Stoics, that school of philosophers whose tradition lasted five hundred years, adopted a generous portion of Aristotle's metaphysics and ethics. The first important formulator of the Stoic doctrine, Zeno of Clitium, came to Athens in 314 B.C., eight years after Aristotle's death. The last great Stoic writer, the Roman emperor Marcus Aurelius, died in 180 A.D. More than a century earlier Epictetus died, the slave-philosopher whom Hegel pitted against the emperor-philosopher in a famous dialogue between master and slave in *The Phenomenology of the Spirit*. It was Epictetus's *Enchiridion* that Stockdale took with him in memory to his prison cell in Hanoi, where the little book which had been to him "an ornament in prosperity" became "a comfort in adversity."

The Stoic cosmology took over from Aristotle (as well as from some of the older Greek philosophers) the doctrine of the inseparability of the "visible unchanging" (the universe) from the "invisible unchanging" (God). The divine element in us is reason or mind. By the proper exercise of our reason we can understand the causes of things through scientific investigation and the contemplation of its results. Aided by this knowledge, we can accommodate ourselves to destiny. There is no chance or free will in the Stoic ordering of things. Freedom consists in knowing that all things and events are determined by the nature of God, who is eternal Mind.

In the seventeenth century in Amsterdam there lived a young Jewish philosopher named Benedict Spinoza. So heretical was his philosophy, summed up in his great book simply titled *Ethics*, that he was excommunicated from the Jewish community of the Dutch city. Spinoza studied Aristotle and the Stoics; the twelfth-century Jewish philosopher Maimonides, who was an Aristotelian; and Descartes, the great geometer. (The *Ethics* is written *more geometrico*, its contents arranged in the form of axioms, postulates, and theorems.) Like the Stoics, Spinoza believed that there is no separation between God and the physical universe. Sometimes he refers to *Deus sive Natura* (God or Nature). More often he calls God "Substance," in order to avoid what he considered anthropomorphism and to emphasize his belief that there is only one truly independently existing thing—God (all other things being attributes or modes of Substance, or God). Substance (God), which is infinite, reveals itself to us through two infinite attributes: Extension (matter) and Thought (mind). From these there follows (as the conclusion of a syllogism follows from its premises) "The Face of the Whole Universe," the Infinite Mode. From that in turn follows the aggregate of finite modes—people, things, every individual entity—the whole mortal show, including Socrates, you, and me. All modes follow by divine necessity from Infinite Substance through the infinite attributes of Extension and Thought, matter and mind.

Spinoza's ethics, like that of the Stoics, is an ethic of knowledge. He believes that the highest happiness lies in mounting the grades of knowledge, with science as model and purpose. Going beyond and above the sciences of mathematics, geometry, and physics, and under the strict discipline of separating false from true knowledge, we can attain what Spinoza calls the Third Kind of Knowledge, in which our minds, imperfect though they are, can understand something of the nature of God (who, as Aristotle taught, dwells in beneficent unawareness of our finite cares and woes).

Can we love this impersonal God of Spinoza, the Infinite Substance which is the cause of all things? Yes, answers Spinoza; it is the love which comes from dedication to knowledge. True love of God (*Amor Intellectus Dei*) is an intellectual love which aspires to the condition of pure geometry. Does God love us? Spinoza says no, and adds, "He who truly loves God shall not endeavor that God should love him in return."

Spinoza never married. Aristotle did. His wife, Pythias, was the niece of Hermias, the benevolent tyrant of Assos, whom some say spent time in Plato's academy. Aristotle and Pythias had one child, a daughter, also named Pythias. After his wife's death Aristotle lived for many years with a lady named Herpyllis. She became the mother of his only son, Nichomachus. In the last years of his life Aristotle returned to Chalcidice in the north, near his native city of Stagira. He died in 322 B.C. Aristotle had freed many of his slaves and left instructions that the rest were not to be sold. The philosopher speaks fondly of Herpyllis in his will and makes generous provision for her. But he directs that his wife's bones be buried beside him in his last resting place.

5

Kant and the Metaphysics of Morals

> Two things fill the mind with ever increasing admiration and
> awe . . . the starry heavens above and the moral law within.

> Kant, *Critique of Practical Reason*

> One must do one's duty without thinking of the consequences.

> Princess Marie de Cröys
> (before a German military
> tribunal, Brussels, 1915)

Immanuel Kant (1724-1804) has always been of special interest
to the military, particularly in Germany. Count Gerhard von
Scharnhorst, founder of the Prussian general staff and of the
Prussian war college, L'Ecole militaire, made Kant required
reading for his students (Carl von Clausewitz among them). The
philosopher and the military aristocracy shared the ideal of duty
as its own end, not done for profit or preferment. Scharnhorst
lived at a time when the merchant class in the German states was
growing in strength and power. Military officers (and this was
true down to the Second World War) were for the most part
drawn from the noble classes. In the eyes of the nobility and the
higher military, the merchants' growing power exalted the profit
motive rather than the ideal of duty for duty's sake. In their turn,
the affluent merchants of the old Hansa cities developed a
patrician class of their own which did its best to combine the
profit motive with a stern Protestant ethic of righteousness.
(Thomas Mann's novel *Buddenbrooks* (1901) dramatizes the conflicts that resulted from this combination of motives.)

Kant's powerful thought belongs to that great swing toward
the subjective, the centering of inquiry on the self, the *I*, which
emerged in the seventeenth century, that age of genius. The
French philosopher-geometrician René Descartes, for example,

put aside the encyclopedic volumes of the Scholastics, saying that we should begin afresh in our search for that kind of knowledge which is certain, reliable beyond doubt. Descartes' source of certainty is the immediate experience of the self, the famous "Cogito ergo sum" ("I think therefore I am"), which in our language might be, "I know that I exist for it is an immediate fact of experience, neither permitting nor requiring proof." Since I cannot possibly doubt my own existence, philosophy should begin with that first certainty and then move on to other secure ground that follows. For example, I find that I have in my mind the idea of a perfect being. I would not have such an idea were there not a perfect being to produce it. I cannot produce it myself, for I am imperfect; I doubt. Therefore the idea is caused by something outside me, the perfect being itself, which is, of course, God. Now God, being perfect, is all-good and would not deceive me; he would not permit the image of the world that I have to be a mere phantasm. So the external world, the world in which we live and move and act, is roughly what it appears to be. *Roughly* because I, as an imperfect being, have certain limitations on my knowledge of the world outside me.

Kant was attracted to another champion of the primacy of the self, Jean-Jacques Rousseau, whose name is associated with the Enlightenment movement that ruled eighteenth-century thought. To Rousseau, knowledge of oneself is the beginning of wisdom. People who think this way are apt to write autobiographies, and Rousseau, like Augustine ages before him, wrote his own *Confessions*. On the very first page of this testament of personal individualism we read, "I may not be better than other men but at least I am different!" Like Rousseau, but with far less self-indulgence, Kant proclaimed that the essence of the moral self is freedom.

Although Kant was a child of the Enlightenment, the roots of his thought go deeper and farther back, back to Luther, a former Augustinian monk. Kant is the philosopher of Protestant heroism, his moral doctrine marked by inwardness (*Innerlichkeit*), that concern with the inner self so characteristic of the philosophy and literary works of the eighteenth, nineteenth, and even the twentieth century in the German-speaking states.

Kant taught that our knowledge of the external world is limited, conditioned, contingent on the concept-forms of space, time and causality; while our will, our good will, the foundation of moral philosophy and ethical action, is unlimited, unconditional. We find this doctrine anticipated in Luther and Augustine's distinction between the order of grace, which is unbounded, unlimited, independent, and the order of necessity, which is bounded, limited, conditioned rather than unconditioned. Or, to put it more simply: just as Kant insisted that the inner nerve of the act of true moral worth lies in the purity of the *motive*—described as a sense of duty for duty's sake rather than seeking beneficial *results*—so we are reminded of Luther's primary emphasis on *faith* rather than *works*.

*

Kant's life was not a colorful one. A bachelor whose career was that of a university professor, he never travelled more than a hundred miles from Königsberg, in East Prussia. (After the Second World War Königsberg was incorporated into Soviet territory and renamed Kaliningrad.) As to Kant's career, we U.S. Americans are always interested in stories of how a young person rises from poverty and humbleness to success and eminence. Kant was the child of a poor leather worker who made saddles and stirrups. His mother was a simple woman, a small part of that great wave of uncomplicated devotion, the Pietist movement of the eighteenth century. Pietism had its American counterpart. The German immigrants of colonial times brought with them to the New World their unadorned religious devotion and plain style of life. Kant does not as a rule write with emotion, but he makes an exception in favor of his mother; he speaks of her with love, and of how much he owes to her.

How did Kant rise from his humble circumstances to the position of eminent professor whose fame brought so many scholars to little Königsberg? There were only two ways that a poor boy could mount the tightly stratified social ladder of eighteenth-century Germany: he could study for the clergy or for a scholar's position in the small but prestigious academic world. Kant studied hard and made his way through gymnasium and university, gaining the academic credits required for a teaching position. His high aim was a professor's chair at the University of Königsberg.

Kant's first job was assistant librarian at the university library. The library was situated in a castle of Frederick the Great, who personally signed every appointment connected with the university. Kant complained that the greater part of his duties consisted of sweeping the floor and keeping the unheated library clean. In due course he became a docent (a member of the faculty paid by fees from students), then an associate professor (*extraordinarius*), and finally a full professor (*ordinarius*). And there he worked for the rest of his life, producing a series of essays that were to issue forth in his great book, twenty years in the writing, *The Critique of Pure Reason*.

Apparently Kant was a good teacher, a dapper little man who wore a wig and a small gold dagger, the emblem of his office. His habits were so regular that it was said that the housewives of Königsberg could set their clocks to the exact time by observing Professor Kant's mile or two walk after his classes. (At least we have that story from Heinrich Heine, who studied philosophy under Hegel in Berlin and admired Kant's teachings. But Heine was a poet, and poets, as Plato has taught us, are not to be trusted with the truth of their stories. Besides, Heine was a bit of a cynic. Wasn't it he who said, "However great the tragedy, however deep the sorrow, it always ends up by one blowing one's nose"?)

The Critique of Pure Reason is sometimes referred to as the *First Critique* because Kant wrote three. This book revolutionized the course of philosophy and the theory of knowledge and science. It is a difficult book (some say that even Germans have a hard time understanding it), and it warrants a brief digression in order to sketch a bit of background.

*

Descartes said that our knowledge of the world outside us is, approximately speaking, reliable. But by no means 100 percent so. Descartes and Galileo conducted some experiments in physics that seemed to indicate that certain qualities of objects in the world outside us do not exist "out there," but rather they are *effects* produced in us by these objects. Consider a blue flag or a red sunset. The colors are not "out there." Instead, there are certain movements of the constituents of matter which produce in us the effect of blue or red. Similarly, the fragrance of a tree does not inhere in the tree. Rather, the tree has certain bodies in it, quite minute, and it is their activity that produces in us a sense of a particular fragrance.

So we can see that the new science of the seventeenth and eighteenth centuries has begun to whittle away certain aspects of our knowledge of the external world, moving from objective independence to a partial dependence on our faculties of perception. The new science admitted, indeed, required the supposition that physical objects exist "out there" independently of us. Their physical being is real. But their hue, their sound, their scent, and other so-called secondary qualities are subjective responses to their being.

Now certain British philosophers picked up this point and made more of it. Seventeenth-century John Locke had read Newton as well as Descartes, and he was well aware of the distinction between primary and secondary qualities, that is, between the physical objects which exist independently of us and the effects produced in us by their being (yielding us sensations of color, scent, sound, and the like). To the silly question "If a tree falls in the forest and there's nobody around to hear it, is there any sound?" the sensible Locke would have replied, had he the patience to answer, "If you mean by *sound* certain motions in the air produced by the tree striking the ground, the answer is yes. But if you mean by *sound* the noise-perception we would expect to experience if we were in the vicinity of the tree, the answer is no, for the organ of perception, the ear, human or animal, is missing."

Like a good British philosopher-scientist, Locke held that the most reliable method of testing the reality or truth of anything is EXPERIENCE (he capitalized the word in just this way in his *Essay on Human Understanding*). His emphasis on the primacy of experience as the ranking test of truth got him into a little trouble with this problem of our knowledge of the external world. Consider a tree (hemlock, if you like things that remind you of Socrates). Locke believed that we do not experience the tree directly; we infer its existence from what Locke called our *idea* of tree (the sum of our perceptions—shape, hardness, greenness, fragrance, et cetera). It is the perception of tree and not the tree itself that we experience. The objective tree is really "out there," independent of us, and it *causes* our perceptions of it.

All this was a bit too fine for George Berkeley, a divine of the Church of Ireland who came to Newport, Rhode Island, in the mid-eighteenth century with plans for founding an institute of higher education in Bermuda. This college was to be for the American colonists, who would sail out to it for their lectures and study, and for the Indians, who would paddle out in their canoes from the Carolina coast. But Berkeley had failed to take proper account of the distance between Bermuda and the mainland, and the plan for the college had to be abandoned. For three years Berkeley lived in the Middletown section of Newport in the residence named Whitehall (now open to the public). He preached at Newport's Trinity Church and donated to the church the original part of its pipe organ. He also gave libraries of books to Yale (The College of New Haven) and Columbia (King's College). Berkeley then returned to Britain and, as a reward for his labors, Queen Caroline made him a bishop.

Berkeley's *Alciphron* was written at Whitehall, but his most startling books were published when he was still a young man at Trinity College, Dublin. He had read Locke's *Essay on Human Understanding* with admiration, but he asked how Mr. Locke knew that the perceived tree corresponded to the supposed physical tree, for it is impossible to prove such a correspondence. The truth is, wrote Berkeley, that our perceptions of objects *are* the objects. We don't need an independently existing material or physical tree to create a perceived tree in us; the perceived tree is enough. Why have two trees, a perceived tree and a material tree, when the perceived tree will do everything the supposed material tree will do? Conclusion: The external world is not material at all, only an elaborate series of orderly perceptions with God as its ultimate cause. Berkeley thought this commonsense theory would refute materialism and add support to religious belief. The world is entirely a mental story, as it were, told to us by God, and the order of God's mind is projected in the sensations which come to us. This doctrine came to be known as a form of *idealism*, the belief that all things are more of the nature of mind than of material bodies. To Kant, Berkeley's doctrine was a radical "mentalism" that led to insuperable difficulties.

The Scottish philosopher David Hume (1711-1776) pointed out that one of these difficulties was that Berkeley's theory led to *solipsism*, the untenable belief that I alone exist. For if material bodies are perceptions residing in consciousness, how do I reach beyond them to know that back of that bundle of perceptions that I call "you" is another *mind* like my own? And what happens when two solipsists meet each other in the street? Embarrassing!

Hume was willing to admit that "mind" is no more than a bundle of perceptions. But he insisted that the belief that there is something back of these perceptions that *causes* them is no more than habit, repeated associations of A with B which lead us to jump beyond the experience of particulars to state universal principles, like "A causes B" or "All As are Bs," when all we know is that a great many of them do or are. Experience, says Hume, does not give us those universal and necessary relations which inhere in generalizations. "A body in motion tends to remain in motion in a straight line," or "Gases when heated expand"—we make up these "laws" by the repeated association of particulars. "All our different perceptions," he says, "are distinct existences, and the mind never perceives any real connection among distinct existences." Here is a stone in my garden. When the sun is shining, the stone is warm. After repeated experiences of "sun shining" and "warm stone," I go beyond what experience gives me and I say, "The sun warms the stone." That is, I assume that there is a causal relation between the sun shining and the warming of the stone. I *believe* that myself, says Hume, but I cannot *demonstrate* it; it's all a matter of distinct and different perceptions linked together by habit.

So much then for the so-called universal and necessary foundations of the "laws" of science, which Mr. Newton had so beautifully arranged in his famous *Principia*!

*

It was to this challenge of the "laws" of science that Kant addressed himself in *The Critique of Pure Reason*. "It was the warning voice of David Hume," said the professor at Königsberg, "that awoke me from my dogmatic slumber." Kant solemnly suspended all metaphysicians from their tasks until they had answered Hume's question. How do we justify our belief in the reliability of universal "laws" such as the principles of science? If experience furnishes us with particulars only, what right have we to make generalities out of them? How can we show that universal and necessary relations connecting things and events—such as causality—have their foundation in something more than habit, association, repeated coincidence? Or, in Kant's difficult language, "How can I demonstrate that *a priori* synthetic judgments are possible?"

Kant replies that first of all we must give up the belief we have that we can know the external world, the world outside us, as it really is. We must content ourselves with admitting that we can know the world *only as it appears to us*. Kant's is not a skeptical conclusion. The world as it appears to us has a relative but nonetheless real "thereness." It is a world experienced by us as the result of an unknown flux out there ("the world-in-itself") filtering through certain categories or concept-forms of the knowing mind. The world we know, the *phenomenal world*, is conditioned by the concept-forms of space, time, and causality inherent in mind. It is as if mind lays down a grid upon the unknown flux and arranges it in such a way as to make orderly common experience and the laws of science possible.

Kant's emphasis on the crucial role of mind (cognition) in ordering the objective (that which is "out there") is not as outlandish as it may seem on first encounter. We are well aware, for example, that the year 1492, 50 A.D., or 2001 is not really "out there." Calendar and clock time are instances of the grid-laying operation of mind as it orders the seamless, moving web of experience.

Let's draw a diagram. Kant would not like it, for it seems to turn his theory of cognition into something like a box, and he thinks of mind not as a container, not as an attic to be furnished, but as a living, forming process.

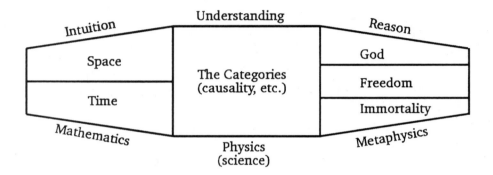

First, says Kant, we order experience by the "pure Forms of Intuition" (*Anschauung*), that is to say, *space* and *time*. We tend to think of space and time as entities "out there"; we cannot help but experience things and events as if they were located in a certain space and at a certain time. But suppose, by an effort of the will, we agree with Kant that mind is equipped with certain inherent forms that orient what is "out there" as happening in space and time. That space and time are rooted in mind is shown by the fact that we cannot imagine them away. Indeed, Kant argues, the fact that mind orders things in space and time is what makes mathematics possible. (Kant tended, in a rather old-fashioned way, to think of the foundations of mathematics as geometrical in nature.)

Now we come to a further refinement in Kant's concept of mind's operation. (By the way, we must not confuse *mind* with *brain* in this analysis; Kant would refuse to identify the high concept of mind with three pounds of matter.) Having considered the pure forms of Intuition (space and time), Kant then describes that power of mind he calls Understanding (*Verstand*). It is the *categories* of the Understanding that make physics (science) possible. These categories, which include the concept-forms of universality, totality, and causality, sort things out in such a way as to supply those universal and necessary connections which Hume found lacking. The categories of the Understanding project outward onto the unknown flux—that orderly universe-picture described by Newton.

There is one other great power of mind, and here comes even more trouble. That power is pure Reason (*Vernunft*), and against its pretensions Kant is going to level his most incisive analysis, one that will give his book its title—*The Critique of Pure Reason*. In pure Reason there are three dominant ideas: God, freedom, and immortality. We cannot help but think in terms of these three ideas. We cannot wave them out of our thought; they are there. And they lead us to the metaphysical foundations of ethics.

In his *First Critique* Kant lists three great questions: What can I know? What should I do? For what may I hope? I cannot help but believe in God. I am also conscious of myself as a being capable of freedom of choice, not a puppet pulled by strings over which I have no control. Then too, there lies in my breast the inextinguishable hope that this life is not all there is, that the human soul is immortal. Kant addresses the first question in his theory of knowledge and deals with the second question in his ethical writings. The third question points toward the realm of religious belief. Kant planned to write a book on that, but did not have time to do so.

God; freedom; immortality. How valid, how firm a foundation are these ideas of pure Reason? Unlike the forms of Intuition and the categories of the Understanding, which have material of an unknown kind to work on, to shape, the ideas of pure Reason have no material to order; there is no data from the realm of sense experience that relates to them. The ideas of pure Reason, says Kant, are *empty*; they do not have experiential content, as we would have when we form the idea of a causal relation or a universal law in physics or chemistry. These ideas are dialectical, for Reason by its very nature is dialectical. The term *dialectical* refers in this case to two notions that contradict each other. Reason, says Kant, will produce a thesis and immediately counter it with an antithesis; and *each proposition can be argued as cogently as its contradictory.*

Let's take the idea of pure Reason that Kant designates as God. In Kant's century there was an argument for the existence of God which was popular not just among the clergy but among the educated, literate public as well. It was the *teleological* argument, the proof of God's existence from order and design—that undeniable order and design perceptible in the eye of an animal or in "the starry heavens above." A very powerful statement of this argument was made by Dean William Paley in his *Natural Theology*. The book opens with these words:

> In crossing a heath, suppose I pitched my foot against a *stone*, and were asked how the stone came to be there; I might possibly answer, that, for anything I knew to the contrary, it had lain there forever. . . . But suppose I had found a *watch* upon the ground, and it should be inquired how the watch happened to be in that place; I should hardly think of the answer which I had before given, that for anything I knew, the watch might have always been there. . . . [rather] the inference, we think, is inevitable that the watch must have had a maker.

Paley goes on to argue that if we examine the complicated mechanism of the watch, we do not hesitate to conclude that it was made by an intelligent designer, namely, a watchmaker. How much the more then should we be persuaded that the universe itself, a mechanism almost infinitely more marvelous than the watch, is the product of a Creator, whose powers surpass those of a mortal watchmaker in like proportion.

This reasoning seemed convincing to many, but not to those who had read David Hume's earlier response to a similar argument. When we come upon a house, complete with rooms, stairs, fireplaces, kitchen, we believe without hesitation that it is the product of an intelligent designer, namely, a house-builder. Why should we not argue by analogy that the celestial array of the universe is the product of an immensely greater intelligence and skill than that of the house-builder, and that this artificer is none other than God? The answer, said Hume, is that the analogy is bad. We conclude that the house was built by an intelligent designer, that is, a house-builder, because we have had experience of *both* houses and house-builders. *But we have never had any experience of a universe-maker.* Therefore the argument from purpose and design, resting as it does on the structure of the human eye and that of the visible universe, falls to the ground.

Kant also questioned the validity of the argument from design, though he acknowledged its appeal. His response is at once more complex and simpler than Hume's. More complex because it requires us to accept his teaching that the world as it appears to us is a world conditioned by the concept-forms of mind. We cannot argue from the law-like character of a *conditioned* world to the existence of an *unconditioned* being, God. Or, to simplify, the world order is a product of mind, its law-like character derived from the character of the mind that knows it. Therefore, we cannot demonstrate the existence of anything that *transcends* this order.

Similarly, with each of the other ideas of pure Reason—freedom, immortality—there is no satisfactory proof of their objective foundation. Again, these ideas are dialectical in character; each argument for their reality can be met with a counter-argument. Every argument I use to demonstrate God's existence can be met with an equal and opposite argument for the nonexistence of God. Every argument I use to show that I have genuine freedom of choice can be matched (but not mastered) by a counter-argument that all our actions are determined, that we could not have done other than we did. The idea of immortality has the same dialectical character.

The ideas of pure Reason constitute that realm of philosophy which Kant calls *metaphysics*. He notes that metaphysics is a subtle and dialectical study that will lead you into contradictions, even deceptions, but it has some use. One use is this: Although we know that we cannot prove the existence of God, *we cannot prove God's nonexistence.* Therefore the atheist should shut up; he cannot prove that God does not exist. Similarly, while we cannot demonstrate that we are capable of freedom of choice, nonetheless it cannot be proved that we are completely determined beings, living mechanisms without the power to act other than we do. Libertarian and determinist meet head on, each immovable in the dialectical shoving match.

Another use of metaphysics is that it prepares us for a new discipline, the study of moral philosophy. That is why Kant wrote his second critique, *The Critique of Practical Reason*, which deals with the great question "What should I do?" (in short, ethics or moral philosophy). Kant's *Foundations of the Metaphysics of Morals* was intended as a popularization of his second critique, and it quickly became the most useful handbook on the Königsberg philosopher's moral theory. To that theory we can now at last turn.

*

Kant says that throughout our analysis of knowledge and its limitations, we have been speaking of ourselves as *knowing*, as cognitive beings. But we are not just that. We are *willing* beings as well. We know, but what is more important, we *act*. And every act presupposes a will to act. Moreover, we should note that while we know with part of ourselves, our knowing mind, we act, we will, with all of ourselves. We will with the whole of our being; we know with only a part of it—an important part, to be sure, but a part all the same. Unlike the knowing self, the moral self is not bound, not limited by the concept-forms of mind. Knowledge discloses to us the phenomenal world, the world of appearances; the moral self reaches deeper, touching depths beyond appearances. A purely good will is autonomous and unlimited; it is confined by no conditions. This is not to say that good will cannot be impeded by the drag of the passions, by ignorance, by selfishness. But of itself the truly good will is unconditioned, not constrained by the limitations of knowledge.

Kant does not claim that an act of moral worth has nothing to do with knowledge. It has much to do with it, for every act of moral worth is an act of a rational being. The ethical act is never an irrational act.

Kant's emphasis on the meaning and nature of the act of moral worth allows us to make a certain comparison. There are two ways of approaching the study of moral philosophy. One way is to begin by asking what things in life are good and how these may be achieved. The second way is to begin by asking what actions are right or wrong, and what principles will help us to test an act which purports to be of moral worth. The first is the method of Aristotle; the second is the way of Kant.

To Aristotle, the good man and the good life claim the attention of the moral philosopher. The moral life is a skill, the art of living a life proper to a human. A good cobbler is one who possesses and uses the skills that pertain to making and repairing shoes. A good soldier is one who has the skills proper to the art of warfare and the virtues (particularly courage) that we expect of such a man, considering his role. A good man is one who uses his capacities to live well as a man. Of a good cobbler we expect well-made shoes. Of a good soldier we expect endurance and courage in battle. Of a good man we expect the character and conduct that a good man should have. What that character and conduct should be Aristotle answers with his examination of the moral and intellectual virtues or excellences.

Kant begins his study of moral philosophy by directing our attention to the moral act. He says that the act of true moral worth springs from a good will, and that a truly good will has no strings attached:

> The good will is not good because of what it effects or accomplishes, or because of its adequacy to achieve some proposed end; it is good only because of its willing, i.e., it is good of itself.

Stated simply, our actions are of moral worth when we do the right thing because it is right, and not for what benefit we can get out of it.

Despite his discouraging technical vocabulary, Kant's theory of ethics is simple, direct, and in many ways in accord with the

ethics of common sense. Most of us believe that if we are to do
what is right, we need to have moral *principles* and to act
according to those principles. An example of such a principle
might be "Tell the truth," or "Live and let live," or "Act with the
courage of your convictions." Kant's famous moral principle,
the *Categorical Imperative*, involves the idea of the unconditioned
Ought, the Ought without strings: "Thou oughtst because thou
oughtst."

Let's look at the concept of *ought*. Notice how we use the word
in ordinary language. Sometimes we use it in a sense which has
nothing to do with the moral realm. Suppose I say, "If you want
to drive to Providence, you really *ought* to take Route 24 instead
of 136; you'll encounter less traffic that way." There is no moral
dimension to this use of *ought*; it has nothing to do with the
ethical.

But there are two ways in which we use *ought* that *do* have
something to do with moral right and wrong. For example, if I
say that you *ought* to be honest in your dealings with your
business clients, that's an ethical matter. Now suppose you
ask, "Well, why should I be honest?" I might reply, "Because
honesty in business is the best policy," that is, you should act
ethically because you will profit from it. On the other hand, I
might reply by saying, "Because it's the right thing to do. You
have a duty to your clients to conduct your business that way."
Kant is very much interested in the distinction between doing
the right thing because it will benefit you as opposed to doing
it simply because it is right, period! To him an act of moral worth
must spring from a *motive* of pure duty, not from a motive of
benefit.

But can I not do an act of moral worth, one that produces
good results, that helps other people, even though my motive
may be primarily one of personal benefit? Take the case of a
man giving a large sum of money to a worthy charity—a hospital,
say. The results are good: misery is relieved, and people are
helped. We have been led to believe that the donor gave the
money from a sense of humanity, because he believed he was
doing what was right for the sake of the right. Now suppose we
discover that the donor gave the money primarily to get a

favorable adjustment on his income tax. Is this an act of moral worth? According to Kant, this act may be *in accord* with the moral law, even praiseworthy, but it is not an act of true moral worth. Such an act must arise directly from a will that seeks the good, with no thought of possible benefits accruing to what Kant calls "the dear self." An act of moral worth is *unconditioned*; it has no strings attached, no seeking of satisfaction, not even of happiness (though Kant says a good will *deserves* to be happy).

Kant's point is worth repeating. I give my promise to do something. Why should I keep my promise? So that others will keep their promises to me? For the sake of social harmony? So that I will have and keep my good reputation? If I keep my promise because I am influenced by one or more of these considerations, my promise-keeping is not an act of moral worth. That does *not* mean that it is an *immoral* act. It may be *in accord* with the moral law; it may even be praiseworthy. But it is not an authentic moral act. Only if I keep my promise because it is my duty to do so will the act be one of true moral worth.

Kant's is an ethic of duty, and it is not just a matter for professors of moral philosophy to talk about. Take any senior enlisted aboard a ship who is instructing an inexperienced seaman, and the seaman is protesting, "Why all this?" The senior enlisted replies, "Look, don't ask any more questions like that. It goes with the job, see?" Speaking to reporters about his deployment in the Persian Gulf operations, Airman David Hudson remarked, "We'd all like to go home, but the job is the job."

You may have noticed the name of Princess Marie de Cröys at the head of our discussion. She was one of a group of women in Belgium during the early years of the First World War who covertly assisted Allied soldiers to hide from their would-be German captors and to return to their own lines. Nurse superintendent Edith Cavell was also one of these women. After a brief trial before a German military tribunal, Nurse Cavell was executed by firing squad. Princess Marie de Cröys, summoned before the same tribunal, admitted to sheltering Allied troops and photographing them to make false identity cards. The chief military judge asked, "Did you not know what danger you ran in acting so?" Her reply became a patriotic slogan in Belgium: "One must do one's duty without thinking of the consequences."

In his insistence that an act of true moral worth is based on the motive of pure duty, Kant emphasizes the sovereignty of the moral realm. Ethics is not a branch of psychology or sociology. The realm of the moral is a sovereign kingdom, not just a part of the social sciences.

Kant anticipates certain important steps in twentieth-century moral philosophy by declaring that the moral life comes to us in the form of *commands* ("imperatives") rather than descriptive statements (like "Cavell acted bravely"). He distinguishes between two kinds of imperatives: the *categorical* imperative and the *hypothetical* imperative. Hypothetical imperatives take the form, "I ought to do this for such and such a reason." Categorical imperatives take the form, "I ought to do this because I ought." Kant says,

> There is one imperative which directly commands a certain conduct without making its condition some purpose to be reached by it. This imperative is categorical. It concerns not the material of the action and its intended result but the form and the principle from which it results. What is essentially good in it consists in the intention, the result being what it may. This imperative may be called the imperative of morality.

Again we must note that Kant does not hold that the results or consequences of an act are of no importance. He knows that good intentions are not enough: the road to hell is paved with them. He *assumes* that an act of moral worth is the act of a rational being and must therefore have some good end in view.

Hypothetical imperatives include counsels of prudence. "Be attentive to your duty so that you will earn preferment and promotion" is as much an instance of the hypothetical imperative as Kant's own example: "Thou shalt not make a false promise so that, if it comes to light, thou ruinest thy credit."

Kant admits that it is hard to rule out benefit to "the dear self" in any of our acts that aim to be of true moral worth. In fact, he says, it cannot be demonstrated that there ever was an act completely pure in motive. But, he would add, moral philosophy is not concerned with how people *do* act but with how they *should* act, and we are *capable* of acting according to motives of pure duty.

Kant offers two formulations of the categorical imperative. Here is the first: "Act only according to that maxim by which you can at the same time will that it should become a universal law." Suppose I am faced with a moral problem which calls for decision and action. Can I honestly at that moment say to myself that I truly *will* that what I am about to do should be done by *everybody*? Or am I making an exception in favor of myself? Kant believed that most moral rules derive from the categorical imperative. While this imperative cannot tell us what to do or how to decide in a particular situation, it serves as an indispensable guide as to what we *ought* to do.

To will that our act should become universal law. Note the element of universalization as a characteristic of ethical rules. Commonsense morality confirms that universalizing is a useful method of testing the moral character of judgments or acts. Take, for example, the mother who says to her child who has pocketed some store candy without paying for it, "What if *everybody* did that?" Since the mother wants to wake the child up to the destructive social consequences that would follow if "everybody did that," Kant might say that her judgment is prudential rather than purely moral. Kant would admit that such a test may properly be used, that it is in accord with the moral law, even if it does not spring from a precept of pure duty. Many of us believe that children cannot understand the meaning of right and wrong unless it is explained that to do right will be beneficial to them and others. But Kant believed that even young children can understand the meaning of duty for duty's sake, and that the motive for acts of moral worth should never be represented to them in terms of reward in this world or the next.

Kant's second formulation of the categorical imperative follows from the first: *Treat persons as ends in themselves, never as things, never solely as means or instruments.* Kant states it this way:

> Now I say man and, in general, every rational being exists as
> an end in himself and not merely as a means to be arbitrarily

used by this or that will. . . . Man . . . is not a thing and thus
not something to be used merely as a means; he must always
be regarded in all his actions as an end in himself. Therefore
I cannot dispose of man in my own person so as to mutilate,
corrupt, or kill him.

This follows from the first formulation of the categorical imperative because if I recognize myself as a sovereign person, capable
of stating to myself "the moral law within," then I must recognize
and respect your similar moral sovereignty. This being so, I
cannot treat you as if you were—as Aristotle says of slaves— "a
living tool."

Our ethical common sense recognizes the power of this
principle and how easy it is to *use* other people. To Kant one of
the worst forms of immorality is to use a person as an instrument
while making the person believe that you are doing good to him
or her for that person's own sweet sake. Aristotle considered
business friendships quite all right so long as each party *knows*
that the other cultivates the friendship for its utility. But he
would have as much contempt for concealing our use of a person
as Kant had.

Apropos business, one could object that life could not go on
if we treated persons only as ends in themselves. The factory
manager needs workers to turn out quality computer parts. The
navy needs "hands," that is, men and women to work, whether
it's navigating a ship, chipping paint, or operating a word
processor. To this Kant would reply, "Understood! You may use
persons as means, provided that they know and you know that
they are primarily ends in themselves, possessed of all the
sovereign dignity of a rational being, each capable of acting
according to 'the moral law within.'" So if an employee in a
paper-box factory falls ill or has problems at home, it would be
the ethical duty of his superior to regard him as what he is, an
end in himself, and treat him accordingly.

It is a curious thing that in the society in which Kant lived
there were no agencies, or very few, that by law protected people
who fell into misfortune. In the last couple of centuries, particularly in our own, we have seen that burden shift from the

private sense of duty toward one another, often religiously motivated, to, "Well, let Medicare or welfare take care of it; that's what we pay taxes for." True enough, but thereby the possibility of our choosing to do good to others is reduced.

This concept of persons as ends in themselves is reflected in Kant's social philosophy. Consider for a moment his idea of the Kingdom of Ends. If we were to sit down to construct a model of a just state, we might with Kant think of a community of men and women acting out of right reason and good will, and receiving the moral law from within as sovereign individual ethical beings. In this realm of ends, each autonomous self would move in harmony with every other autonomous self, according to the same principles. All moral law would come from within; law would not have to be legislated from the outside. Good will and right reason would hold sway over greed, selfishness, evil teachings, and the drag of the passions, with each person a law-giver to himself as well as a legislator to all.

Such would be the Kingdom of Ends, a moral idea that Kant puts forth as a model of what could be and should be rather than what is. (For Kant was very well aware that ours is a world of moral and political conflict where external law, backed by force, is necessary to prevent men from injuring their fellows through greed, passion, and ignorance.) Kant's constructed community is an enlightened philosophical *anarchism*. Our own Henry David Thoreau would subscribe to this form of philosophical anarchy.

Once again it is striking to see how Kant, moving in the philosophical order, recalls Luther, who moved in the religious dimension. In Luther's treatise *On Secular Authority* we find this passage:

> We must divide all the children of Adam into two classes; the first belong to the kingdom of God, the second to the kingdom of the world. . . . if all the world were composed of real Christians, that is, true believers, no prince, king, lord, sword, or law would be needed. For what were the use of them, since Christians have in their hearts the Holy Spirit, who instructs them and causes them to wrong no one, to love everyone.

So the state is necessary, and it must be ready to use force to protect the innocent from the wicked. Kant wrote a little book, hardly more than a pamphlet, called *Perpetual Peace*. Like Hobbes, he believed that the natural condition of the human is war, not peace. But he held that peace can be achieved if nations will work for it. His model for peace is an arrangement we are not unfamiliar with—a sort of league or federation of nations in which the strong powers join together, agreeing that they will maintain order; and the weak powers, when they get out of line, will be brought into line by the strong powers. By giving up their "savage lawless freedom," humanity can ultimately form a federation "which will be ever increasing and would finally embrace all the peoples of the earth." But that day will be a long time in coming, and until that day, Kant believed, each nation should keep its hand on the hilt of its sword.

*

Kant could never quite put away his belief that there is something about war that compels our awe. "War," he says, "provided it is waged with due regard to the sacred rights of civilians, has something sublime about it, while too long a peace leads to a purely commercial spirit." But war belongs not to the order of grace, but to the order of necessity.

You in the military profession may know better than others the meaning of the distinction between the order of grace and the order of necessity, for you must often suppress in yourself the gentler side of your nature in order to carry out the stern summons of duty. As the sixth Dalai Lama said hundreds of years ago, "The demons and serpentiform gods rest on your severe and powerful shoulders."

There is a story told in the *Bhagavad Gita*, itself a part of the great Indian epic, the *Mahabharata*. Prince Arjuna leads a great army, and he faces, opposing him, an armed host in which there are many of his relatives. Arjuna holds a bow in his hands, and all await his raising of the bow, the signal for the battle to begin. He hesitates. And his charioteer, who is really a divinity in disguise—Krishna—hears Arjuna say,

I wish no victory, Krishna. I will not slay them, even though they slay me.

Krishna replies,

For a warrior there is no finer thing than a fight required by duty. On action alone be thy interest, never on the fruits of action. Let not the fruits, the consequences of action be thy motive. Natural-born action, O Son of Kunti, though faulty, should not be abandoned.

Arjuna answers,

By thy grace, O changeless One, I stand firm, all doubts removed. I shall do thy word.

He raises his bow, the signal for the engagement to begin.

And there we must leave him . . . to the wisdom of Vishnu . . . to the mercy of Brahma.

6

Utilitarianism: John Stuart Mill

Utilitarianism, empty of all ideal content, a vague cosmopolitanism, a leveling of a bastard democracy, will achieve, with this, its ultimate triumph.

J.E. Rodó, *Ariel* (1900)

In the Golden Rule of Jesus of Nazareth, we read the complete spirit of the ethics of utility. "To do as you would be done by," and "to love your neighbor as yourself" constitute the ideal perfection of utilitarian morality.

J.S. Mill, *Utilitarianism* (1863)

For a very long time utilitarianism had a bad press. It was linked with a doctrine advocating a narrow form of selfish expediency and with attempts to justify some of the cruel economic excesses that grew out of the Industrial Revolution. The first lines above are from José Enrique Rodó's *Ariel*, an essay which portrayed the ethos of Latin America in terms of the blithe spirit of Shakespeare's *The Tempest*, with the United States, the giant of the north, assigned the role of Caliban, its dominant values being materialism and a utilitarianism so heartless and mean that John Stuart Mill, the sober champion of the doctrine, would have recoiled from it in horror.

In his novel *Hard Times* (1854), Charles Dickens offered copious material to those who interpreted the book as an attack on utilitarianism, again taken in the narrow sense of self-serving expediency, profit-taking by heartless bosses and grinding down the workers to increase those profits.

In the academic world, Mill's utilitarianism endured a century of attacks. Some conservatives saw in it a weapon that secular rationalists could use to weaken or destroy religious faith, and many professional philosophers gleefully counted Mill's technical errors. Indeed, it has often been said in university philosophy

departments that the history of late nineteenth and early twentieth-century British social philosophy is the history of the correction of John Stuart Mill's mistakes.

Mill belonged to that impressive British tradition of brilliant
philosophical amateurs. Kant was a true professional, a professor of philosophy in a German university who had his own
special technical vocabulary which did not always serve to make
his ideas clear. His great successors—Fichte, Schelling, Hegel
among them—were university professors as well. They too required mastery of a formidable technical vocabulary if their
difficult doctrines were to be understood. Britain, on the other
hand, was served from the seventeenth century onward by a
band of knowledgeable amateurs whose thoughts were usually
expressed simply and clearly, as readers of Locke, Berkeley, and
Hume can attest. Mill had no university training in philosophy,
and his real or alleged technical mistakes may have owed something of their origin to that lack.

Utilitarianism has stimulated much revisionist interest in the
past twenty years, partly because it is one of no more than a
half-dozen models of the just state. Social philosophers have
found that even if they reject the utilitarian model, whether in
Mill's formulation or in some other, the burden is upon them
to show why utilitarianism is unacceptable.

On an early page of his *Utilitarianism* Mill defines the doctrine
in terms of the meaning of moral right and wrong:

> The creed which accepts as the foundation of morals "utility"
> or the "greatest happiness principle" holds that actions are
> right in proportion as they tend to promote happiness, wrong
> as they tend to produce the reverse of happiness. By happiness
> is intended pleasure and the absence of pain; by unhappiness,
> pain and the privation of pleasure.

Mill states that he does not mean just the happiness of you or
me, but "the greatest amount of happiness altogether." Unlike
Kant, who finds the nerve of the act of moral worth in the *motive*,
Mill finds it in the *results* or consequences. Mill uses this example:
Suppose a person is drowning, and a man jumps in the water
and rescues the person from a motive of pure duty; the man

swam to the rescue because he believed it the right thing to do. Now here is a second case: the rescuer swam to the drowning person in hope of reward. According to Mill both actions are of equal moral worth, because the good consequences are alike: a drowning person is saved in each instance. What we can judge *not* to be alike is the moral worth of the agent, that is, the man performing the act.

We remember that Aristotle identified the highest good as happiness. Later the Epicureans defined happiness in terms of pleasure. Mill's acceptance of happiness as pleasure got him into trouble. His father's friend, Jeremy Bentham, had earlier preached the doctrine of "the greatest happiness for the greatest number," cheerfully arguing that "higher" or "better" pleasures could be calculated simply in terms of *more* pleasure. Mill insisted that there was a *qualitative* as well as a *quantitative* difference among the pleasures—between the pleasure, say, of listening to a Beethoven piano sonata and getting drunk in the tavern on Saturday night. But he seemed unable to tell just what it was that made the first "higher" than the second.

Another difficulty that Mill's utilitarianism formula ran into was this. Suppose it were possible to increase the general happiness of 90 percent of a given society on the condition that 10 percent of the members of that society would be enslaved or otherwise oppressed. It would seem that in this arrangement the utilitarian goal of substantial net increase in general happiness is achieved, and by a wide margin. But what about the 10 percent who are oppressed? Such a society would not be a just society, and Mill was passionately convinced that justice was the virtue of virtues, the "mother-virtue" of the good society. Mill seems to have sensed what was wanting in his opening definition of utilitarianism, for in the last chapter of his essay he argues that the principle of utility requires that each person count for as much as the next, and that therefore not one single man or woman should be made to suffer injustice in order to increase the happiness of all the rest. Splendid! But is this admirable principle contained in or derivable from the definition of utilitarianism that Mill provides in the beginning of his essay?

Mill's teaching that liberty and equality are essential to the good society has been more pleasing to his critics, particularly those inclined to liberal views. Taking *Utilitarianism* and *On Liberty* together, we find two basic rules for a just society: first, maximum liberty for everyone until the exercise of that liberty conflicts with someone else's liberty; and second, no one should be rewarded more than anyone else unless his services work to the good of all. In his book *A Theory of Justice* (1971), John Rawls states that his doctrine of justice is not a form of neo-utilitarianism, but rather a quasi-Kantian construct of what a truly just society would be like. Yet Mill's two rules appear in Rawls's book under the heading "Two Principles of Justice": first, each person is to have an equal right to the most extensive liberty compatible with a similar liberty for others; and second, social and economic inequalities are to be arranged so that both are (a) reasonably expected to be to everyone's advantage and (b) attached to positions and offices open to all. So utilitarianism is like Captain MacWhirr's *Nan-Shan* in Conrad's tale *Typhoon*. Like that storm-battered ship, it has taken a number of quite visible hits, but it sturdily sails into its port of Fu-chau.

*

Socrates taught by inquiry, precept, and example that philosophy is not just doctrine taught but a life lived. The Socratic axiom that "the unexamined life is not worth living" may not be true for all, but Mill believed it his duty to examine his own life (why else would he write his *Autobiography*?). We too should examine Mill's life, which many readers have found more to their interest than his writings.

One must draw back a generation to understand Mill's circumstances, and look for a moment at the bootstrap rise of his father, James Mill, who with Jeremy Bentham constituted the first generation of utilitarians. U.S. Americans like to hear a story of upward mobility, of the poor boy who by dint of hard work, application, and grit rises to success. James Mill, John Stuart's father, was born in Northwater Bridge, Scotland, of a family in humble circumstances. Like Kant's father, James Mill's father worked in leather. The German was a saddler, the Scotsman a cobbler.

As a boy James Mill was singled out by a perceptive clergyman; and James's mother, anxious as every Scottish mother is to see her son go to "univairsity," wept with joy when Lady Stuart, wife of the local laird, Sir John Stuart, gave the lad money from a fund set up to send poor but deserving boys to Edinburgh to study for the ministry in the Church of Scotland. James did well in his studies, took his degree, and left Scotland behind forever. There was no clergyman's living available to him, and besides, he had begun to doubt the truth of the church doctrine he had been taught.

So he went to London to seek his fortune, and there he married a woman who eventually bore him nine children. With hungry progeny and little money, the Mills could hardly have survived without the help of Jeremy Bentham, legal scholar, reformer, and inventor. James Mill earned a meager living writing for the reviews, those periodicals which had come into existence in response to the demands of the new affluent business and industrial classes (for England was now turning from an agrarian into an industrial society). The poor young man wrote indefatigably for the *Anti-Jacobin Review*, the *Encyclopedia Britannica*, and the *Edinburgh Review*; and he edited the *Literary Journal* as well as the *St. James Chronicle*.

Then James Mill took a big chance: he decided to write a history of India. These were the early golden years of the East India Company, and Britain was fascinated by this faraway land and its multitudinous people. James Mill had never been to India, but he considered this an advantage in that he could carry out his task with greater objectivity. So while his growing family almost literally starved, he wrote his history in three years, and the multivolume work proved a popular success. Still, without the help of Jeremy Bentham it is difficult to see how the Mills could have managed.

*

Bentham deserves a word or two. As the co-founder of utilitarianism, it was he who popularized this name for the greatest-happiness doctrine. He invented a number of other words, among them *international*, so familiar in usage today that it is almost as if Adam, after naming the animals, proceeded to use Bentham's word for relations among nations. Less admirably, he invented the word *maximize*. (The unfortunate word *prioritize*, however, was devised in the bureaucratic circles of Washington, which also produced the barbarism *finalize*.)

But Jeremy Bentham was far more than an inventor of words. A legal scholar and reformer, he managed to get the number of capital crimes in Britain reduced from two hundred to fifty. No more would a poor rural mother live to see her son hanged for stealing a sheep. An educational reformer, Bentham played a leading role in the founding of the University of London, the first college for the sons of the working people who were coming up in the world. (Oriel-bred John Henry Newman sniffily referred to it as "that college in Gower Street.") Bentham's legal tradition was positivist—law and morality are not identical, though the second may have in the beginning fructified the first. The tradition known as "natural law" he regarded as "nonsense on stilts."

And Bentham was also an inventor. He constructed the *frigidarium*, a refrigerator built under a mound of earth to keep food fresh. Better known was his famous prison design, for he was interested in penal reform: the *panopticon*, octagonal in shape, had cell-blocks radiating outward from a center where guards and supervisory personnel could watch over their charges with less need for brutality in correction. The British government, at first interested in this humane design, finally reneged but bought Bentham out for £23,000. With that and other means that came to him he was able to enjoy life on a large country estate, to which from time to time he would invite the Mill family.

At Ford Abbey the great reformer was free to indulge his passion for study and his personal eccentricities. His favorite walking stick he named Dapple. And one of his tricks was to take an uninformed guest for a walk in his garden and there to pause before a small stone house, at which point he would brandish his stick over the shoulders of the astonished guest and shout,

"On your marrow bones, sir!" so that the visitor would know that here Milton wrote his poems. He had a collection of lowborn cats, the top cat named (for some reason) Sir John Langborne.

Perhaps Bentham's most remarkable invention was the *auto-ikon*. The science of embalming had advanced considerably by his time, and Bentham had access to a new high-grade varnish (possibly through his brother Samuel, who was an officer in the Royal Navy). So he conceived the idea of persuading wealthy families to replace the classical statues lining their driveways with *auto-ikons* of their elders. Why not take one's deceased forebears, one's parents, grandparents, for example, and with proper embalming treatment plus several coats of good varnish, stand them up on pedestals, so that as you drove into the estate you would enjoy the edifying spectacle of your forebears preserved in perfect, or nearly perfect, condition? This project, enthusiastically entered upon, did not prove to be a commercial success.

But loyal to his idea, Bentham required in his will that an *auto-ikon* be made of himself, and you can see it to this day if you visit the University of London. There he is in a glass case, dressed in his favorite suit and holding Dapple, his walking stick. His embalmed head did not stand up well to the effects of time and was replaced with a wax likeness; and moth damage to the clothes has required periodic changing or cleaning.

*

James Mill enlisted the aid of Jeremy Bentham in planning and conducting the education of his first child, John Stuart Mill, who was born in 1806. Mill père believed that the mind at birth is a clean slate, a *tabula rasa*, to be written upon by experience, habit, and training. When the boy was three, the two learned eccentrics put him to the study of Greek and mathematics. At the age of six he could read in the original Greek six of the Socratic dialogues of Plato (but later confessed in his autobiography that he did not always understand the substance of what he was reading). At eight he was ready for Latin. By ten he was reading history and formal logic. At thirteen he began the study of the new science of political economy. At fifteen he was prepared to learn French.

For that language he was sent off to France to the home of Sir Samuel Bentham, now retired from naval service. Sir Samuel had served Catherine the Great in Russia's conflict with Turkey, distinguishing himself by sinking an entire Turkish fleet bound for the port of Chalcis. The sinking was done by unloading a shipment of new recoilless cannon and turning them against the Turks. For this quick thinking and efficient action he was promoted to brigadier by Catherine and given a jeweled sword as a royal present.

Sir Samuel showed his young charge all possible benevolence, and deserves much of the credit for making the boy a Francophile. John Stuart's French was excellent, and in later life his favorite philosopher was Auguste Comte, the positivist founder of the science of sociology. (According to Comte, order and progress were to be the chief attributes of the societies of the future, and those words appear today on the flag of Brazil: *Ordem e Progresso*.)

Young Mill returned to Britain at the age of sixteen, and James Mill, now chief examiner of the East India Company, installed the boy as a junior clerk in the company's offices, where he would rise in the ranks until, like his father, he attained the grade of chief examiner. John Stuart was also made responsible for supervising the education of his younger brothers and sisters. At seventeen he had an article in the *Westminster Review*, a periodical that the Mills, father and son, were eventually to take over in a merger with the *London Review*. He also had a little trouble with the law at this time. A young friend had shown him a dead baby that had been left in a trash barrel; and the shock of this, combined with his reading of Malthus' essay on the dangers of overpopulation, led him to join his friend in distributing birth-control pamphlets in a public park in London. Young Mill was brought before a magistrate and could have been sent to jail for his offense. But the judge, who knew the Mill family, considered the matter no more than misplaced youthful zeal and dismissed the case. To the end of his life John Stuart Mill remained a staunch advocate of birth control. Like so many

reformers of his time, he believed in the Malthusian principle—
that the population of the earth increases at geometrical proportion while the food supply grows only at an arithmetical rate,
and that the larger part of the planet's inhabitants will eventually
go hungry or starve to death. Therefore, population control
must begin at the source of its increase.

Most of young Mill's friends were older men belonging to his
father's generation. He admired the legal scholar John Austin
and attended his course, which was marked by a strong emphasis
on the positivist tradition of law. George Grote, author of a large
History of Greece, became a lifelong friend and admirer of James
Mill's brilliant son. Grote also wrote a book on Plato which was
recommended to us at Harvard by Professor James Haughton
Woods. (The multivolume *History of Greece* came into the world
this way: When Grote married, his wife considered her young
husband somewhat lacking in ambition. So, to make something
of himself, she ordered him to sit down at a table and there to
write a definitive history of Greece. Thirty-two years later he rose
up from the table, his great history completed. But he disap-
pointed his wife by going off with a young woman sculptor, Miss
Durant. "Old men do these foolish things," said Mrs. Grote.)
David Ricardo, the brilliant economist who was the senior Mill's
friend, gave much time to the boy. And later Mill met Jane and
Thomas Carlyle, and a lasting relationship developed with the
roaring Scotsman.

Years of unrelenting study and intellectual labor, with no
allowance for relaxation and play, took its toll on young John
Stuart Mill. At the age of twenty he had a severe nervous
breakdown—deep depression, a loss of pleasure and interest in
anything, a sense that life was not worth living, and a temptation
to suicide. The acute phase of the depression lasted four months;
the chronic, four years. Relief from the acute phase began with
his reading of the memoirs of Marmontel. When the French
writer was a boy of eight his father died, and the little lad
announced to his mother and sisters that from then on he would
be the support of the family. On reading this Mill burst into
uncontrollable tears, a release of emotions too long pent up.
Later a good friend, John Stirling, persuaded Mill to read certain

plays of Shakespeare and above all some poems of Wordsworth, whose ecstatic reaction to the presence of earth and sky, to the interfusion of all things in nature, caused Mill to realize how much of the aesthetic side of his nature had been neglected. But there was stronger medicine in store for him.

*

Harriet Taylor, the young and comely wife of John Taylor, owner of a prosperous pharmaceutical business, approached a Unitarian minister, W. J. Fox, and confided to him that she was troubled because her husband, a good man whom she loved, could not talk with her about intellectual matters, particularly about her concerns for social reform and the condition of women. To whom could she turn to discuss these things? Mr. Fox said he would consider the matter.

John Taylor was forty-one years old to his wife's twenty-three. Already she had borne him two children, and was expecting a third. Harriet Taylor was just a little over five feet in height, but her posture was so perfect that she appeared taller. Great brown eyes, which could assume a piercing gaze, looked out from a delicate heart-shaped face of the sort that graced the heroines of Victorian novels. Her soft low voice and gentle manner did not conceal a fierce anger at social injustice, a formidable will, a detestation of conformity, and a resolve to do everything in her power to improve the conditions of less privileged members of society, particularly women.

Mr. Fox concluded that he had just the man for her, and she arranged a dinner to which John Stuart Mill, now twenty-four, was invited. At the table and afterwards they talked and regarded each other, and almost instantly, as a friend said, a passion sprang out of the bushes like a hundred Ashantees and carried Mill captive away. He fell deeply in love with her, and she with him. Soon they were meeting frequently in her house to discuss matters of needed social improvement dear to the minds and hearts of both of them.

Kind John Taylor noticed that John Mill was underfoot, and he asked Harriet if Mr. Mill, distinguished as he was, need come quite so often. She then confessed to her husband that while she still loved him, she was also in love with John Stuart Mill. John Taylor suggested a trial separation of six months—not from him, but from Mill. The lovers agreed to try it, but Harriet came back to her husband saying it was no good, that if he insisted on separating her from Mill, even for a time, she would have to leave him, her husband. If he permitted her to go on meeting Mill, she would continue to love him, John Taylor, and she would be at his side as much as she could. Whereupon the good man accepted the situation, even providing her with a house in Kent for her own use. Here John Stuart Mill would come to her on weekends to discuss matters of social concern; and from time to time John Taylor himself would pay amiable visits to the house.

The earnest pair travelled together to France, which they loved, and to Italy, where they found at Sorrento a little inn, La Serena, from which they could look out over the sea to Capri. All that *bellezza* seemed but a benediction to their love, and John Mill pronounced Harriet Taylor to be the most admirable person he had ever known. They returned to England with Mill in a state of exalted personal beatitude.

Were they lovers in the physical sense of the word? John Mill says no, and he was a man with an almost exaggerated respect for truth: not while John Taylor was alive were they more than soul mates. And Harriet herself says that from the time of her meeting Mill she was a *Seelenfreundin,* a soul-friend, to both men.

The pair spent hours discussing what they would write together. In his later writings, particularly in his autobiography, Mill insists that whatever he wrote after meeting Harriet was inspired by her ideas, and that in the case of certain works—*The Subjection of Women,* for example—he acted as her amanuensis, jotting down her thoughts and editing and developing them a bit. Most scholars believe that Mill exaggerated his dependence on her out of love's blindness, but agree that Harriet did have a marked influence on his thought and writings, and that he owed much to her.

Mill says that only the two-volume *System of Logic* was written without her influence. That work, published in 1843, proved to be a very widely used text. The first volume is devoted to deductive logic of the traditional Aristotelian sort and the second volume to inductive logic, where Mill sought to make his original contribution. His goal was to find a method of testing inductive inference that would compare in rigor to the demonstrations of the Aristotelian syllogistic. Scholars agree that he never quite achieved that, but there is no one trained in inductive logic who has not read Mill's treatise; and his so-called Canons of Induction constitute tests that we find today in more sophisticated form in the methodology of the sciences and the statistical disciplines.

Harriet Taylor's hand is visible in certain sections of Mill's second large book, *Principles of Political Economy*, which appeared in 1848. A two-volume text, its wide use was rivaled only by the popularity of the *Logic*. Mill did not set forth any original ideas of economic theory but offered a clear exposition of classical economics, at that time a new discipline owing much to the foundation work of Adam Smith and David Ricardo. From the point of view of the acquisition of wealth we find familiar principles, drawn from Smith and Ricardo: the wealth of a nation does not lie in what can be dug out of the ground, but in the productivity of its citizens (today we can think of Japan, if you like); the token nature of money; the axiom that profit is a function of the cost of labor; the need for free trade and a balance of trade in a nation's economy. From the point of view of the distribution of wealth we find a strong reform element, no doubt reinforced by Harriet's touch: a call for a wider distribution (sharing) of wealth in the name of justice; no inheritance of wealth beyond the first generation; and the extension of the franchise, the right to vote, to women and certain other sections of the citizenry (although Mill did not dispense with a property qualification in order to vote). Harriet Taylor was responsible for two major alterations in the manuscript: she made Mill add a chapter on the condition of the working classes and the need to do something about it; and she persuaded him to delete a polemic he had written against socialism and communism.

Communism? Eighteen forty-eight, the year *Principles of Political Economy* appeared, saw the publication of Marx and Engels'

Communist Manifesto and the outbreak of violent revolutions on the continent of Europe. Britain escaped the worst of the disorder, for she had years earlier instituted the first of a series of reform bills that ran from 1820 to 1867. (The Reform Bill of 1825 included the Catholic Emancipation Act. This act extended the franchise to Roman Catholics, who had hitherto been subject to a number of civic disabilities, including debarment from higher education.)

*

In 1849 John Taylor, Harriet's husband, died of cancer. His wife attended him faithfully, hardly moving from his side in his last days. There seems little question that she did love him, after her fashion. Mill and Harriet waited nearly two years before they were married in an obscure registry with only two witnesses, both of them Harriet's children. The couple settled in Blackheath, outside of London, seeing few friends and then seldom. Mill developed an almost insane sensitivity to what he considered "insults" to his wife, particularly from members of his own family, his mother and sisters. Estrangement inevitably followed and was never repaired.

Visits from the Carlyles were accepted. The bellowing Caledonian had come down from the north to make his way in the literary world of London. His *Sartor Resartus* impressed the critics but brought in little money. Citing his father's success in writing a history of India, Mill suggested to Carlyle that he write a history of the French Revolution, the vivid remembrance of which was still close to the reading public. Carlyle accepted the suggestion and set to work. When the manuscript of the first volume was finished, he entrusted it, the only copy, to Mill to read over. In a fit of absence of mind, Mill dropped it in his wastebasket and it was burned. Mill went to Carlyle with trembling limbs and blanched face to confess his carelessness. Carlyle looked at him in astonishment. "John Mill," he cried. "What ails ye, man? Have ye gone off your heid?" Mill told him of the loss, and Carlyle took it very well: "Aye, well, I'll do it again. It won't be the same, but it may be better." And he did it again. That and the second volume completed, the work became a great success, enabling Carlyle to put needed money into his and Jane's home at Craigenputtock.

John Mill and Harriet now settled down to work out a schedule of works to be written: *On Liberty*; *Utilitarianism*; *On Representative Government*; an essay on the subjection of women; an autobiography; some essays on religion—all to be guided by their shared enthusiasm for reform and the radical movement. But the physical health of each left much to be desired. Mill endured another bout of depression as well as a severe tubercular infection, with which he almost certainly infected his wife. Her troubles were put down at first to "neurasthenia." On medical advice Mill took a Mediterranean trip to Greece, while his muse installed herself in Torquay, an English seaside resort with a mild climate thought to be good for her "nerves."

The year 1857 saw the flames and cannon shot of the mutiny in India, which cost so many lives, British and Indian. It was time for reform in the great subcontinent, heretofore governed by the East India Company with the support of British troops. The Better Government of India Act was passed and the East India Company told to dissolve itself. Disraeli, the prime minister so admired by Victoria, proudly presented to the queen empress the imperial state of India, the "jewel in the crown." Mill retired from the office of chief examiner of the company with a handsome pension. He rejoiced in the freedom to take his wife to their beloved countries to the south, France and Italy, maybe even as far as Greece, before picking out some beautiful site to enjoy their retirement and write their books.

And so they set out. But Harriet soon showed that the journey was too much for her. Once before in France she had suffered a hemorrhage of the lungs and had been treated by a resident English physician. Now she collapsed at Avignon. Her frightened husband sent to Nice for the doctor who had helped her before, but he came too late. "Day and night now made no difference," writes Mill's biographer Michael Packe in describing the scene:

. . . her coughing was quieter and her spirit still, and then suddenly another paroxysm, a little gasp, and the beautiful dominant genius lay dead in the face of her uncomprehending lover.

Mill's grief was savage. To the mayor of Avignon he sent a thousand francs to give to the poor in her name. Distracted, he ran to the masons to order the purest marble from Carrara in Italy to build a beautiful memorial for her grave; on that marble would be written an inscription pronouncing the lost loved one to have been the sum and repository of all human virtue. He bought a little house as near as he could possibly get to the Avignon cemetery and planned to live there in retirement. But how could he go on living without her?

*

With Harriet's daughter Helen, Mill returned to England to work on the manuscripts that the loving pair had planned to revise and publish. *On Liberty*, appearing in 1859, opened with a passionate inscription:

> To the beloved and deplored memory of her who was the inspirer, and in part the author of all that is best in my writings—the friend and wife whose exalted sense of truth and right was my strongest incitement, and whose approbation was my chief reward—I dedicate this volume.

There was more, much more, of a sort that one critic said only one of John Stuart Mill's reputation could survive.

On Liberty was not a hit when it first came out. It was upstaged by Darwin's *Origin of Species*, which nearly everyone was talking and shocked about. And Britain's social consciousness now focused on democracy, teamwork, community, and unions rather than the radical individualism celebrated in Mill's small volume. The educated public did not want to read a paean of praise for individualism pushed to the point of exalting eccentricity. But in a few years the book achieved a belated vogue, and to this day *On Liberty* is a wine that will stand much watering.

We can ourselves afford a minute or two to read Mill's comment on his axiom of maximum freedom for everybody until that freedom infringes on the freedom of someone else:

> The object of this essay is to assert one very simple principle, as entitled to govern absolutely the dealings of society with the individual in the way of compulsion and control, whether the means used is by physical force in the form of legal penalties, or the moral coercion of public opinion. That principle is, that the sole end for which mankind are warranted, individually or collectively, in interfering with the liberty of action of any of their number, is self-protection. That the only purpose for which power can rightfully be exercised over any member of a civilized community against his will, is to prevent harm to others. His own good, either physical or moral, is not a sufficient warrant. He cannot rightfully be compelled to do or forbear because it will be better for him to do so, because it will make him happier, because, in the opinions of others, to do so would be wise, or even right. These are good reasons for remonstrating with him, or persuading him, or entreating him, but not for compelling him, or visiting him with any evil in case he do otherwise. To justify that, the conduct from which it is desired to deter him must be calculated to produce evil to someone else. The only part of the conduct of any one, for which he is amenable to society, is that which concerns others. In the part which concerns himself, his independence is, of right, absolute. Over himself, over his own body and mind, the individual is sovereign.

Note the last two sentences of this passage: "In the part which concerns himself, his independence is, of right, absolute. Over himself, over his own body and mind, the individual is sovereign." These sentences apply to many problematic cases debated in our society today. A motorcyclist refuses to wear a crash helmet, saying, "The law has no business forcing me to wear a crash helmet just because it's for my own good." What would Mill say? The cigarette smoker objects to the increasing number of restrictions on smoking, arguing, "I know smoking is probably harmful to my health. But the lungs are mine. I'll take the risk." Again, what would Mill say? The sufferer contemplating suicide says, "It is my life, not yours." Would Mill's axiom justify that position? Or consider the "pro-choice" versus "pro-life" controversy over abortion: a woman says with Mill, "Over myself, over my own body and mind, I am sovereign." Would Mill agree that his principle of liberty applies in this case?

In answer to these questions, a commonsense person might say, "Circumstances alter cases." Surely Mill would agree that the death or serious injury of a motorcyclist involves others besides the rider—his family, the effect on insurance rates, the public medical expense of long-term hospitalization. In the matter of cigarette smoking, does not the issue sometimes pass beyond the individual who likes to smoke—in crowded office spaces or in aircraft, for example, where smoking may cause discomfort or even physical harm to others?

The term *suicide* covers a wide range of cases. Mill would agree that force should be used to prevent a minor from suicide. More difficult is the question of ending life because of a terminal illness with intractable pain. Who "pulls the plug"? In such situations the patient may ask the help of another in doing this. But in most states of our nation, the person who assists a suicide is guilty under law of culpable homicide, even murder. We know that in certain cultures suicide was considered morally permissible, even praiseworthy under some conditions. In old Japan suicide compensated for serious personal disgrace. Under old Roman law a slave could not be punished for an unsuccessful suicide attempt, for even a slave was considered to have sovereignty over his own life. But the Judeo-Christian moral tradition, generally speaking, has agreed with Socrates in Plato's *Phaedo*: "A man should wait and not take his own life until God summons him, as he is now summoning me."

On the matter of abortion, so forcefully debated in our country today, would Mill agree that "over herself, over her own body and mind, the woman is sovereign"? Or would he hold that two sovereign beings, woman and fetus, are concerned? And if so, would he give priority to the woman or to the fetus? Although Mill and his wife were vocal advocates of birth control, Mill says or writes nothing about abortion (probably because in his time, and indeed until the 1950s, abortion in Britain was a criminal offense, and he would not have wanted to encourage others to commit a serious breach of the law with the severe penalties such an action would incur).

Utilitarianism, first published in *Fraser's Magazine* in 1863, was well received. Rather than concentrating on individual liberty and expression, this essay spoke of the whole, of the community. Here Mill begins, as Aristotle does, with the question of human desire for the good. Like the Greek philosopher, Mill identifies the highest good as happiness, for—as Aristotle said—happiness is desired as an end in itself and not as a means to some other good. Neither Aristotle nor Mill denies that there are other "goods" that we desire as ends in themselves, things we want for their own sake—health, family, honor, for example—but Mill avoids (or tries to avoid) inconsistency by insisting that these "goods" are *parts* of happiness.

Mill's *On Representative Government* (1861) conveyed by its title what kind of polity he held to be the best—a constitutional democracy in which the majority rule with due respect for the rights of the minority. The primary criteria for a good government, Mill says, are order and progress (Comte's slogan), though Mill is quick to point out that a despot's idea of order is not that of a liberal Englishman like himself. Basic to Mill's idea of order is obedience to just laws, while the criterion of progress tests a government's continued working for the greater good of its people. As for the right to vote, Mill argued for a substantial widening of the franchise to include certain minorities and above all women. Mill would keep certain property qualifications for voting and would exclude from the franchise certain classes of society—those continually in debt, for one. With even the most liberal-minded of his time, Mill believed that Britain's rule of India was fully justified; but he held that its goal should be to help the Indian people to form a good government of their own.

Always a good friend to the United States, Mill gave much thought to the American form of democracy. He had read and admired De Tocqueville's *Democracy in America* and had noted the Frenchman's observation that liberty and equality do not necessarily increase in direct proportion to one another—indeed, one often grows at the expense of the other. Some of Mill's own thoughts on our political manners may seem odd to us. He believed, for instance, that our political parties did not put their best men forward at election time:

> . . . at the election of the President, the strongest party never dares put forward any of its strongest men, because every one of these, from the mere fact that he has been long in the public eye, has made himself objectionable to some portion or other of the party and is therefore not so sure a card for rallying all their votes as a person who has never been heard of by the public at all until he is produced as the candidate.

This has certainly been true in some instances. In 1920, for example, the Republican party chose as its presidential nominee Warren Gamaliel Harding, a weak but successful candidate who had never been heard of by most Americans.

*

Mill himself was persuaded to stand for Parliament in 1866 in the district of Westminster, the tough political heart of London. His candidacy had not been his idea, and he kept his campaigning to the absolute minimum required. A poor public speaker, he was the last to be thought of as winning over the working class. Still, he earned their respect. Once Mill stood before a crowd of working men, soberly reciting principles of political economy, when a group pushed forward bearing a large sign with a quotation from one of Mill's writings: THE WORKING CLASSES, THOUGH HABITUAL LIARS, ARE ASHAMED OF THEIR LYING. A workman shouted, "Did ye say that, Mister Mill?" Dead silence. Then Mill said, "Yes, I did." And instead of the traditional vegetables being hurled at him, he received a round of cheers.

What got Mill elected to Parliament? First, his reputation for honesty and fairness. Second, unlike most prominent Englishmen, he had defended the Union cause against the Confederacy in the American Civil War. Right-thinking minds in Britain had favored the Southern cause and had cited, among other high-sounding matters, the right of self-determination. The truth, said Mill, was King Cotton. The Lancashire mill owners needed the South's cotton, and it was that rather than admiration for the gallantry of the South that secured British support for the Confederacy. With the assassination of Lincoln and the end of the war, the British public turned toward Mill's position. Third, there was Mill's unrelenting pursuit of social reform and justice for Ireland. That land, he said, had been miserably misgoverned, against her will, as an oppressed colony of Britain. So Mill won the support of the Irish benches in Parliament and the Irish laboring classes in England. Result: Mill found himself elected as M.P. from Westminster, and set about the task of working for reform.

Reform included a just government for Ireland and the broadening of the franchise. Mill's first motion in Parliament was the extension of the suffrage to women. He also championed the navy, which was then being radically drawn down. In a speech which his biographer has compared to the oratory of Winston Churchill, he proclaimed, "We have put away the natural weapon of a maritime nation: it is a national blunder. . . ."

Mill was no pacifist. He saw war as an evil, but not as great an evil as "systematic submission to injustice":

> War is an ugly thing but not the ugliest of things: the decayed and degraded state of moral and patriotic feeling which thinks nothing worth a war is worse. . . . A man who has nothing which he cares about more than his personal safety is a miserable creature who has no chance of being free, unless made and kept so by the exertions of men better than himself.

Mill condemned aggressive war, whether waged for an idea or to take over territory. But he says that "there are assuredly cases in which it is allowable to go to war, without ourselves having been attacked or threatened with attack." It is the responsibility of nations, he adds, to determine the circumstances in which going to war is justified. Mill was much concerned with the question of intervention, and in his writings he urged that nations carefully consider what would justify one nation's intervention in the affairs of another. He believed that the only way to keep peace in the world was international arbitration backed by force—a United Nations, as it were, with teeth in it. And he hoped for some kind of universal national service, convinced as he was that voluntary enlistment was not enough if a nation needed a large armed force for its defense.

Mill was defeated for Parliament in the elections of 1868, despite the fact that the Liberals, headed by Gladstone, had beaten the Conservatives over the issue of the disestablishment of the Church of Ireland (Protestant). Why was he rejected after two years of vigorous service in the House of Commons? One reason was Mill's support of the commutation of the death sentence passed upon two ringleaders of the Irish rebellion of 1867. Another was his highly publicized effort to prosecute Governor Edward Eyre for the draconian measures used to put down the Jamaica rebellion of 1865 (in which hundreds of Jamaicans were hanged or otherwise done to death). Mill also aroused hostility by backing Charles Bradlaugh as a candidate for Parliament. An able man with enlightened views of social questions, Bradlaugh was an evangelical atheist, given on occasion to standing in a public place, watch in hand, and allowing God ten minutes in which to strike him dead (not realizing perhaps that the Deity had more important concerns). Bradlaugh aside, Mill had a tendency to irritate fellow members of Parliament by interfering with committee work beyond his responsibilities, and by making unsolicited judgments about the moral worth of certain candidates for those bodies.

*

In any case, Mill was defeated, though most expected him to be swept into office on the coattails of the victorious Liberal Gladstone. Mill gave a sigh of relief. Like Aristotle's model of the good citizen, he had served well, but reluctantly. Now he was free to enjoy his retirement. High on his list of things to do was to return to the little house he had bought near Harriet's grave in Avignon. His stepdaughter, Helen Taylor, accompanied him, for by now she had in large measure taken over the role of her dead mother—seeing to Mill's modest wants, arranging his papers, getting his manuscripts ready for publication. Imperceptibly the same encomiums once pronounced on Harriet descended on Helen, with few words changed save "my daughter" in place of "my wife." To paraphrase Proust's Marcel on meeting the granddaughter of an old love,

> The soul of Harriet Mill had gone, but the charming head of the departed bird, with its piercing eyes, had come and taken its place on the shoulders of Helen Taylor to plunge her stepfather, the aging philosopher, into dreamy musings.

Mill tidied up *The Subjection of Women* for publication in 1869. This essay, which grew out of his conversations with Harriet, was the least successful of Mill's books at the time of its appearance. It had to wait years for its day in the sun, but it is now an irremovable classic in the feminist canon. Mill then prepared the seventh editions of *Political Economy* and the *Logic* (each had fourteen editions all told, seven on either side of the Atlantic). And he turned to finish his autobiography (all that happened after Harriet's death is given only a quick summary). The *Autobiography* and *Three Essays on Religion* were published posthumously. His views on theism no longer held in check by Harriet, Mill wrote that Jesus occupies a place "in the very first rank of men of sublime genius of whom our species can boast," and he even found a good word to say for the argument for God's existence from design. In a letter written by Mill in 1862 we find this passage: ". . . that the world was made in whole or in part by a powerful Being who cared for man, appears to me, though not proved, yet a very probable hypothesis."

The "Saint of Rationalism," as he was now known, found happiness in hearing that a motion to give the vote to women had actually been debated in Parliament; although the motion was defeated, one-third of the House supported it. It would take fifty more years and a world war before the franchise was extended to women, and then despite extreme and rowdy anti-feminist demonstrations designed to discourage it.

Mill found a good friend in Avignon in the person of Henri Fabre, the entomologist. Mill had an amateur's competence in botany, and the two savants spent pleasant hours together hunting for interesting specimens in field and farm. Fabre lost his job as supervisor of a natural history collection at the abbey of St. Martial, because he took to offering lectures in Avignon in which the sexual practices of arachnids were described in detail. Strange. Sixteen hundred years before, the great church father Clement of Alexandria had no trouble mentioning the deplorable sex habits of the female hyena. But Fabre's peasant brusqueness had offended certain members of the community. Mill gave Fabre three thousand francs to tide him over.

Mill also made friends with a young couple who had all the courteous manners of the English aristocracy. Lord and Lady Amberly were young, beautiful, noble—right out of the cast of *Upstairs, Downstairs.* They had a nice new baby and asked Mill if he would be godfather to the little fellow. Mill consented, and sent the traditional silver mug. Since the baby was thought to be in delicate health, he was brought up on asses' milk. It must have done him good, for he lived to his hundredth year as Bertrand Russell. So John Stuart Mill was godfather to Bertrand Russell, and I (*Moi!* as Miss Piggy would say) attended Russell's lectures in New York. I even had the chance of asking him a question: "How does your philosophical position differ from that of the logical positivists?" His reply: "They reduce everything to syntax. I don't *quite* reduce everything to syntax."

Mill died quickly and quietly in May 1873. An attack of erysipelas, endemic in the Avignon area, brought on pneumonia that could not be controlled. He was buried by the side of his wife's remains, with the marble memorial engraved with his proclamation of her virtues towering above. Fulsome praise, but at least one line of it is touching:

WERE THERE BUT A FEW HEARTS AND INTELLECTS
LIKE HERS

THIS EARTH WOULD ALREADY BECOME

THE HOPED-FOR HEAVEN

Not to end on too elegiac a note, let us go back just two or three years before Mill's death, when the students of St.

Andrew's University in Scotland elected him to the honorary office of chancellor. For his acceptance speech Mill took for his topic the humanities, and how they stood at the base of all science and culture: this ancient wisdom and these shining ideas were not to be treated as objects of contemplation, but as instruments of action. And at the end he recalled that when the Athenian populace listened to the glorious speeches of the orator Demosthenes, they did not say, "What an eloquent speaker!" No. They cried, "Let us march against Philip of Macedon!"

7

Existentialism: Sartre and Camus

Mean something? You and I mean something? Ah, that's a
good one!

Samuel Beckett, *Endgame*

We may make of our own history a hopeless inferno, a junkyard
of events, or an enduring value.

Simone de Beauvoir

The important thing is not what they've done to you, but what
you do with what they've done to you.

Jean-Paul Sartre (as POW, 1940)

Our sermon today tells the story of two young Frenchmen
of our century who wanted to be philosophy professors:
Jean-Paul Sartre and Albert Camus. Sartre made it, but left the
classroom early for wider activities, preferring near the end of
a long life to be known as *"homme de lettres"* rather than as
philosopher. Camus was barred from a teaching post, for he had
tuberculosis. He did not die of it, but of an automobile accident
at the age of forty-six. The two men became friends in Paris
during the Occupation of World War II, and somewhat belatedly
took part in the Resistance. After the war they quarrelled
bitterly, separated, and only the sudden death of Camus healed
the breach between them.

The pair became famous through their writings, associated
with the cultural movement popularly known as existentialism.
The postwar popularity of existentialism was immense, and for
a few years it spread to many countries, including our own. But
intellectual chic has a way of dropping off quickly, and in no
country is this more clearly true than in France. At the peak of
the high popularity of the so-called existentialist writers in this

country, French writers, academics, and intellectuals had already moved on to other enthusiasms: the New Novelists (Butor, Simon, Sarraute), the Tel Quel group, Lévi-Strauss, structuralism, semiotique, neo-Marxism, neo-feminism, and other areas of intellectual excitement.

In the past few years there has been a certain revisionist interest in Sarte and Camus. In the period 1988-89, four large books about Sartre appeared in English, including Annie Cohen-Solal's excellent biography. And Herbert Lottman's large biography of Camus (1979) plus Patrick McCarthy's shorter one (1982) helped many readers to take a second look at the author of *The Stranger* (L'Etranger), which sold millions of copies in English-speaking countries alone.

Existentialism derived much of its novelty and dramatic impulse from the background of the Second World War in Europe, and it expressed itself most appealingly in novels and dramas rather than philosophical essays (although Sartre's bible of existentialism, *Being and Nothingness* (L'Etre et le Néant) was written as a treatise on philosophy). Existentialism exalted the virtues of individualism, particularly with reference to moral choice. Individualism in one form or another has had a long history. In France, Rousseau was its great eighteenth-century prophet, and we have had our own brand of it in this country— the teachings of Emerson and Thoreau, for example. So while the philosophy of individualism did not begin with the existentialists in France, the originality of their exposition lay in the dramatic timing and form of their publications, and in the personal character of these (then) young prophets of the sovereignty of the individual self.

Spreading widely as it did during the war and postwar years, existentialism had a special interest because of its apparent pessimism, its proclamation that we are what we are because we have so chosen to be, that we are the sum of our acts, those acts in turn the products of free choice, a freedom we are reluctant to accept. Freedom is a heavy burden; we will do almost anything to put it down. It is much easier for us to assign our fate to external circumstances over which we have no control. We like to talk about our freedom as a precious possession, but we would really prefer that somebody else take care of things for us.

Basic to the Sartrean brand of existentialism is the axiom that moral choice is *irrational*—not in the sense of insane, but that no reason can be given for our choosing one or another alternative in ultimate situations. "Moral *reasoning*" is a bogus conception; reason has little or nothing to do with what we choose when the chips are down. We act first, then look around for reasons afterwards.

The First World War stimulated a cultural movement which dethroned reason and made the irrational king. Known as Dada, it was organized in Zurich in 1915 under the leadership of the Rumanian poet Tristan Tzara and the painters Picabia and Marcel Duchamp. (The latter's *Nude Descending a Staircase* was jeered by the untutored at its New York exhibition as "Explosion in a Shingle Factory.") Dada espoused the irrational on the ground that the educated nations of the West, with all their heritage of reason and logic, had created the supreme horror of world warfare; truth, therefore, must lie not in reason and logic but in the unreasonable, even the crazy. Dada dramas were delightfully nutty. A man would come out on the stage and read a newspaper article aloud while an electric bell did its best to drown him out. Or a bizarre character would appear on stage and point a banana at the audience: "Bang!" Curtain!

Dada was indeed minor art, but it flowed into a more significant tradition, one we know as *surrealism*. The life of this tradition's godfather-poet, Guillaume Apollinaire, played itself out like a Dadaist drama, though one of superior quality. Apollinaire returned to Paris from the trenches in 1916, wounded and ill. He lay dying on the day that the Armistice was declared, and he heard from his bed the joyous mobs in the streets shouting "A bas Guillaume!" ("Down with William!"). They meant the kaiser, but Apollinaire thought they meant him. So he sadly turned his face to the wall and died, poor man. In happier days he had been in love with a young English governess named Annie. When the family that employed her moved to Texas, Annie accompanying them, he wrote a poem for her, imagining her somewhere in that vast America he knew little about. Its first lines:

Sur la côte du Texas
Entre Mobile et Galveston . . .

His geography is a little inaccurate, but they are all good people down that way, are they not?

*

What books did Sartre and Camus admire? Who were their literary heroes? They read Dostoyevsky and applauded the Russian's Underground Man, who in a state of continuous bad temper and ill will stood for the irrational against reason, who denounced as pious hogwash the Socratic axiom that every person desires his own good and aims for that, even though he may be mistaken, even criminally so. No, said Dostoyevsky's angry misfit, there are those, and they are many, who go head down straight to their own destruction, and they know what they are doing. That is their "irrational" choice.

Sartre and Camus read Kierkegaard, that eccentric Danish theologue who was the first to use the word *existence* for the actual, the concrete, the individual, the man of flesh and bone, as opposed to the abstract, the system, the universal, the essence.

They read Kafka, that strange, haunted man of Prague who derived from his work in an insurance office the conviction that reality itself is like an enormous business complex where the filing system is both completely illogical and totally inaccurate. You pick up the telephone and get either no answer or someone who says, "That's not my area of responsibility; phone X." But X doesn't answer because there is no central telephone system, or if you do get his office you are told that your inquiries may reflect unfavorably on your personnel file. Most of us have had Kafka's experience: we have called the Internal Revenue Service or Blue Cross, only to be connected to a talking machine that tells you in a clear, friendly voice something that you positively do not want to know, since it has no relation to the inquiry you are desperately trying to make. Kafka constructs a pessimistic metaphysics out of this experience. (Our own Thoreau calls it a life of "quiet desperation.")

They read Nietzsche, who said that man is not a rational animal, that a human person is not a creature that looks to preserve its being. No, the human is an animal that seeks to expend itself, not save itself. Nietzsche punctured that false sincerity that passes for authenticity when we account for our actions. Freud would use it as an instrument of therapy:

> "I did that," says my memory.
> "I could not have done that," says my pride. . . .
> Eventually, memory yields.

American writers were also prominent on their reading lists. Sartre devoured "private eye" novels by the dozen, particularly those of Dashiell Hammett, Raymond Chandler, and James Cain, author of *The Postman Always Rings Twice*. This accounts for much of the tough-guy language that we find in Sartre's fiction. Albert Camus pronounced Herman Melville's *Moby Dick* as "one of the five or six books I call great"; and in 1960, the year of Camus' death, his dramatization of Faulkner's novel *Requiem for a Nun* had been running on the Paris stage for over a year. To these two would-be philosophers and men of letters, literature was more than fine words and beautiful characters.

*

Of the two men, Sartre was the older by nine years. His family was Alsatian bourgeois, and his granduncle was Albert Schweitzer, humanitarian and author of *The Quest for the Historical Jesus* (its conclusion: abandon the quest!). Sartre was born in 1905, the year of the first revolution in Russia and in France the law of separation of church and state. Sartre's father, who died young, was a naval officer. At the time of Jean-Paul's birth he was at sea as the executive officer of the destroyer *La Tourmente* (Turmoil). Young Jean-Paul followed the classic French education track of students of good family: first to the Lycée Henri IV, followed by two years at a good public school at La Rochelle (where his guardian uncle lived), then back to Paris to study for the baccalaureate examination, and finally to the prestigious L'Ecole Normale Supérieure, the government training ground for lycée and university professors. Pompidou and Raymond Aron were *normaliens*, as was Simone de Beauvoir, Sartre's lifelong friend and companion, who placed second in the entrance examination for the women's division in her year (top honors went to another extraordinary character, Simone Weil). *Normaliens* were held in great respect, despite the rude saying, "They know everything, but that's all that they know!"

Next came the examinations for the *agrégation*, a certificate of practical studies strange to U.S. Americans. These examinations were as difficult as those for scholar-field marshals in medieval China (one reason for the popular name "Mandarins" given to this learned crème de la crème). The top graduate schools in France today offer more avenues of higher studies: besides L'Ecole Normale Supérieure, Les Grands Ecoles include the Polytechnique, Commerce, Politique, and Administration.

In the early 1930s many French philosophy students, Sartre among them, went to Germany to study the philosophical methodology known as *phenomenology*, associated with the work of Edmund Husserl and the metaphysics of his pupil, Martin Heidegger, who succeeded to his teacher's chair in 1928. Husserl's method was a kind of Teutonic cartesianism: concern with the distinction between appearance and reality is abandoned; what you philosophize about is the immediate data of consciousness. Phenomenology, says Sartre's brilliant pupil Maurice Merleau-Ponty, "tries to give a direct description of our experience as it is, without taking account of its psychological origin and the causal explanations which the scientist, the historian, or the sociologist may be able to provide."

Although his large unfinished treatise *Being and Time* (Sein und Zeit) is dedicated to Husserl, Heidegger prefers to begin philosophy with a division of being and its kinds. The sort of being that concerns him most is what he calls *Dasein*, which may be translated as *human reality*. The reality that we know directly in immediate experience is "our kind of being," and it worries us, makes us anxious (*Angst*) when we realize that we do not have to exist, but only happen to exist. We humans are *thrown* into existence, and this sense of "thrownness" (*Gewerfenheit*) is the source of our metaphysical uneasiness. We stand too close to nothingness to feel at ease with existence, as the nonhuman animals do. By *nothing* (das Nichts) Heidegger, following Plato's later dialogues, means not a metaphysical zero, but simply "other than being."

Some of us may remember a program from the Golden Age of Television: Sid Caesar's "Show of Shows." In one of his classic vignettes Sid plays the part of a German philosophy professor, just off the Lufthansa plane, being interviewed by American reporters. They question the famous scholar about the big book he is working on. What is it about? In his best Teutonic accent Sid replies, "Es ist about Nothing!" This leads the baffled reporters to ask how a book, even a famous metaphysical one, could be about nothing. In impressive pseudo-Heidegger-deutsch, Sid answers, "Mein Buch ist about der Nothingness of Nothing, und how it Nothing-Makes der Nothingness of Something."

Sartre's career as a teacher of philosophy began with an appointment to a lycée in the port city of Le Havre. In the classical lycée, the senior year was known as the "philosophy year." Not until the students had reached the approximate age of nineteen did they have access to this prestigious discipline. The lycée professor of philosophy was an important character. So often in French literature this professor appears as a personage who makes an indelible mark on his young students, their characters not yet completely formed. Sartre made his own mark at Le Havre. The students were pleased with his camaraderie and his contempt for rules and authorities.

He moved on to a lycée in Auteuil and then to one in Paris itself, where Simone de Beauvoir attended some of his classes. The two had met while they were preparing for the *agrégation* exam, for she herself took the path leading to teacher of philosophy. Gradually the relationship turned into a fifty-one year "morganatic marriage" as they playfully called it. Twice during these long and adventurous years Sartre offered to marry her, and twice she refused.

Sartre planned to produce his books in pairs—one would be a fiction piece and the other a philosophy essay. The first pair appeared in 1938. The philosophy book was a monograph, *The Transcendence of the Ego*, making the case that there is no such thing as a *self*, that the word is a mere label for a bundle of impressions of mental and physical events. (French philosophers have often been attracted to David Hume's skeptical analyses.)

The fiction piece, *Nausea* (La Nausée), attracted more notice. It is the story of a young historian who comes to a town to do research on the life of a certain historical character. The name of the town is Boueville (Mudville), and the town itself bears a close resemblance, fogs and all, to Le Havre. The historian, Roquentin by name, experiences a horrible vision, a dark epiphany in which, gazing at the root of a chestnut tree, he suddenly sees all the tree's qualities, all its universal attributes, like color, shape, and the rest, stripped away, leaving him the shocking perception of existence itself. Bare existence has a kind of viscous quality that is so close to the atmosphere and spirit of the foggy town that he abandons his research and leaves, without saying a decent goodbye to an acquaintance, a self-taught man who believes in the reality of universals, essences, general attributes (we want brides to look very bridey, senators quite senatorial, generals to look like generals). The self-taught man believes above all in "human nature." That's enough for Roquentin. He has his shattering vision, the metaphysical counterpart of the stripping away of hypocrisy from the framework of accepted morality. Simone de Beauvoir said that Sartre wrote *La Nausée* while suffering the aftereffects of a single shot of mescaline.

Nineteen-forty brought the war and the German invasion and occupation. Every able-bodied man was called up for military duty. Sartre served in a meteorological unit of the French army and found himself a prisoner of war confined in a stalag in Trier. The German program was to return the French soldiers to civilian life as soon as possible, except for those deemed politically unreliable. The Germans wanted to get France back on its feet and running, with due subservience to the occupying authorities. France was divided into the occupied sector and the quasi-autonomous Vichy-governed area. French POWs were released batch by batch as their documents were processed and passes issued. Sartre escaped his POW camp on a phony pass unchallenged, while his comrades with legitimate passes were further detained.

Not long ago I talked to a Frenchwoman, well into her nineties, who lives in Adamsville, Rhode Island. I asked her about life in Paris during both world wars. Her answer: in the first war, the men were all away; in the second, they were all at home.

The German authorities kept French artists, authors, and intellectuals on a rather loose rein, provided that they did not make trouble or get involved with the Resistance. In France in 1943, eight thousand books were published and several memorable films were made, including *Children of Paradise* (Les Enfants du Paradis) and *Visitors of the Evening* (Les Visiteurs du soir). Book censorship was in the hands of a Goebbels protégé, Gerhardt Heller, a youngish Francophile who enjoyed French literature and laid a light hand on new literary works. A French author seeking to publish his novel was told, "Yes, a very good tale you have there, and of course it should be published. But look, you have two bad German businessmen in your novel, and that won't do at all. But it's easily fixed. Just change them to two bad *Dutchmen* and the whole thing fits beautifully."

By this time Sartre had written a number of dramas, some of which were staged in Paris. German officers with an eye for culture thought it chic to attend Sartre's plays, such as *No Exit* (Huis clos) and *The Flies* (Les Mouches). While neither Sartre nor Beauvoir were in any sense collaborators with the German authorities, they did not antagonize them, and in one case each they contributed to German-controlled publications (though the substance of each contribution had nothing to do with the political or military situation).

Meanwhile Sartre was plugging away on his big book, the bible of existentialist philosophy, *Being and Nothingness* (L'Etre et le Néant), the title of which reflects the ontological categories of Heidegger. Sartre's magnum opus sets out a philosophy of *man* in the generic sense of *human being*. It is the predicament of the human, the human situation, that claims Sartre's attention. *Man* in this usage is neither Aristotle's rational animal nor John Dewey's intelligent problem-solver. It is, rather, the individual human of flesh and bone, the hero of the Spanish philosopher Unamuno's *The Tragic Sense of Life*.

Human reality, Sartre writes, is incomplete, filled with the consciousness of a lack, an emptiness, at its base. We yearn for wholeness, for the four-square completeness that physical objects and even nonhuman animals have, whether domestic tabby or magnificent tiger. The nonhuman animal is complete, all there, lacking nothing; and that is what contributes to the impression of calm beauty when we observe such an animal at rest. The lack that we sense in our own being comes from the nothingness that is part of us. The nonhuman animal is completely *made*. We must make ourselves, and we do this by our acts, acts of true free choice. Our character is no more than the sum of these acts. As Unamuno says, we are not born with a soul; we die with one we have manufactured.

The authentic choice in the moral sphere is *irrational*, in the sense that no reason can be given for why we choose one alternative or another in the ultimate situation: to shoot or not to shoot at the solitary figure of the enemy soldier cleaning his mess kit; to join the priesthood or to leave it; to marry or to divorce. Sartre believes that in most cases the reasons for one choice run head on into equally cogent reasons for another. In a sense, then, the authentic act is pre-ethical. True, in questions of important moral choice—say, for example, to remain in the naval service or to take retirement to be with one's family—we go around to ask friends for advice, for counsel; but we've already made up our mind, says Sartre. To make out that our decision rests on "moral reasoning" is a cover to make it look good. We act, then we fish around for reasons afterward. (The existentialist act as the product of irrational choice is not without precedent in moral philosophy. For example, both David Hume and Thomas Jefferson believed that moral choice does not have its principal origin in the rational side of our nature, though they presented the case in a less dramatic way than Sartre.)

How is it that Sartre can say that we are the sum of our acts? He uses a metaphor which more than one French writer has employed. Each of us, he says, is in the process of painting a self-portrait, and every act is a brush stroke—not like an oil painting, more like a fresco, for an act once completed cannot be erased. Only at the moment of death, when we lay down the brush, is the portrait complete. Then for the first time we become essence, *what* we are, rather than existence, *that* we are.

Sartre and his circle were fascinated by what they considered the absolute lack of reason for human existence. An instance points this up. One day, in a preparatory class for the L'Ecole Normale entrance examinations, Simone de Beauvoir approached Simone Weil because she was moved to hear that Weil had been weeping at the news of the thousands dying in China of famine. Weil said to Beauvoir, "I think the most important thing is to answer the question, How can we prevent these people, all people, from going hungry and dying of it?" Whereupon Beauvoir incautiously replied, in the vocabulary of her beloved tutor, "I think the most important thing is the reason for our existence." This produced a chilly stare from Weil, who said, "Well, it's easy to see you've never gone hungry." Beauvoir later confessed that she felt she had been dismissed as a bourgeoise with nothing to show for it.

We say that the freedom to choose is a boon, but it is really a burden, says Sartre. All our instincts drive us to lay the responsibility for our acts on circumstances we did not create, while at the same time we rejoice in our alleged liberty. How often do we make excuses, particularly for those acts we are not proud of. We say, in extenuation of what we have done, "I got no sleep at all last night," or "It's that traumatic experience I had when I was thirteen years old," or "It's my boss," or "My commanding officer is really nuts." This is self-deception, inauthenticity: we put the responsibility for what we are, for what we have chosen, on others—rarely on ourselves.

It was in the POW camp at Trier that Sartre responded to this very human habit by saying, "The important thing is not what they've done to you, but what you do with what they've done to you." And there couldn't be a better example of this than Stockdale. What was done to him in the Hanoi prison was terrible, at times unbearable. But the important thing was not the solitary confinement, not the starvation or the torture or the beatings, not the psychological and physical pressure employed by his captors. No. The important thing was what he did with what was done to him. ("Everybody breaks sometime," he says. "The important thing is to make them do it all over again the next day. And they don't like that!")

Our freedom of choice, this burden we carry, this care, this deep-rooted anxiety, comes from one very simple cause: it is up to us. We must act out of that element in our being which is nothingness. Out of that nothingness we create what we are. We are the sum of our acts, and we cannot erase what we have done. (Conrad's Lord Jim could never escape that one act of cowardice; it pursued him to his death.)

But there is a sense in which we can annihilate our past, and this is what the nonhuman animals cannot do: we can make a 180 degree turn, set an entirely new course in life. You could leave this lecture room, and the college as well. You could resign from the service to become a monk or a fish farmer. You could leave spouse and family, never to return to them. Many have done this. You are free to turn your life around, though "free" does not mean "easy." Old volumes of the lives of the saints bulge with chronicles of scarlet rakes and sinners who suddenly—on the road to Damascus or in a Paris hospital bed—pick themselves up and, with a new moral compass, create a second biography. There is a French saying: "Out of the stuff of the greatest sinners comes the stuff of the greatest saints." (Sartre played the role of sinner with a certain philosophical flair but did not become a saint. Albert Camus was no saint, but he was made into one by an adoring public.)

*

How did the two meet? Camus came to Paris in 1943, the year Sartre published his *Being and Nothingness*. Sartre had read *The Stranger* (L'Etranger), published the year before, liked it, and welcomed the young Algerian Frenchman to his circle that met at the Café Flore. Unlike Sartre, Camus came from a working-class family. His father, a hardworking *pied noir,* had turned over the dirt in the vineyards of Mondovi with his own hands. In 1914, the year of his son's birth, Camus père was killed in the first battle of the Marne. Eventually his widow received a packet containing her husband's Croix de Guerre and a fragment of shrapnel that had been dug out of his skull. Camus cherished a lifelong devotion to his mother. Of Spanish origin, she worked as a cleaning woman. Partly deaf, and illiterate, she could never read her son's books. She was a silent loving presence in her gifted son's life.

After the death of Camus' father, a tyrannical uncle took charge and moved the small family to the tough Belcourt district of Algiers, inhabited by white French Algerians of the working-class. (The Arabs had their own quarters, including the famous Casbah.) Camus remained proud of his "Belcourt boys," the tough, street-wise French kids. They had a code of ethics which included, See that your mother is respected in the street; Show consideration for pregnant women; When you're after a guy, don't two of you jump him at once (it looks bad). Yet all his life Camus was haunted by the image of the young French Algerian worker: married, two kids, a job, and at thirty he has already played every card in his hand.

Teachers quickly recognized talent in little Albert and, with some difficulty, persuaded his uncle to let the boy continue in grammar school so he could go on to the university. The University of Algiers was then a small school, and Albert said he preferred the soccer field to the classroom. His intense extra-curricular activities included writing for the school paper as well as active membership in the dramatic society. Journalism and theatre were to form an important part of his life. "In a theatre I find myself happy," he declared later, and he remembered the drama club group (L'Equipe) and the plays that he and his comrades had made out of the novels of Dostoyevsky, Kafka, Gide, Malraux, Faulkner.

Since Camus wanted to be a philosophy professor, he had to write a graduate thesis for his certificate in higher studies before he could take the brutally difficult examination for the *agrégation*. Augustine and Plotinus formed the subject of his thesis. Camus appreciated the *quietism* in the Greek philosopher's teaching, the conviction that all action is inferior to contemplation. There is more than a touch of quietism in French thought. The eighteenth-century preacher Fénelon, for example, declared that all action is an insult to God. In later life Camus came to believe that political action, particularly revolution, carries within it the seeds of its own corruption. That is one reason why he left the Communist party, which he had joined briefly while a student at the university.

As for Augustine, much of the life and thought of this greatest of the Latin church fathers drew Camus' attention and sympathy. There is the African background (Augustine was born in Tagaste in 354 and died as the bishop of Hippo in 430, both in present-day Algeria). There too is the early Manichaean and neo-Platonist connection, the sinner-saint personal individualism so "existentially" expressed in the *Confessions*. And there is the underlying Augustinian concern with the problem of evil. To Augustine's cry "Death is the enemy!" and his search for what can be done about it, unbeliever Camus would attempt a reply in the language of the absurd in *The Myth of Sisyphus*.

Because of the discovery of his tubercular condition, Camus was not permitted to apply for the *agrégation*. For a while he eked out a precarious living as an investigative reporter for an Algiers newspaper and a clerk in the government's meteorological office. Then came a lucky break: a job offer from the newspaper *Paris Soir* that would take him to France, leaving behind a wife he divorced, the daughter of a physician unable to cure the girl's drug habit. (It would also take him away from another job offer that came at last—to teach at Sidi bel Abbès. One visit to that desert gateway sent Camus fleeing from it.)

Another stroke of luck took the form of Andre Malraux's reading of Camus' manuscript of *The Stranger* (L'Etranger). Malraux recommended the book to Gallimard of Paris, the prestigious publisher of France's literary great, and Gallimard published it immediately. Success snowballed. Camus' American publisher, Alfred Knopf, would later report that three and a half million copies of the work were sold in the Vintage edition. *The Stranger* tells the story of a young clerk in Algiers who doesn't give a damn, a kind of literary James Dean of *Rebel without a Cause*. Camus wanted the title to be *L'Indifférent* (The Indifferent One), but was talked out of it. The clerk, Meursault, goes to work every day simply out of habit. He neither likes nor dislikes his job. His girl asks him one day if he loves her: "I mean, do you *really* love me?" Meursault thinks for a moment and replies in effect, "On the whole, no." One day he gets into a bit of trouble at the beach. A friend asks Meursault to hold a pistol for him, for it seems that some Arabs are after this friend for an offense allegedly committed against the sister of one of them. As Meursault walks idly down the shore along the burning sand, he encounters a group of Arabs, one of whom half-pulls a knife. Meursault shoots him. He fires not one shot but four. Why? He does not know. Maybe the molten sun exerted pressure that pulled the trigger. Maybe not.

The rest isn't far from Kafka. At his trial on a capital charge (unthinkable in the case of a white French Algerian), Meursault asks his lawyer why the prosecution keeps bringing up things like Meursault didn't cry at his mother's funeral. "What's that got to do," Meursault asks, "with whether I deliberately killed the guy or did it in self-defense?" His lawyer replies, "The fact that you don't know what your failure to cry at your mother's funeral has to do with your guilt shows that you know nothing about the law." Meursault is found guilty, sentenced to death, and awaits the guillotine. When a priest comes to offer him consolation, Meursault loses his indifference and throws the priest out: "All his certainties are not worth one strand of a woman's hair." At the end he realizes all that he is going to lose—the swimming, the salt spray, the smell of coffee in the morning, the light on the silver earring of a pretty girl. All this wonderful world of sense will be gone, rubbed out. As his death-time nears, all that remains for him is the expectation that when he is led out to the place of execution, he will be greeted by howls of execration from the mob. ("Like a dog!" says Kafka's Joseph K. as he feels the executioners' knives sinking into him.)

Also published in 1942 was Camus' philosophy essay *The Myth of Sisyphus,* which helped to make the idea of the absurd fashionable in international cultural circles. Bad philosophy, said the critics, but it caught attention all the same. *Absurd* has at least two meanings: first, funny; and second, contradictory. If I ask, "What are you doing in that absurd jacket?" I mean first that its effect is comic, and second that its character is totally inconsistent with your own. So Camus elevates this ordinary use of *absurd* to a metaphysical level in order to apply it to the human condition: lucid common sense tells us that there is no transcendent reality, nothing up there to make it right with us, but there lives within us the unquenchable longing for immortality; we long with every bit of our being for that which transcends us, and yet we know that time and death is all there is.

Camus makes a hero of what he calls the absurd man—and there is more than one type of him. Such a man knows, consciously or not, that he is under a sentence of ultimate annihilation, so he crams as much living as he can into the time allotted to him. There is the actor, who, by the roles he plays, packs a hundred lives into one, his own. Says actor Jack Nicholson, "The actor is Camus' ideal existentialist hero, because, if life is absurd . . . the man who lives more lives is in a better position than the guy who lives just one."

There is the Don Juan, who presses many lives into his own, burning, burning into the flame. Camus was a bit of a Don Juan himself. Good-looking in his Humphrey Bogart trench coat, he attracted women; and a former friend, who felt betrayed, said, "Camus is a man who steals other guys' girls!" But Camus may have taken his Don Juan philosophy less from his own amorous adventures than from the Don Juan section of Kierkegaard's *Either-Or.* Art more often imitates art than life.

Don Juan is a conqueror under the banner of eros. Those who conquer under the sign of the cross or the sword also deal in their own way with the predicament of the absurd. They change the shape of the world, packing their multiple conquests into one single life.

Ranking high among the representatives of the absurd is the artist, particularly the writer of imaginative literature. Such humans give increase to their lives by staging the drama of the absurd. Like François Mauriac, Camus sees the artist as a creator of worlds: there is the planet Dostoyevsky, the planet Balzac, the planet Faulkner. Like the God of creation, the artist gives life to his own creatures, guiding their destinies or leaving them to find their own. Thus the artist (in Mauriac's words) is "the ape of God."

Camus' second novel, *The Plague* (La Peste), appeared shortly after his postwar visit to the United States, a lecture tour financed by the new French government. A plague breaks out in the Algerian city of Oran; it is uncontrollable, striking dead innocent and guilty alike. The hero of this rather traditional novel, Dr. Rieux, remains in the stricken city, sealed off by quarantine, to do what he can with his small stock of medicines. He can't do much. He knows his serums do no good, but he applies them anyway, visiting the sick and dying at the risk of his own life. Asked why he does this, he says something about common decency (*honnêteté*): "I don't know what that means to other people, but to me it means doing my job." Dr. Rieux is Camus' absurd man. He knows he's licked, but he fights back anyway.

In 1951 Camus' *The Rebel* (L'Homme révolté) appeared. It was a big, badly written, poorly organized semi-treatise, full of misplaced erudition and stuffed with proper names—Nietzsche, Hegel, Chestov, Saint-Just, Baudelaire, Rimbaud, Marx, Sartre, and a baker's dozen more. It took as its basic theme the innate tendency of all revolutions to devour themselves, with the Russian version the current shattering example. The U.S.S.R., said Camus, had become a police state, "the biggest Lie of the century." All this contrasted with the *artist's* revolt, which was authentic. *The Rebel* was a Cold War book, a "God-that-failed" book as Patrick McCarthy calls it. Camus' magisterial stumbling into the arena of political philosophy had nothing of the impact of Arthur Koestler's powerful novel *Darkness at Noon*. But few have noticed the consistency of *The Rebel's* theme with that Camusian quietism familiar to close readers of his work, that suspicion of action which is present even in the early North

African essays, not to mention *The Stranger*: all action, particularly revolutionary action, tends toward its own corruption.

Sartre and his editorial circle at *Les Temps modernes* blasted *The Rebel* as the work of a man who was afraid to dirty his hands. Sartre called his comrade of the Café Flore a self-appointed "high priest of morality" and jeered at his acceptance of the office of moral spokesman for the West, gleefully pointing out his mistakes in philosophy as well as "that pomposity which is natural to you." A bitter exchange of letters torpedoed their friendship.

A further source of estrangement between Camus and the leftist intellectuals was his attitude toward the Algerian revolt and its success in making a nation independent of France. Camus' father had lived close to the land. How could the FLN's idea of "independence" call forth such cheers of support from those who had never been there, never known what it was to be born there, to grow up there, to have been a part of French Algeria's sun and sky? To throw that away in the name of "justice"!:

> I have always condemned the use of terror. I must also condemn a terror which is practiced blindly on the Algiers streets and which may any day strike down my mother or my family. I believe in justice, but I will defend my mother before justice.

Camus' last novel, *The Fall* (La Chute), appeared in 1956, and it puzzled nearly all its readers. The book is quite small in size, smaller even than *The Stranger* (of his three novels, only *The Plague* comes near to middle-size). *The Fall* consists simply of four monologues. We are standing at a bar in Amsterdam called the Mexico City, and we hear the cultured voice of a familiar of the place, a Frenchman talking to a compatriot he has button-holed. The compatriot utters not one word, at least in our hearing. The monologist, it seems, has exiled himself from France, where he had won fame in Paris as a lawyer who delighted in getting the worst criminals and the most hopelessly abject out of trouble. As he chatters on, we gather that his motive for helping the helpless was his own glory. Like Satan, he promised in effect, "I will do unlimited good for you, if only you fall down and adore me." Why he left Paris for Amsterdam and the Mexico City remains unclear. Some critics have seen in *The Fall* an admission by Camus that Sartre and his circle were not altogether wrong when they accused him of electing himself the high priest of postwar Western morality.

The Nobel Prize came in 1957, at the moment Camus stood at the peak of his fame. Everybody read him, including people who don't normally read books, like university presidents and corporation board members. Preachers on Sunday would take their text from Camus, and the *Atlantic Monthly* proclaimed that Albert Camus was "a good man."

But he did not have long to live. It was not his tuberculosis, steadily worsening, that cut him down, but a violent automobile accident. He was returning to Paris from his new house at Lourmarin in the south of France, riding in his publisher's sporty Facel Vega, when a tire blew at ninety miles (not kilometers) an hour. The car climbed halfway up the bare trunk of a tree, throwing everybody out but Camus. He alone died.

That was in 1960. And there was not an obituary writer on either side of the Atlantic who failed to use the word *absurd* in regard to the manner of Camus' death. A wave of sorrow swept over France, with Sartre writing a healing eulogy:

> Insofar as Camus's humanism contains a human attitude toward the death that was to take him by surprise, insofar as his proud and pure quest for happiness implied and called for the inhuman necessity of dying, we shall recognize in that work, and in the life that is inseparable from it, the pure and victorious attempt of one man to snatch every instant of his existence from his future death.

*

Sartre lived on another twenty years. He finished the first volume of his *Critique of Dialectical Reason*, an attempt to give Marxist materialism its due in contrast to the excessively individualistic *Being and Nothingness*. This obscure work was not well received, particularly by Marxists. He wrote a three-hundred page preface for Genet's plays. Material circumstances, he wrote, made Genet a homosexual and a thief; but he was also Genet. Sartre's immense biography of Flaubert, although unfinished, made a similar point: every circumstance of the novelist's life conspired to make him into a model bourgeois; he became a bourgeois, but he was also Flaubert.

For the rest, there were the left-wing causes—Algeria, Cuba, Indochina, "U.S. Imperialism." Sartre and Beauvoir were threatened with arrest for distributing anti-government pamphlets, but President de Gaulle raised his hand: "One does not arrest Voltaire." Sartre's reputation and that of his loyal consort declined, in France and abroad. Concerning Beauvoir's last novel, *Les Belles Images* (1962), a London critic sniffed, "Sartre and Mme de Beauvoir have long been regarded as specialists in how not to be a human being, and Mme de Beauvoir more particularly in how not to be a woman."

A noted French bookseller said that during the last eight years of Sartre's life, the booksellers could not move his books. Students, the young, the intellectual left wing had deserted him: "On ne parle plus de lui" ("One does not speak of him any more"). Existentialism was *vieux jeu* (old stuff); it had been succeeded by structuralism, post-structuralism, semiotique, and the rest. Asked by a reporter how the decline in his readership affected him, Sartre replied, "I am not Shakespeare. I am not Hegel. But I have produced my books with as much care as I could. Some have been failures, surely. . . . Others less so. Some have succeeded. That is enough."

Alcoholism, sleeping pills, and assorted drugs dragged down what health Sartre had left. In 1965, without Beauvoir's knowledge, he formally adopted a young woman, Arlette Elkäim, as his daughter. Beauvoir bravely accepted the blow and continued to nurse Sartre in the long years of his continuing decline.

He died on April 15, 1980, in the Broussais hospital, his adopted daughter Arlette by his bedside. Beauvoir asked to lie beside the body through the night, but the doctors forbade it because of the gangrenous sores on the corpse. Throughout the world flashed the news of the death of "the last master of French thought," and fifty thousand people crowded into the area around the cemetery at Monparnasse. A news photographer caught a look of agonized sorrow on Beauvoir's face. An old woman selling newspapers at a kiosk said, "Now God will have to figure out what to do with him."

Strange that this avowed atheist-genius wrote a little play to celebrate the birth of Christ. In 1940, while he was in the German prison camp, a fellow POW, Father Marius Perrin, approached him with a request to write a Christmas play for the prisoners. He consented, and he called his Nativity play *Bariona*. Bariona is the chief of a village, and the despair and revolt of his fellow villagers cause him to order them to express their predicament by refusing to have any more children. When Bariona hears the news that a child who is a sign from God has been born in Bethlehem, he does not change his mind. But one of the three kings, the magi, persuades him that we humans are always more than we are. Our lot is freedom, at once our despair and our hope. Bariona embraces this freedom, consents that his own child shall be born, enlists in the service of the little king in Bethlehem, and though life is suffering, he will die in joy.

In his little autobiographical book *Les Mots* (The Words), Sartre tells how he lost his religious faith when he was young. "I needed God," he writes. "He was given to me. I accepted him without realizing I was seeking him. Failing to take root in my heart, he vegetated in me for a while—and then he died. Today when somebody mentions his name to me, I reply with the easy assurance of an old beau who meets a former belle: 'Fifty years ago, if it hadn't been for that little misunderstanding, that accident, that mistake that separated us, why, there might have been something between us.'"

8

Lenin and Soviet Philosophy

We have always said that a long period of "birth pangs" lies
between capitalism and socialism, that violence is always the
midwife of the old society.

Lenin, 1918

The principle of co-evolution of man and nature . . . involves a
moral imperative which is based on the principles of all-human
morality such as "Thou shalt not kill" and "Love thy neighbor."

N.M. Moiseyev, *Voprosy filosofii*, 1989

On the morning of August 23, 1991, in the newly independent republic of Estonia, a work crew removed the
statue of Lenin which had stood before Communist party head-
quarters in Tallinn, the Baltic nation's capital. The *New York
Times* correspondent on the scene reported the sarcastic remark
of one of the spectators. "It was done with respect," said retired
economist Aino Siiak. "A crane came, they put a chain around
his neck, and took the great philosopher away."

Vladimir Ilyich Ulyanov (1870-1924)—known to the world as
Lenin—was not a great philosopher like Hegel or even a great social
theorist like Marx. He was a powerful revolutionary activist,
responsible for the seventy-four-year rule of the Communist
party over the vast land known as the Union of Soviet Socialist
Republics, and the inspirer and idol of revolutionaries, large and
small, from China to Cuba.

But Lenin was a friend of philosophy—philosophy in the sense
of an academic discipline as well as in the broader meaning of
ideology. He read philosophy voraciously; and though he
pronounced Hegel's "idealism" as "incorrect," he came down
hard on those Soviet theorists who neglected the German
philosopher: "It is impossible to understand completely Marx's
Capital, and especially its first chapter, without having thoroughly

studied and understood the whole of Hegel's *Logic*." In the wake of the October revolution, it was Lenin who saved philosophy as an academic discipline, who rescued it from being thrown out of the universities and the higher technical schools in the early years of the Soviet Union.

Soviet academic philosophy had a strange, isolated history. Western philosophers paid little or no attention to it, and those few who did look into it were puzzled, baffled, and in most cases scornful of what seemed to them little more than propaganda with academic pretensions. It's a curious and interesting story all the same.

Quite soon after the Bolshevik revolution, those Soviet academicians who took the positivist line favored the elimination of philosophy from higher education. Following the French father of sociology, Auguste Comte, they proclaimed that the most important truths are best expressed in the language of positive (i.e., physical) science. Now that we have science, argued the Bolshevik positivists, philosophy is useless; furthermore, philosophy is dangerous, for it has a close affinity to religion. So, "Overboard with philosophy!" ("*Filosofiu za bort!*").

But Lenin held up his hand. No, he said, we need philosophy; we need philosophy in order to synthesize, clarify, and even to criticize the conclusions of science. As a result of Lenin's intervention on behalf of the discipline, philosophy occupied an important place in the teaching and writing of the higher echelons of Soviet academia.

Lenin established a philosophy journal titled *Under the Banner of Marxism*. It never achieved intellectual respectability because it made indefensible claims, such as the existence of a "class character" differentiating Western bourgeois from Soviet socialist science. The editor, A.M. Deborin, a man of some intellectual ability, was ultimately removed from his post as a "Menshivising idealist," one of the more lethal weapons in the arsenal of orthodox Soviet invective.

Not until after the Second World War did Soviet academic philosophy try to take on a posture that would qualify it intellectually as a competitor of Western thought. In 1947, while Russia was still pulling herself together after the shattering experience of "the Great Patriotic War," Stalin ordered his cultural hatchet-man, Andrei Zhdanov, to assemble the academicians and scientists and to tell them that they'd been hiding behind protestations of loyalty and devotion to Marxist-Leninism for too long, that it was time for them to produce Soviet material of intellectual merit. In 1948 the first respectable journal of Soviet philosophy appeared: *Problems of Philosophy* (Voprosy filosofii), which continues to be published to this day.

*

Stalin showed a curious though limited interest in philosophy late in life. He had none of the intellectual brilliance of Lenin (to whom reading and discussing philosophy was a treat), but he developed firm convictions on the relation between language and thought. A series of Stalin's articles were bound together before his death in a little book, *Letters on Linguistics*, in which he criticized certain Soviet scholars for their theories of language which he believed to be incorrect.

The first of these scholars was an odd figure named Nikolai Yakovlovich Marr, a Russified Scot. Marr had what we find in many Russians long before the Bolshevik revolution: a pleasurable interest in Utopias. He believed that the language of the future would not need to be spoken or written, that our thoughts would emanate from our separate psyches like radio waves, producing instant and reliable communication. Under these circumstances, there wouldn't be differences in language; there would be a universal language constructed from mathematics and deductive logic. Though unappreciated by Stalin, poor Marr was no more than a humble representative of a long tradition that dreamed of a universal language, including great scholars as different as the German philosopher-mathematician Leibniz and the Italian historian and polymath, Giambatista Vico.

Stalin was particularly angered by Marr's claim that language is not part of the *base* of a society but part of its *superstructure*. In Marxist theory, the base elements of a society would include its means of production. Ethics and religion would be part of the superstructure, because they are functions of the society's material conditions and modes of exchange. In one of his letters on linguistics, Stalin pronounced Marr's theory incorrect on the ground that language belongs to neither the base nor the superstructure, but to something quite different, presumably a special plane of its own. Little was heard of Marr after that.

A more intellectually formidable linguistic scholar was removed from Stalin's wrath by illness. Lev Semenovich Vygotsky, who died of tuberculosis in 1934 at the age of thirty-eight, was one of the founders of cognitive psychology. Vygotsky held that language and thought come from two different roots, while Stalin responded that this was nonsense, that thought and language arise from a common root. Stalin's linguistic theories were closer to those of Pavlovian behaviorism and the American psychologist John Watson, who declared that thinking is no more than subvocal talking. Vygotsky claimed that the relation between language and cognition is far more complicated than that. He believed, for example, that a child's language development moves from a prelinguistic stage to external speech, and then to the far more mature level of "internalized speech."

Vygotsky conducted empirical investigations to see whether socialization or lack of socialization had any important effect on thought. He would give dolls to city children and country children, and he would ask them questions. And he found enough empirical evidence to satisfy himself that the development of a child's mind and language ability is to an important degree dependent upon early and continuing socialization.

One of Vygotsky's disciples, Alexander Romanovich Luria, carried out some of these experiments in the steppes of central Asia. Approaching a peasant, Luria would give the fellow the premises of a simple syllogism: "In the far north, where there is eternal snow, the bears are white. Now Novaya Zemlya is in the far north, where there is eternal snow. What color are the bears there?" Instead of the expected reply ("white"), Luria received a variety of different responses: "Well, there are many kinds of bears," or "Look, your honor, if you want to find out about the color of the bears, why don't you go up there and see for yourself?" or even "You have your tsar and we have ours. Why don't you just go your way?" (this spoken nearly twenty years after the revolution).

*

Over the years Soviet scholarship has reflected the changes in the limits of government tolerance of art, science, and philosophy. Here is an excerpt from a 1950 Soviet textbook on the history of philosophy:

> The tasks of this chapter are to subject to partisan Bolshevik criticism the reactionary, bourgeois ideology of the imperialist period; to show its connection with the general crisis of capitalism and with the corruption of all contemporary bourgeois culture; to pull to pieces with particular severity the reactionary philosophical and sociological doctrines used nowadays by the enemies of Marxism; to show that V.I. Lenin and J.V. Stalin tirelessly attacked the rotten anti-Marxist idealistic doctrines and reactionary social ideas of the imperialistic bourgeoisie and mercilessly exposed every kind of tendency toward idealism and priestcraft; and to emphasize that the contemporary bourgeois ideology is an arsenal of reactionary and odious ideas for the right-wing socialists—the lackeys of the imperialistic bourgeoisie.

Now you will admit that this is not exactly objective criticism.

By way of contrast, let's turn to *Voprosy filosofii* fifteen years after the death of Stalin. Nineteen sixty-eight marked the beginning of a certain degree of easing of government control over philosophy, particularly the philosophy of science. The journal's editor that year, biologist I.T. Frolov, criticized the concept of "party science," with particular reference to the government-backed theories of agronomist Trofim Lysenko (whom we shall discuss later). And the journal's contributors showed a new and somewhat tolerant interest in the work of Western academic philosophers.

Consider a 1968 review of a book by a U.S. American professor of philosophy. Here we can see how careful the reviewer is in trying to make clear the composition and ideas of the book without interposing polemical remarks in disagreement. Indeed, the word *bourgeois* does not occur even once:

> Among the problems central to the main content of contemporary philosophical thought, the author considers the foremost one to be linguistic philosophy; he devotes the first part of his book to this subject. The second part throws light on the problem of knowledge, the third on metaphysical and speculative philosophy, and the fourth on the problem of values. He devotes special attention to the question, "What is philosophy?" The author analyzes various answers—which he considers to be one-sided—which have been given to this question. From his point of view, philosophy contains three basic areas of knowledge: analytical, speculative and moral. . . . Philosophy should go along the path of a synthesis of these three directions, writes the author, but so far it has gone instead along the path of sharp differentiation of them. Traditional philosophy, studying facts (reality) outside of man, is in principle similar to science. This is predominantly "continental" philosophy. "Anglo-American" linguistic philosophy occupies itself with an analysis of the language in which one speaks about these facts. The author's book contains numerous and very well-chosen quotations from philosophers on all these problems, and an excellently compiled reference-bibliographical apparatus.

The book reviewed above is the second edition of *The Meaning of Philosophy* (New York, 1967), and its author, as Miss Piggy used to say, "C'est moi!"

Since 1968 *Voprosy filosofii* has had its ups and downs (the downs represented by articles such as "Following the Glorious Road of the October Revolution"), but generally speaking, its track shows movement away from government-controlled party dogmatism to a widening of philosophical interests to include, if not to approve, the ways of Western academic philosophy.

*

To return to Lenin and earlier controversies in Soviet philosophy, we might first look at his idea of philosophy. It was

a very simple one: there are two kinds of philosophy—
materialism and idealism; the first is correct, the second incorrect. Let's make a brief excursus to look at each of these
important traditions in philosophy.

First, a pair of distinctions in meaning. The ordinary usage of
the term *materialism* refers to undue concern with material
goods—fine houses, stylish clothes, sleek automobiles, wealth
and possessions; whereas the ordinary usage of *idealism* con-
notes priority given to high moral or spiritual aims—pursuit of
ends sometimes hard if not impossible to achieve. The
philosophical usage of the terms *materialism* and *idealism* is quite
different. In philosophy, the materialist holds that reality is
basically physical, that organic life, consciousness, mind, and
thought, are complex organizations or operations of matter, the
physical; while the idealist believes that reality has the character
of mind, thought, spirit, and consciousness—if there are physical
facts, they are secondary to, and functions of, cognition, idea,
spirit.

Western materialism had its origin in ancient Greece, when
certain philosophers turned away from explanations of natural
phenomena in terms of gods and spirits in favor of physical
causes. Democritus, for example, explained reality in terms of a
refinement of Empedocles' earth, air, fire, and water. Everything
that is real, said Democritus, is made up of invisible particles of
varied shape and weight called *atoms* (uncuttable; indivisible).
All that exists is composed of these minute particles, which are
forever in motion. (Karl Marx, by the way, wrote his doctoral
dissertation on the materialism of Democritus.) The Stoics
picked up this thread and wove it into a cosmology that is frankly
materialist: God, soul, mind, reason—everything that exists is
corporeal. (Yet in describing these things, the Stoic vocabulary
refines matter to the point of spirit.)

There was no place for materialism in the religion-connected
philosophies of the Middle Ages, but the doctrine revived in
modern times is an extrapolation of some of the discoveries and
methods of the new physical sciences. Seventeenth-century Descartes was no materialist, but his sharp dualism between mind
and body opened the way for a thoroughgoing materialist

doctrine. To Descartes, the soul resides in a body which is a "machine designed by the hand of God." Descartes' successors in France, the eighteenth-century *philosophes*, found that the machine was enough, that there was no need for a soul whose nature was completely other than matter. This was the philosophy of La Mettrie, set forth in his treatise *Man a Machine* (L'Homme machine). Nor was there any further use for that pure spirit, God. Approaching the astronomer Laplace (author of *Celestial Mechanics* (Mécanique céleste)), Napoleon is said to have remarked, "Admirable! But where is God in your system?" To which Laplace replied, "Sire, I have no need for that hypothesis."

Nineteenth-century biology stimulated the doctrine of organic evolution, culminating in Darwin's conclusion in *The Descent of Man* (1871) that we humans are descended from nonhuman animals. Darwin's admirer, T.H. Huxley, declared that mind, thought, spirit represent *epiphenomena* of the body. Just as a great electrical machine may give rise to an aura of vivid colors radiating from it, so soul, consciousness, mind, thought are the products of the matter in motion which constitutes the body. Biological materialism has continued into our own century. In 1951, the discovery of the genetic code in the DNA molecule by Watson and Crick seemed to many to confirm materialist philosophy. James Watson's attitude remained frankly materialist, though he declared that philosophical questions interested him not at all. To him, it was a question of what could be observed on a slide under the microscope or submitted to physical examination by more delicate means.

Now let us turn to philosophical idealism. Its great exponent in ancient Greece, Plato, taught that reality cannot be of the nature of this world of matter, a world where perceived things come into being and go out of being, but never really *are*. True being must be something far closer to the character of mind, thought, soul, idea than to matter. Hence the label *idealism*, here Platonic idealism.

With idealism we again have a spin-off from the brilliant scientific work of the seventeenth century. Locke, who read Newton carefully, says in his *Essay on Human Understanding* that if we are to take the test of experience as primary verification, then we must admit that we do not know objects in the external world directly; what we experience are our perceptions of these objects; what we know directly are ideas (sensations) of things. To this George Berkeley responded that there is no way of comparing our perceptions with the external world. Therefore, the world is composed of our perceptions; it is a mental, a spiritual world, with no need of a material, physical backing. The world is a panorama of our perceptions, its order (as in science) a product of the continuous creation of God.

Immanuel Kant believed that Berkeley's idealism was too simple. Kant held that there is an external reality, but our knowledge of it is conditioned by the concept-forms of space, time, and causality. The world has a rational, orderly character because of the rational, orderly character of the mind, which lays down its grid upon the unknown flux of the world-in-itself, the better to control and master that world.

With Fichte and Schelling clearing the way for him, Hegel took Kantian idealism to its nth degree of complexity, holding that reality is the continuous unfolding of the consciousness of Absolute Spirit, the continuous, ever increasing self-awareness of God—that is to say, Aristotle's self-thinking thought carried to its logical world-historical conclusion. So that history, Hegel taught, is the operation of Absolute Spirit in the world it has made, and is still making.

Marx was strongly attracted to Hegel's method of *dialectic*, and concluded that this method could be combined with materialism to give the latter the life and movement it needed. After rereading Hegel's *Logic*, Marx said that his task was to "extract the rational kernel of dialectic from the mystical shell of Hegel's idealism."

Hegel did not invent the dialectical method. That method is as old as Socrates' way of reaching for a sound definition by exposing inner contradictions. But Hegel's dialectical method was far more elaborate than the early Socratic version, since, for one thing, the German had the work of his predecessors—particularly Kant, Fichte, and Schelling—to profit by.

Discussion of Hegelian dialectic would take us too far afield, so let us content ourselves by accepting the simple definition implicit in Marx's reading. Dialectical materialism is the philosophical teaching that matter lies at the root of all things; it is the really real. But matter is not an aggregation of dead lumps. Rather, matter moves progressively. It has its own powerful dynamic, relentlessly moving to overcome the one-sidedness of things by exposing the contradictions that dwell at the heart of every stage of becoming. This is true whether we are talking about chemistry, the labor theory of value, or the relation of morality to a given society's control of the means of production. In sum, matter moves and develops according to the laws of dialectic inherent within it, so that at various stages it produces organic life, consciousness, mind. History itself—be it art, religion, politics, economics—is produced by the dialectical drive of matter.

Marx and Engels did not actually use the term *dialectical materialism* in their writings, though they had the idea and related words for it. The term appeared in the first textbook of dialectical materialism, written by Lenin's friend G.V. Plekhanov. At one point Plekhanov got into trouble because he was a Menshevik, but he was never harmed because of his known friendship with Lenin, who said, "Nobody can understand, I mean *understand*, dialectical materialism who has not read and thoroughly digested Plekhanov's book."

*

What about Lenin himself? He wrote a book on philosophy entitled *Materialism and Empirio-Criticism*. Published in 1908, it was a product of those halcyon years spent down in Capri with his friend Gorky, a fellow exile. The pair talked and read philosophy, and Lenin's pondering of Hegel's writings reinforced his conviction that philosophy was needed to supply a critique of the sciences (since science was too important to be left to the scientists). Like all of his writings, Lenin's *Materialism and Empirio-Criticism* is polemical in style. Basically, it is a fierce attack on the theories of Ernst Mach, professor of physics at the

University of Vienna. (Jet pilots are familiar by experience with the meaning of the "Mach number," the ratio of the speed of an object through a gas to the speed of sound.) Mach's influential *Analysis of Sensations* (1898) was *positivist* in character (truth is best expressed in the language of the empirical sciences) and *phenomenalist* in its claims (sensations alone are real). All physical objects and events are collections of sensations. We experience colors, tones, spaces, textures, and these alone are real. The rest are constructs made by us. The concept of *atom*, for example, is a useful fiction. Such concepts enable us to handle, indeed to exploit, the variegated flux of sensations.

Lenin will have none of this, for this is idealism, the enemy of materialism, the true philosophy. Mach's phenomenalism, says Lenin, is just as idealist as that of Berkeley, who held that this is a world composed of minds and the thoughts minds generate, that matter is never an object of experience; anyone who holds that what we know are sensations or perceptions must hold that the world is simply an aggregate of mental events, and that is false.

Lenin then turns to attack the Russian A. Bogdanov, an admirer of Mach and a writer of Utopian novels. (His *Red Star* tells of a visit of intelligent beings from Mars and their critique of our societies.) The title of Lenin's book was a take-off on Bogdanov's *Empirio-Monism,* which argued that what is real is fundamentally *one*, and that is the grand orderly procession of sensations we receive (which science orders and codifies in the form of laws, by means of which we can predict future occurrences of sensation). Lenin pulled Bogdanov's theory to pieces as miserable Machist idealism. (Bogdanov got into political trouble before and after Lenin's death, and eventually died in prison.)

Finally, Lenin takes on his admired senior Plekhanov—very gently in comparison to the job he did on Bogdanov. Plekhanov's thesis read that there is an objective material world out there which is real, and we understand this world and are able to manage it through our sensations, which may be compared to hieroglyphics. Such glyphs are not exact pictures of what is real but are sufficient to communicate to us by a system of signs the meaning and nature of external reality. Lenin disagreed: "*Hieroglyphics* is just another name for sensations, and your theory of knowledge, my dear Plekhanov, is all too reducible to Mach's idealistic sensationalism."

Now Lenin offers his own theory of our knowledge of the external world. He liked to call it objectivism, or realism. His position amounts to this: Our sensations are simple copies (*kopii*) of what is outside us. We stand in direct relation to the world. We know it directly, and we know it as it really is. Only approximately, granted, only roughly, granted, but we know it basically as it is. Truth is objective.

Lenin knew that the slightest touch of epistemological *relativism* would pose a political threat to the revolutionary theories upon which the Soviet state was based. Those theories were held by Lenin—and Marx before him—to be objectively true, scientifically unassailable. In like manner, then, Lenin's theory of our knowledge of the external world had to convey that our perception of the world as it comes to us through the senses is essentially a true copy of the world. Such is the thesis of Lenin's little book, *Materialism and Empirio-Criticism*.

*

After Lenin's death Soviet academicians, under Stalin's sharp eye, watched the sciences and the scientists carefully for any straying from ideological orthodoxy. Of government interference during and after Stalin's rule, the best known example—the Lysenko controversy—had little to do with dialectical materialism. The question was whether external alterations made to plants—for example, grains like wheat—could be passed on through the genes to following generations. Lysenko's answer was yes; and he pointed to his own experiments with winter wheat which proved, he claimed, that if you modify winter wheat, then plant it and take cuts from it, the change you make externally will be passed on through the genes. This biological doctrine practically did away with genetics as Western and many Soviet scientists knew it. Lysenko's theory revived the discredited claim of the French biologist Lamarck that acquired characteristics could be inherited through the "germ plasm." At the notorious Soviet genetics conference of 1948, intimidated biologists bowed to party power when Lysenko informed the assembly that the Communist party's central committee had approved his report. There was nothing more to be said. Even after Stalin's death, and particularly under Khrushchev's ascendancy, Lysenkoism hung on, despite increasing opposition from competent Soviet biologists. It was not until 1965 that Lysenko—in whose character we find a combination of genius and charlatan—was finally discredited.

Certain interesting controversies in Russian physics had a closer relation to dialectical materialism. Some Soviet scientists, though none of the first rank, criticized Einstein's relativity theories on the ground that he had imported his teacher Mach's phenomenalist doctrine into physics. But most Soviet physicists found no contradiction between Einstein's theories and dialectical materialism, and at the celebration of the centenary of the great man's birth, they offered tributes to his genius. (In fact, the special theory of relativity contains nothing more harmful to morals and politics than the claim that physical processes occurring in a closed system are not affected by the non-accelerated motion of the system as a whole, that the speed of light (186,000 miles per second) is independent of the velocity of its source, and that the relation between matter and energy can be expressed in the famous equation $E=mc^2$.)

An important controversy in Soviet physics concerned quantum mechanics. Schrödinger and de Broglie had first raised the question of uncertainty in the prediction of subatomic events, which had the dual properties of particle and wave. Carried further by the German physicist Heisenberg and the Danish physicist Niels Bohr, quantum mechanics asserted that we cannot disassociate our measurement of a subatomic event from the event itself.

Andrei Zhdanov fired the first shot at quantum mechanics in his 1947 address to the academicians: "The Kantian vagaries of modern bourgeois physicists give free will to the electron, say that matter is nothing more than a collection of waves, and other devilish tricks." In a word, quantum mechanics was idealism. For if a micro-event is inseparable from our measurement of it, we must admit the Bohr-Heisenberg claim that it is not nature we know but *nature as known by us*. Berkeley's "Esse est percipi" ("To be is to be perceived") thus becomes "To be is to be measured," which is incompatible with the Marxist-Leninist principle of objective reality.

Not all Soviet physicists accepted this view of quantum mechanics. Throughout the controversy, the physicist V.A. Fock sturdily defended the principle of Bohr and Heisenberg, though he had reservations about some of Bohr's wider claims. The core of quantum mechanics, said Fock, does not eliminate objective reality; it simply provides an objective description of quantum states. By 1960 government opposition had faded, and quantum mechanics was completely rehabilitated; in that year the *Great Soviet Encyclopedia* pronounced it one of the most brilliant achievements of twentieth-century physics.

Fock was one of a number of older Soviet scientists who claimed that dialectical materialism had helped them formulate their creative and critical apparatus. But as the century moved into its later decades, dialectical materialism lost considerable ground as a fundamental theory of objective reality. Although older scientists (the "ontologists") still clung to it as a fruitful description of reality itself, younger Soviet investigators (the "epistemologists") were prepared to admit only that dialectical materialism was a helpful theory of cognition, of knowing rather than of being.

By the late 1970s Communist party members outside the Soviet Union had almost completely lost interest in dialectical materialism. Raymond Jean, the senior intellectual of the French Communist party, called for the "demythologizing" of Soviet Marxist-Leninist dogmas, among which dialectical materialism occupied a prominent place. Bright young philosophers in France, such as Henri Bernard-Levi, led the university faculties in total revolt, and Marxism found itself no longer fashionable in intellectual circles. One anonymous voice denounced dialectical materialism as an "intellectual mummy," and was cruel enough to refer in this connection to the embalmed body of Lenin in Red Square, Moscow.

*

Any Westerner who has joined the long line waiting to be admitted to Lenin's tomb will not easily forget the experience. One sunny day in May 1970, a friend and I joined the quarter-mile queue in Red Square, willing to settle down for a long wait while watching the handsomely uniformed young soldiers stiff-leggedly changing the guard at the entrance to the red granite mausoleum. A plainclothes guard approached us: "You have papers?" (meaning passports from an important country of the West). Having produced them to his satisfaction, we were discreetly led to a position very near the head of the line; and we soon descended into the eerie interior, lighted in pale blue, where we gazed for a moment into the crystal coffin at the embalmed remains of this extraordinary man. A relief to emerge into the sunshine and to read the names of those entombed in the Kremlin wall, Stalin among them. (Stalin's body had been removed from its place beside Lenin not long after Khrushchev's revelations of the Stalinist rule of terror.)

Looking on the great revolutionary's remains, embalmed and enshrined, one could not help marvelling at what the man must have suppressed in himself in his ruthless pursuit of power. He had little personal life. He loved music, but controlled that. Once with his friend Gorky he listened to a young woman pianist play Beethoven's *Apassionata Sonata*, the great opus 57. Turning to Gorky, Lenin said,

> I don't know anything greater than the *Apassionata*. . . . I always think with pride what marvelous things human beings can do. But I can't listen to music too often. It affects your nerves, makes you want to say stupid, nice things, and stroke the heads of people who could create such things while living in this vile hell. And you mustn't stroke anyone's head—you might get your hand bitten off. You have to hit them over the head, without any mercy, although our ideal is not to use force against anyone. Hm, hm, our duty is infernally hard.

On Sunday, September 8, 1991, the line of visitors waiting to see Lenin's tomb nearly reached the one-mile mark. People had

heard that the Soviet authorities were considering a proposal to
bury Lenin's remains in the city formerly known as Leningrad,
now once again St. Petersburg.

*

Although Lenin was deeply interested in philosophy, he concentrated on the methodological or epistemological aspects of
the subject. Ethics, moral theory, he left alone. He rarely, if ever,
talked about his personal ethic, for that would have seemed to
him sentimental. He was not like the cultured Russian gentry of
pre-revolutionary days, who loved to talk about God, the soul,
freedom, and to turn as many problems as possible into moral
questions. Not until after the Second World War do we find
Soviet academicians taking much interest in what Western
philosophers would classify as ethics or moral philosophy, as
opposed to party-related morality.

After Stalin's death, Khrushchev decided that a code of public
morality governing personal conduct was needed, and in 1961
the Communist party published such a code as part of its party
program. While "loyalty to the Communist cause, love of the
socialist motherland and of the other socialist countries" headed
the list of ethical principles, the code also exalted "humane
relations. . . . honesty and truthfulness, moral purity, modesty
and unpretentiousness in social and private life."

With the passing of the Brezhnev period and the ascendancy
of Gorbachev, with his revolutionary program of *glasnost* (openness) and *perestroika* (restructuring), Soviet philosophy journals
began to feature articles with strong humanist rather than party
emphasis. Titles such as "The Notion of the Nature of Man in
an Ethical System" and "Spirituality as a Factor of Restruc-
turalism" were typical, though an occasional scholarly attack on
"imperialism" could still be found in the pages of *Voprosy filosofii*.
In 1988 a new textbook on philosophy appeared. Prepared as
always by a committee, it called for Marxist treatment of "man's
existence in the world." By 1989, amidst the general unravelling
of the Soviet structure, dialectical materialism itself had lost its
place as the official academic philosophy of the Soviet Union.

Here is part of a letter from the U.S. Russian scholar Loren Graham (the friend who stood in line with me on the 1970 visit to Lenin's tomb):

> I was in Moscow a month ago [September 1989] and visited the Institute of Philosophy a number of times. The new trend in Soviet philosophy is interested in the philosophy of social sciences, ethics, and "the problem of man." A definite lessening of interest in dialectical and historical materialism is occurring. In fact, the old department of "Dialectical Materialism" has been abolished, replaced by one on "Logic and Cognition." However, most of the personnel are the same, and many of them seem to be working on the same sort of problems as earlier, including the philosophy of biology and physics within the framework of what they consider a more sophisticated form of dialectical materialism. And I am told that in provincial universities not much has changed.

The reader should not be deprived of Graham's description of certain aspects of the Moscow scene:

> Moscow itself was a fascinating place for me because of the intellectual and cultural (as opposed to economic) changes. I had been there only 10 months earlier, but the political evolution since then was remarkable. Moscow in September 1989 was simply not the city politically that I have known all these years. While I was there a group of monarchists held a demonstration downtown calling for restoration of the Romanov autocracy; the demonstration was shown on television without adverse comment. The anarcho-syndicalists did the same a few days later. All the intellectuals that I talked to were delighted with the political changes but, oddly enough, all critical of Gorbachev, saying that he really didn't know what he was doing, and fearing that he would lose control.

> The changes in Moscow were sometimes comic. This repressed Victorian society has found out that glasnost includes more sexual questions. I saw a woman on one of the main streets of Moscow who had set up a card table and was selling pictures of nude men and women. She had two separate stacks of photos, one of men and the other of women.

Everybody buys everything in Moscow by standing in line, so there was a line of men in front of the stack of pictures of nude women, and a line of women in front of the stack of nude men. There is also a brisk trade in pornographic videocassettes. . . .

Moscow right now has a Dada-like atmosphere, with many people talking wildly about extrasensory perception, aliens from outer space, astrology, coming cataclysms. Two taxi drivers told me the end of the world was coming soon. One said it would happen in 14 months. I asked why not 13 or 15, and he said he had reliable information that it would be exactly 14 months.

Atheism, the official theology of the now defunct U.S.S.R., was never the concern of the best brains in the Soviet bureaucracy, nor did it ever awaken much interest among top Soviet scholars. And in the final years of the Soviet Union, when religious worship was no longer unlawful, Soviet leaders publicly expressed their religious tolerance. On September 6, 1991, President Mikhail Gorbachev of the Soviet Union and President Boris Yeltsin of the Russian Republic appeared on a television talk show moderated by newsman Peter Jennings. Asked about his personal religious beliefs, Gorbachev said,

I am an atheist. But I—and I've never concealed this—I respect the feelings and the religious beliefs of each citizen, of each person. This is a question of personal sovereignty, and we have done a good deal so as to, in a legislative sense, guarantee each person the right to call himself what he wants, to allow each person to select his own religion. . . .

Yeltsin's remarks were more positive, his ingenuous tag line engaging:

The service, the ritual aspect, I don't really observe those, although I've been in church quite often, because during the service there's a kind of internal feeling of moral cleansing, as it were. And I certainly make a point of attending church, not to mention my respect, of course, for believers. . . . I'm also superstitious, by the way.

Perhaps we should let Yeltsin have the last word on Soviet communism:

> I think this experiment which was conducted on our own soil was a tragedy for our people, and it was too bad that it happened on our territory. It would have been better if this experiment had been conducted in some small country, at least, so as to make it clear that it was a utopian idea, although a beautiful one.

Or is this too ingenuous?

*

Our reflections on Lenin and Soviet philosophy should not end on a light note. The sufferings and greatness of the Russian people merit our high admiration and respect for them, if not for the melancholy series of autocratic governments and tyrannies that they have endured for centuries. Their rich culture has produced a galaxy of creative spirits that include, among others, Pavlov and Mendeleev; Solovyov and Berdyaev; Pushkin and Gogol; Tolstoy and Dostoyevsky; Chekhov and Turgenev; Tchaikovsky and Rimsky-Korsakov; Stravinsky, Prokofiev, and Shostakovich. And despite the uncertain future of the new Russian commonwealth (*Sodruzhestvo*), the genius and culture of the Russian people will survive.

With the breakup of the monolithic Soviet Union founded by Lenin and his followers, we have seen the shattering of faith in communism, the end of Soviet domination of Eastern Europe and the Baltic states, the reunification of Germany, and a flood of new nationalism, long suppressed, among the many fragments of the Soviet empire. We have seen the end of the Cold War, and sensed the massive diminution if not the final extinction of the threat of intercontinental nuclear war. For these changes, continuing to accelerate at this moment, we must be grateful. At the same time, we might realize with a certain humility that a heavy burden of moral as well as political responsibility now rests upon the shoulders of the surviving superpower, our own country, the United States of America.

9

Evolution and Ethics

If you teach children that they are evolved from apes, then they will start acting like apes.

From legislative testimony on Louisiana's law concerning teaching of evolutionism versus creationism (1986)

Those who adopt the spiritual explanation are right when they defend a certain transcendence of man over the rest of nature. But neither are the materialists wrong when they maintain that man is just one further term in a series of animal forms.

Teilhard de Chardin (1951)

Our discourse on evolution wanders from old bones to the DNA molecule, from "survival of the fittest" to the improvident Irish, from *homo erectus* to Tennessee Williams. But isn't that the way of moral philosophy? Plato taught that you cannot talk about ethics as if it were separate from other things: in order to make sense of it you need a sound theory of knowledge and metaphysics; in short, you must be a "friend of ideas."

So I thought we'd start with Thomas Jefferson and moral philosophy. In August 1787, from his ministerial post in Paris, Jefferson wrote to his nephew in Virginia, who had asked his uncle's advice about college education. After recommending close attention to Spanish (since "our future connections with Spain and Spanish America will render that language a valuable acquisition"), Jefferson wrote,

Moral philosophy. I think it lost time to attend lectures in this branch. . . . Man was destined for society. His morality therefore was to be formed to this object. He was endowed with a sense of right and wrong merely relative to this. This sense is as much a part of his nature as the sense of hearing, seeing, feeling; it is the true foundation of morality. . . . The moral sense, or conscience, is as much a part of man as his leg or arm. It is given to all human beings in a stronger or weaker degree, as force of members is given them in a greater or less degree. It may be strengthened by exercise, as may any particular limb of the body. This sense is submitted indeed in some degree to the guidance of reason; but it is a small stock which is required for this: even a less one than what we call Common sense. State a moral case to a ploughman and a professor. The former will decide it as well, and often better than the latter, because he has not been led astray by artificial rules.

Jefferson had a strong interest in paleontology. Among many other items, man-made and natural, he collected old bones; and he was well aware that much plant and animal life that once existed on earth no longer does. When he talked to Lewis and Clark before they set out to cross the country and to explore the Northwest, he instructed them to keep a sharp eye out for any surviving mammoths that might be roaming the area we now call Montana and Idaho. As you know, Lewis and Clark did not sight any mammoths, but they did see many other wonderful things beyond the frontier.

Jefferson would have been a stout champion of the theory of organic evolution. He belonged to the generation of the European Enlightenment, and his firm belief in separation between church and state would have colored his view on the controversies we have seen in our time on the teaching of evolution in the public schools.

The 1980s produced a number of court decisions on the teaching of evolution that were appealed and brought to the Supreme Court of the United States. In these cases *evolution* meant the Darwinian theory of it, particularly with reference to human descent from animal forms (usually depicted in the media illustrations as ineluctably ape-like). The Texas Department of Education tried to keep Darwin's name out of the textbooks, while permitting the mention of evolution. Louisiana and Arkansas wanted "equal time" for the teaching of evolution and creationism in the public schools. Arkansas' definition of "creation science" included the teaching that the universe was created from nothing and that humans were not related to apes.

Louisiana's "equal time" law was struck down by a federal district court on the ground that "creation science" was a thinly disguised version of the creation account in Genesis and therefore a religious doctrine. The Supreme Court sustained this decision in Edwards versus Aguillard (1986).

In ruling on this case, a federal appeals court remarked that Louisiana's law "continued the battle William Jennings Bryan carried to his grave." That battle was fought at the famous Tennessee "Monkey Trial" of 1925, when a high school biology teacher was recruited by a liberal group to openly defy a state law that prohibited teaching "any theory which denies the story of the creation of Man as taught in the Bible." John Scopes, the teacher, was tried, found guilty, and a small fine was levied. William Jennings Bryan assisted the prosecution against a brilliant defense led by the renowned trial lawyer Clarence Darrow (who had managed to prevent two callous young murderers, Leopold and Loeb, from being sentenced to death). The Scopes trial attracted international attention and generated a circus atmosphere in the small town of Dayton, where vendors sold little toy monkeys you could pin on your shirt. The heat was so terrific that the judge allowed the lawyers to plead in their shirtsleeves. Worn out by his labors, Bryan died in Dayton shortly after the trial ended. The Scopes trial inspired the Broadway drama *Inherit the Wind*, starring Paul Muni as the liberal lawyer. Later a film was made of it with Spencer Tracy in the same role. Both actors made the most of the scene that ends the drama: the defender of the teaching of evolution picks up two books from the courtroom table—the Bible and Darwin's *Origin of Species*; he looks at them for a moment, then claps them together and leaves the empty courtroom with the two great volumes under his arm; no exit line needed.

*

Today scientists agree that humankind has had a long foreground on planet Earth. But just how long is a matter of hot debate. How old is *homo sapiens*? How far back can we trace the evolutionary line that led to our species? A relatively recent phase of the controversy began with a discovery in 1974 by the anthropologist Donald Johanson. Near the Kenya border, in the Afar district of southern Ethiopia, Johanson and his team turned up a 40 percent-complete skeleton of a young female, about four feet tall, with a head like a chimpanzee and legs on which she could walk upright like a human. Johanson named her Lucy, after the Beatles' popular song "Lucy in the Sky with Diamonds." A drawing of Lucy, with ape-like head and humanoid body covered by furry hair, illustrated Johanson's book, written with Maitland Edey and titled *Lucy: The Beginnings of Humankind*. The scientific name selected for Lucy was *australopithecus afarensis*.

The name *australopithecus* dates from 1925, when Dart and Broome, working in East Africa, uncovered fragments of the pre-hominid "Taung child." Much more evidence of the existence of *australopithecus* in Africa was dug up by the Leakey family. Mary Leakey discovered fossil remains of *australopithecus* in Olduvai Gorge, Tanzania; these bones were believed to be about 1,750,000 years old. In 1972, shortly before Johanson turned up Lucy's skeleton, Mary Leakey's son Richard unearthed fossil remains pronounced closer to *homo sapiens*; this pre-human's age was estimated at 2.6 million years. Johanson upstaged the Leakeys by asserting that Lucy dated from 3.2 million years ago, thereby claiming credit for discovering the remains of the oldest pre-human. Johanson claimed that Lucy was the ancestor of *australopithecus* and of a pre-hominid line that led to a proto-human which in turn led to our own ancient ancestors. Richard Leakey retorted that his *australopithecus* had two lines, one of which led to hominids and eventually to *homo sapiens*, while the other line led to types like Lucy, a dead end, which went nowhere at all.

A new method of estimating the age of human beings and their ancestors came into the picture in the early 1980s with the application of molecular biology to the problem. The findings of this discipline suggested that hominids had been around millions of years earlier than first suspected, and that we humans are more closely related to chimpanzees than many of us would like to believe. Allan Wilson and Vincent Savich compiled an "index of differentiation" based on their study of similarities and

differences in the mitochondria of human and animal DNA mole-
cules. Their differentiation figure for cows was 20; for new world
monkeys, 4; for old world monkeys, 2; and for gorillas, 1.7. A
mere 1.6 represents the difference between ourselves and chimpanzees. Wilson's co-workers identified the common ancestor of
humans as a woman who lived less than 250,000 years ago in
Africa. The sex of this reputed mother of us all was determined
to be female because the relevant DNA could have been passed
on only through the female line.

Contemporary paleontologists have their doubts about all
this, since their findings indicate a common human ancestry
dating from half a million years ago. But molecular biologists
point to the limited size of the paleontologists' hard evidence.
"Most of those old bones would fit on the top of a billiard table,"
said one. And in 1988 Nobel Prize laureate Luis Alvarez
remarked, "I don't like to say bad things about paleontologists,
but they're really not very good scientists. They're more like
stamp collectors."

*

Belief in evolution, the transformation of living forms, plant
and animal, developed into scientific doctrine in the eighteenth
and nineteenth century, although some scholars claim that
pre-Socratic Greek philosophers had an intuitive glimpse of the
idea. The rapid growth of the modern concept of evolution is
probably inseparable from the intense interest in progress and
development that gripped the Western world in the late seventeenth and eighteenth century. By that time many things had
happened: kings had been executed; travel was easier; new
continents had been discovered; machinery was being
developed; manufactories were being established; the Industrial
Revolution loomed. Reason, progress, development, positive
change moved to center stage. Now when you study the idea of
progress and development you find that not only does it look
ahead, but it looks back to see where it all came from. The
movement we call the Romantic turned with nostalgia to times
long ago. Amateur naturalists in Britain and on the continent of

Europe were studying old bones, bemused by a sense of a lengthening past. In the last quarter of the seventeenth century, an Oxford don, a clergyman, had a fair collection of fossil bones that indicated strange animal forms as old as Noah's flood, perhaps even older. Then the exploration of a Belgian cave yielded the skeletons of twenty iguanadons. And the question arose, how do we explain this transformation? In our hands we hold the remains of animals, living forms that are no longer here. What are we to make of this?

One explanation, quickly rejected, was that God had put these bones here to test our faith, to find out if we would succumb to the false belief that there really were creatures like that in the past. Another explanation claimed that the fossil bones of strange animals were vestiges of God's experiments, the "clay models" which the Almighty had weighed and found wanting. More plausible was the catastrophe theory, and the logical candidate for that was Noah's flood: the strange animals to whom these fossil bones belonged actually did exist before the flood, but perished in the waters that covered the face of the earth. A later theory held that an age of cold temperature put a comparatively abrupt end to the dinosaurs once widespread over the globe.

In our day the catastrophe theory was revived, but in a different form. Luis Alvarez supported the hypothesis that long ago a straying star or asteroid came so close to Earth that it ignited a large portion of the planet's surface. He named this star Nemesis, and as part of the evidence he pointed to unexplained deposits of soot as well as abnormal deposits of iridium, a metal found in many meteorites. According to the Nemesis hypothesis, then, the dinosaurs died not from ice but from fire.

But what about the emergence of new forms of plant and animal life? How did they come to be? Numerous fossil remains indicated that many animal and plant forms had for millions of years hardly changed at all. (The familiar horseshoe crab, which strands itself on our beaches at egg-laying time, has been around virtually unchanged for three million years.) Yet there have been fantastic changes in other animal and plant forms. How did this happen?

Charles Darwin's grandfather, Erasmus Darwin (1711-1802), developed a monistic explanation: all life emerged from a single source, a primordial biological first cause. His book *Zoonomia* anticipated certain evolutionary ideas of the nineteenth century, but it did not explain how evolutionary changes occurred. The great French naturalist Jean-Baptiste Lamarck (1744-1829) explained these changes in part by the inheritance of acquired characteristics, his too-famous example the neck-stretching giraffe who passed on its gains in inches to its progeny through the "germ-plasm." We noted earlier that the Russian agronomist Trofim Lysenko held that cuttings grafted onto winter wheat could result in modified progeny with advantageous results. The Darwin-Wallace theory of evolution rejected this notion; their explanation of the factors energizing evolutionary change was quite different.

*

Although we hear much more about Darwin than about Wallace, they both arrived independently at the same explanation for the cause of the evolution of plant and animal forms. Like so many brilliant amateur naturalists of the nineteenth and early twentieth century, Alfred Wallace was an Englishman. Apparently he had money enough to wander through the world at will, and he particularly loved the East Indies. He spent many years in Malaysia, particularly in the islands of what he called the Malaysian archipelago. While sweating out an illness he read Thomas Malthus's *Essay on Population*, the thesis advanced that population tends to outrun food supply, thereby resulting in a fierce struggle around the feeding trough. Wallace concluded that this helps to explain why some life forms survive and others perish, that the struggle for existence leads to what he identified in a famous phrase as "the survival of the fittest."

Darwin preferred "natural selection" to "survival of the fittest," although he used the latter as a synonym of the former in *Origin of Species*. Darwin was uneasy with "survival of the fittest" for he believed that those who survive are not always the best. In Darwin's *Descent of Man*, in a passage you would not want to read at the annual meeting of the Friendly Sons of Saint Patrick, the great naturalist argues that

> . . . the reckless, degraded and often vicious members of society tend to increase at a quicker rate than the provident and generally virtuous members of society. Or as Mr. Greg puts the case, "The careless, squalid, unaspiring Irishman multiplies like rabbits; the frugal, foreseeing, ambitious Scot, stern in his morality, spiritual in his faith, sagacious and disciplined in his intellect, passes his best years in struggle and celibacy, marries late, and leaves few behind him. Given a land originally peopled by a thousand Saxons and a thousand Celts—and in a dozen generations, five-sixths of the property, of the power, of the intellect, would belong to the one-sixth of the Saxons that remained. In the eternal 'struggle for existence,' it would be the inferior and less favored race that had prevailed—and prevailed by virtue not of its good qualities, but of its faults."

Odd that Darwin did not seem to notice the inconsistency in the passage he quotes. Like the "squalid Irishman," the "frugal Scot" is a Celt, not a Saxon.

Most of the scientific community in the nineteenth century agreed that evolution of plant and animal forms had happened. Evolution was a fact; everyone agreed on that, except for a few flat-earth types. The big question was *how*? Was evolution the result of direct intervention at the hand of God? Or was Lamarck right in believing that environmental pressures caused an animal or a plant to modify itself in some favorable way and that this modification could be passed on through the "germ plasm" to its offspring? Darwin and Wallace agreed on several factors. The pressures of environment—short food supply, for one—tend to favor the survival of living forms, plant or animal, that best adapt to the environment. We know that animal and plant forms tend to vary; some are stronger or better adapted to their environment, while others are weaker. Of a litter of dog pups, some will be more aggressive than others; often the weak runt of the litter will be pushed out of the way of nourishment by his tougher siblings, who will have a better chance to survive and pass on their sturdy genes. Here we have a process of natural selection, although this example may mislead one to think that the way to successful adaptation is the way of brute strength. This is not always the case: the dead-leaf butterfly's success in adaptation lies in its camouflage, not in its muscle.

Like the comic-strip character Andy Capp, Darwin belonged to a pigeon club, and there he observed how by *artificial* selection a desired strain could be produced by managing the breeding; and he noted the same, changing what is to be changed, for dogs and horses. Wallace made similar observations, and, like Darwin, the younger man hit on the idea of *natural* selection: given that natural variations are random, those that lead to successful adaptation tend to favor survival, and over millions of years minute changes lead to substantial transformations. (If Darwin and Wallace had known more about the important part that mutations play in the game of life, they would have felt confirmed in their thesis of random variation plus adaptation.)

As guest naturalist on H.M.S. *Beagle* (1831-36), Darwin observed the correlation between isolated land masses (Galapagos, Tahiti, Australia, New Zealand, Mauritius, for example) and the flora and fauna indigenous to them. Wallace too had ample time to consider the same type of evidence of evolution by adaptation. "Wallace's Line" divides Borneo and Bali from Celebes and Lombok, each area with its own animals and plants peculiar to itself.

Darwin believed his theory strengthened by the study of comparative morphology: the hand of the human with its clever opposable thumb, the wing of the bird and the bat, the fin of the fish and the whale—all taking shape along spokes or lines radiating from some central organic source on the road of natural pressures and adaptation to the crucible of environment. Wallace made similar observations, though far less than the multitudinous instances compiled with ant-like patience by Darwin.

Wallace wrote to Darwin from Malaysia, enclosing a paper which summarized his ideas. Darwin replied that this paper could serve as a presentation in abstract of his own theory. In 1858 both naturalists combined their papers on natural selection and made a joint presentation before the Linnaean Society. This joint effort was published in the society's journal that same year, and the following year Darwin published his *Origin of Species*.

*

The Origin of Species does not mention human evolution directly, though it is cautiously implied in the book's concluding chapter. But Darwin's supporters had little doubt about the implications of his theory, and within a year the British scientific community was ablaze with excitement over the applicability of evolution to humans. At a meeting at Oxford of the British scientific association, a paper was read about certain properties inherited by a bird species, including some observations on what Mr. Darwin had written touching the subject. The harmless ruminations of this paper seemed far from the dangerous thoughts implied in Darwin's book, but somebody raised the question of the place of humans in all this. The atmosphere of the Oxford hall became electrified, and everybody began talking at once. Samuel Wilberforce, bishop of Oxford (named by his detractors "Soapy Sam"), asked the questioner on which side he was descended from a monkey, his mother's or his father's? Whereupon Thomas Huxley, "Darwin's bulldog," rose to the question and replied in measured tones that he would not be ashamed to have a monkey for an ancestor, but he would be ashamed if, like His Lordship, he should use great gifts to obscure the truth.

Not until *The Descent of Man* (1871) did Darwin take the gloves off in this famous passage:

> The main conclusion of the whole work is simply that man is descended body and mind from the lower animals. I regret to think that this conclusion will be distasteful to many people who will regard it as inimical to both morality and religion. But we scientists are not concerned with hopes or fears but only with the truth as far as we are able to discover it. Having considered the evidence, it seems to me that we must acknowledge that man still bears indelible and unmistakable traces of his lowly origin. His body is still the body of an animal, and the

mark of the beast is still clearly discernible in all his mental and moral faculties.

That passage, often quoted, quickly captured the popular imagination. One of Rudyard Kipling's scariest stories is titled "The Mark of the Beast." It tells of a drunken British soldier who defiles a holy place in India, and for this he is embraced by a leper. The disease engulfs the soldier, who for the rest of his life wanders around as a beggar, telling the terrible story for pennies to those who will hear him.

Although Darwin softened the passage in subsequent editions, he left untouched his echoing of Huxley's reply to the bishop of Oxford:

> For my own part I would as soon be descended from that heroic little monkey, who braved his dreaded enemy in order to save the life of his keeper . . . as from a savage who delights to torture his enemies, offers up bloody sacrifices, practices infanticide without remorse, treats his wives as slaves, knows no decency, and is haunted by the grossest superstitions.

The public, of course, took shivering pleasure in the controversy. If you look at the illustrated London papers of the time, you will find sheaves of cartoons and artists' reconstructions of "Darwin's Ape-Man," quite similar to the rendering of Lucy in Johanson's book—furry pate, hair-covered body, receding chin (all the ape-like characteristics that made some crude fellow say of Lucy, "You've come a long way, baby!"). In America, prelates and college presidents took sides in the evolution controversy. President Barnard of Columbia declared in 1873,

> If organic evolution were true, then the existence of God is impossible. . . . If the final outcome of all the boasted discoveries of modern science is to disclose to men that they are more evanescent than the shadow of the swallow's wing upon the lake . . . give me then, I pray, no more science. I will live on in my simple ignorance as my fathers did before me.

Darwin himself was asked by a young girl if his theory of evolution did away with belief in God and religion. Darwin replied that although he himself was an agnostic, he saw no basic contradiction between his scientific theories and religious life.

*

As a result of the controversy, the search for fossil evidence of human evolution took on new urgency. During Darwin's lifetime only the fossil remains of the Neanderthal Man were known. Not far from Düsseldorf, in the valley of the Neander, human fossil remains were found which appeared to date back fifty or a hundred thousand years. The owners of these bones were human, but they were not quite like us. Artists' renderings revealed Neanderthal Man to be the popular image of the "caveman," complete with furry skin and club, beetling brow, receding jaw. Recently in Israel some handsomely intact remains of this ancient cousin of ours have been found—different from us, but unmistakably human.

In 1902 Eugene Dubois, former lecturer in comparative anatomy in Amsterdam, revealed that he had found in a cave in Java the remains of a man-like creature who was able—so skeletal structure suggested—to stand erect. Dubois dubbed his find *pithecanthropus erectus*. Most scientists agreed that the "Java Ape-Man" was an ancestor of the human, and some suggested that it might well be the "missing link" between animal and human forms. The name for this creature has now been shortened to *homo erectus*—a pity, because *pithecanthropus* has such a nice ring to it. (And we had several pretty specimens of the breed on Long Island school boards a generation ago; perhaps some survive to this day.)

Then in China, in the 1920s, a whole load of *homo erectus* fossil bones was discovered in the caves of Chou-kou-tien, not far from Peking. Just before the Japanese attacked Pearl Harbor, this rich find of fossil remains was put in a cargo vessel to be shipped out of danger. Unfortunately the vessel must have sunk, for neither the ship nor the bones were ever found again. The good news is that casts were made of all the findings, so that we have a good idea of what the originals were like. Today there appears to be tentative agreement among scientists that *homo erectus*, dating

300,000 to 1,000,000 years ago, stands roughly midway in the evolutionary line between *australopithecus* and *homo sapiens*.

At this point the strange tale of the spectral creature *Eoanthropos dawsonii* (the Dawn Man of Dawson) should not be omitted. Commonly known as the Piltdown Man, his remains— or what purported to be his remains—were found in Sussex, England, their existence revealed in 1912 by Charles Dawson, lawyer and amateur naturalist. In that year Dawson brought some skull fragments to Arthur Smith-Woodward, keeper of geology at the British Museum. Dawson told Smith-Woodward that since 1908 he had been picking up fossil remains at a road-worker's gravel pit near Piltdown. The skull fragments resembled those of a human but were much thicker, and they showed signs of deep erosion and stain consistent with great age. Dawson also turned up a jawbone, distinctively simian in character but with teeth worn down in human fashion. Teilhard de Chardin, a young Jesuit scholastic from France studying at the nearby Jesuit college in Hastings, helped Dawson to look for more fossil remnants. In 1913 Teilhard found a canine tooth that fitted the jawbone. Other skull fragments later turned up, with ape-like teeth embedded nearby. These teeth were also worn down like those of a human.

In late 1912 Smith-Woodward announced the startling find to the Geological Society of London, and the epiphany of the bones caused a sensation. Most observers agreed with Smith-Woodward that the remains of a new and very ancient human ancestor had been found. A minority reserved judgment on the ground that the skull and jaw might have come from two different creatures interred together by chance. One elderly scholar pronounced the skull to be that of a degenerate Irishman. One or two distrusted Teilhard's role in the enterprise, particularly his discovery of the missing tooth. (After all, he was a Frenchman, and a Jesuit as well.) In any case, Piltdown's "Dawn Man" held his tenuous place in the ancestral tree of the human until just after World War II, when it was determined that he was a fake. Fluorine and potassium argon tests proved that the fragments were not old. The skull pieces, although abnormally thick, were indeed human, while the jawbone had once belonged to some dear old orangutan who not long before had been glumly brachiating through the rain forests of Sumatra. The teeth had been ground down artificially; and the ancient appearance of the fragments had been secured by filing and by judicious applications of potassium permanganate. Plans for a monument to the Piltdown Man, to be built on the site of the find, were quietly abandoned.

But the question remains, who perpetrated the hoax? All agree that Dawson must have been a participant, but most believe that he was put up to it by some other person. Who was that person, and what was his motive? The usual suspects include W. J. Solas, a bitter enemy of Smith-Woodward, who had disparaged some of Solas's findings as "toys." Motive: to make Smith-Woodward look like a fool when the hoax was discovered (which it wasn't for more than thirty years, and long after Smith-Woodward had died). Another suspect was Sir Arthur Conan Doyle, creator of Sherlock Holmes, who had a considerable interest in paleontology and primal man (as readers of his novel *The Lost World* well know). In a little essay titled "Piltdown Revisited," Stephen Jay Gould identifies Teilhard de Chardin as the "other man." Though Teilhard stands as a godlike figure to many who were fascinated by his posthumous *Phenomenon of Man* (1955), Gould believes that Teilhard was once a fun-loving youth, just ripe for a prank. Besides, the Jesuit had access to old bones from a previous assignment in Egypt, and might well have jumped at the chance "to rub English noses once again with the taunt that their nation had no legitimate fossils, while France revelled in a superabundance that made her queen of anthropology."

My own theory of motive, if not of identity, proposes that Dawson and his confederate were passionate believers in human evolution from simian-related animal forms, and that they thought it no more than friendly to give science a lift, to speed her on her way to complete recognition and full promulgation of the truth of evolutionary theory by adding dramatically to the scant store of human fossil evidence. But I still wonder how Teilhard, with his Ignatian tradition of truth as discipline and his own intellectual brilliance, could have been taken in (if indeed he *was* taken in) by Charles Dawson.

*

Teilhard de Chardin entered the Jesuit order in 1899 and was ordained a priest in 1911. He lectured at the Institute Catholique in Paris from 1913 to 1922, made a visit to China in 1923-24, then returned to teaching at the institute. His superiors were disturbed by his attempts to reconcile Catholic orthodoxy with evolutionary theory, and they sent him back to China. By a remarkable coincidence he arrived in Peking just in time to witness the discovery of the rich remains of *homo erectus* in the Chou-kou-tien caves. Because his superiors had forbidden him to publish anything but purely scientific papers, his works on theistic evolution, including his widely read *Phenomenon of Man*, were not published until after his death in 1955. Teilhard's theistic evolutionism shows the influence of the models provided him by his teacher, the philosopher Henri Bergson, author of *Creative Evolution* (1907), and by C. Lloyd Morgan, author of *Emergent Evolution* (1927).

Bergson taught that living forms on earth resulted from a primal thrust of vital energy, the *élan vital* or "life force." This pure and undifferentiated source of creative energy found itself blocked by matter, which came into being as an indirect by-product of the life force, like dead, spent energy. So the *élan vital* plunged into matter, thereby resulting in a marvelous multiplicity of living forms. The story of evolution is the history of the attempt that the life force has made—and is still making—to overcome the resistance of the matter it has entered, to regain its original undifferentiated oneness, to win through to its original state of freedom. Though Bergson avoids the use of the word *God*, his theory suggests that the name may be justly applied to this primordial explosion of life, which seeks through the channels of various plant and animal forms to break through the wall of matter. Bergson himself says that in the human the life force has come nearest to achieving its former freedom, and that future human evolution will not be physical but moral.

Bergson died on December 7, 1941, the day of the Japanese attack on Pearl Harbor. Shortly before his death he showed that philosophy is not just doctrine taught but a life lived. This distinguished teacher, whose lectures at the Collège de France ranked second to the Eiffel Tower as a tourist attraction, came from an assimilated Jewish family. Late in life he was on the verge of converting to Catholicism when the news came of the Nazi persecution of the Jews in Germany. He abandoned his plan to convert. And though he was exempted by the Vichy authorities from wearing the obligatory Star of David, he stood in line, mortally ill, dressed in a bathrobe, to receive and to wear his yellow star.

The philosophy of "emergent evolution" is associated with the names of C. Lloyd Morgan and Samuel Alexander, Whitehead's teacher and author of *Space, Time, and Deity*. This doctrine claims that organic life is a dimension of being quite different and distinct from matter, though life does emerge and develop from matter. Similarly, mind is quite distinct from organic life, out of which mind emerges by way of consciousness. The diagram and summary below, adapted from the work of Lloyd Morgan and Alexander, illustrates the theory of emergent evolution.

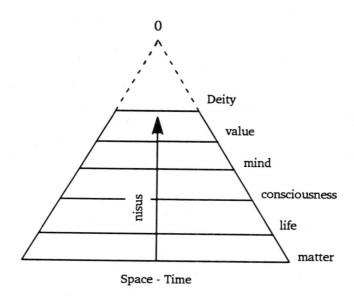

Within Space-Time, the primordial matrix of things, the cosmic womb from which all orders of being emerge, there is at work a creative *nisus* or upward thrust which pushes to the surface, as it were, a succession of qualitatively different emergents. Matter is but one stage in the emergent process; it is the primitive level of physical inorganic being. From matter there arises a new and relatively independent level of being—life. From life emerges consciousness, a more highly organized state of being. From within consciousness, mind separates out to form the next higher realm of being; and value is an emergent level higher still. Value has to do with the emergence of moral standards and relations as well as aesthetic perception and enjoyment. Finally there is Deity, the creative nisus itself, which has been slowly driving upward and outward these various strata of being. Deity has not yet emerged, but is in the process of emerging from the cosmos. Meanwhile Deity operates as the indwelling or immanent creative energy of things.

Teilhard de Chardin's *Phenomenon of Man* offers a highly individual variation on the theme of emergent evolution. His book bristles with neologisms and with a technical vocabulary which fails to mask a religious, even mystical vision, deeply held. Evolution represents increasing complexity—matter, life, consciousness, mind. The materialist account of evolution is correct, but one-sided. "A rocket rising in the wake of Time's arrows that only bursts to be extinguished; an eddy rising in the bosom of a descending current"—such is the materialist's picture of the origin of life, consciousness, mind. But he looks at it only from "the outside of things." Besides the realm of the "outside," there is the "within" of things. From the outside we see matter, bodies, determinism. From the inside, the within of things, we see mind, thought, freedom. To Teilhard, mind was immanent, indwelling in matter from the very beginning and even now only partially emerged. Mind's dimension of being is the "noösphere," which has risen from the "biosphere," the emergent stratum of organic life. "To a Martian," says Teilhard, "a Martian capable of analysing sidereal nations psychically no less than physically, the first characteristic of our planet would not be the blue of the seas or the green of the forest, but the phosphorescence of thought."

Teilhard's "Omega point" is the final goal of evolution, that toward which the universe moves as it throws off successively higher levels of development. The Omega point is the Soul of souls, developing at the summit of the world, the last stage of emergence. We may think of it as God, or as the integration of individual consciousnesses, perhaps akin to the World Soul of certain ancient philosophers. "After all," Teilhard concludes, "is there any other way in which our thought can generalize the principle of Emergence?"

*

When biologists write about philosophy—and they frequently do—they are apt to be very mechanistic. In his *Chance and Necessity*, the late Jacques Monod, Nobel Prize-winning biochemist, refers to Bergson as follows:

> Thanks to an engaging style and a metaphorical dialectic bare of logic but not of poetry, this philosophy achieved immense success today; but in my youth no one stood a chance of passing his baccalaureate unless he had read *Creative Evolution*.

As for Teilhard, the ill-tempered Monod writes,

> For my part I am most struck by the intellectual spinelessness of this philosophy . . . a willingness to conciliate at any price, to come to any compromise. Perhaps, after all, Teilhard was not for nothing a member of that order [the Jesuits] which, three centuries earlier, Pascal assailed for its theological laxness.

In his essay "On Values in the Age of Science," Monod presents his "simple and radical theme" concerning the ethical bases of society:

> The traditional concepts which provided the ethical foundation of human societies from time immemorial all consisted of imaginary ontogenies, none of which remains tenable in the face of scientific enquiry.

Monod is convinced that most of the world's population lies under the spell of false beliefs which he calls "animisms," these ranging from Judeo-Christian "religiosities" to Marxism; and he looks forward with some apprehension to the day when the peoples of the world wake up to the knowledge, provided by science, that there is no transcendent world, that there is no meaning to life except what we give it—a doctrine associated with his friend, Albert Camus. Monod believes that human societies are in for a terrible shock when they finally accept science's attempt to disabuse them of the myths in which they have found answers to questions about the meaning of their existence.

Well, science has its own myths, and human beings are much more resilient than Monod gives them credit for. Douglas Freeman tells the story of a group of Confederate soldiers, adorers like all their comrades of their commander General Robert E. Lee, who were debating the new theory of evolution (*Origin of Species* having then been in circulation for three years). One champion of Darwin cited evidence of the evolutionary theory which he thought was conclusive. After a pause, another soldier rose to say, "Well, you may be right. All of *us* may be descended from monkeys, but I will tell you it took God Almighty to make a man like Marse Robert."

Homer Smith, who for many years taught physiology to New York University medical students, presented a gentler materialism in his little book *Kamongo*. A biologist named Joel and an Anglican missionary priest are returning from Africa aboard ship, sailing slowly through the steaming summer heat of the Red Sea. Joel tells the padre that he is bringing back specimens of lungfish (kamongo) that he found embedded in the dried mud of the shores of Lake Victoria. For millions of years the lungfish have remained unchanged in their environment, having developed a primitive lung to get them through the dry season. Joel is studying their kidneys to see how they manage to survive without excreting lethal toxins. He tells the padre that the kamongo has survived by adapting itself to its environment, but this successful adaptation has made it an evolutionary dead end. The padre shows keen interest in the lungfish, even sympathy; but he wonders how Joel can be so sure that it is a "dead end," for even the humblest of God's creations must have some purpose.

Joel then expounds to the padre a clear and convincing account of the development of living forms, his basic concept that of an updated Darwinian theory of evolution: as Monod would later argue, organic life is all a matter of chance and necessity, natural selection operating upon random variations, much helped along by mutations; there is no meaning to all of this—life itself is no more than a "whirlpool" in the second law of thermodynamics, a temporary push back against inevitable decline and death.

The padre accepts Joel's explanation of biological evolution, but refuses to grant that it is without meaning. Could not God have simply used evolution as a means to fulfill his divine plan, most of it unknown to us? Joel smilingly shakes his head. No, he says. "Your life has no more purpose than that of any other beast. . . . It has no purpose except as you choose to give it one. . . . You are only a branch of the stream that is flowing on, resisting the world about it, trying—" "There it is," the padre interrupts. "Trying different ways of living in order to keep alive. Perhaps in my obscure corner of Africa I am an experiment too. . . . Well, anyway, I hope I don't turn out to be a blind alley." And he gets up to get the biologist a drink in thanks for the fascinating account of the lungfish.

Kamongo ends on a charmingly ambiguous note:

> Joel watched the priest with a puzzled frown as he walked across the deck. His resounding footsteps seemed to echo some familiar phrase, and Joel stopped to listen; but it was not until they had died away that his memory captured it. He chuckled to himself—it was the pulse of life, it had escaped again.

*

So there is the puzzle of *Kamongo*. What difference would it make to our moral selves if Joel were right or the padre? One of the two men sees the evolution of life as the result of chance and necessity, with no transcendent meaning. The other welcomes his instruction in biological evolution as a fascinating glimpse into the mystery of God's creative grace. Scientist and priest are both good men, each doing good in his own way. How can their common ethical character derive from two such different understandings of the foundation of things?

In the strange twilit world of subatomic physics, where tiny invisible not-yet-discovered beasts called "quarks" appear in twelve or more varieties, each with its special and mysterious quality of "charm," a realm where the reality of an event is meaningless without a measurement of it, and exiguous electromagnetic blurs appear now as particles, now as waves, physicists tell us that "this" and "that" are no longer separate entities, but different forms of the same thing.

And remember the words of an old Hassidic Jew, Rabbi Bunim: "A man should carry two stones in his pocket. On one should be inscribed 'I am but dust and ashes,' on the other, 'For my sake the world was created,' and he should use each stone as he needs it."

So, could it be possible that Lucy, poor creature, and "dust" are but two different forms of the same thing? For it is written: "And the Lord God made man from the dust of the earth and breathed into his nostrils the breath of life, and man became a living soul."

Monod would dismiss this angrily as "animism." For him, our presence on this odd planet, colored blue and white as seen from outer space, must be explained as the result of an immense dice roll: "Thus the appearance of life itself and within the biosphere, the emergence of Man, can only be conceived as the result of a huge Monte Carlo game, where our number eventually did come out, when it might as well not have appeared and, in any case, the unfathomable cosmos around us could not have cared less."

*

There is one thing Monod says that we can all agree on: living beings are strange objects, and we humans are the strangest of all. Think of the things we make: war, love, comic books, stealth bombers, chili dogs, the Ninth Symphony, the cathedral of

Chartres, Givenchy dresses, lobster thermidor, string quartets, computers, Dadaist dramas, gas chambers, golf clubs, libraries, radar detectors, the Taj Mahal, pistachio ice cream. Yes, we are strange creatures. And no one has summed up our strangeness better than Tennessee Williams:

> We are the gooks and geeks of creation;
> Believe-It-or-Not is the name of our star.
> Each one of us here thinks the other is queer
> and no one's mistaken since all of us are!

10

Wittgenstein and the Ethic of Silence

Whereof one cannot speak, thereof one must be silent.

Wittgenstein, *Tractatus*

Our final sermon is on Ludwig Wittgenstein, that strange man who for many years of his life lived close to the border of mental illness. Wittgenstein is a person of enormous influence on the philosophy of the twentieth century. Though an Austrian, he was one of that powerful trio of Cambridge-based philosophical prophets, the other two G.E. Moore and Bertrand Russell. If we counted the bales of papers read at meetings of the American Philosophical Association, Wittgenstein's name, like Abou ben Adam, would lead all the rest.

With Wittgenstein we return to the idea of philosophy as a life lived as well as a doctrine taught, to a commitment like that of Socrates, the archetypal example of this rare breed. Indeed, there are similarities—some of them odd—between Socrates and Wittgenstein. Each had a great influence on subsequent generations. In each case, a devoted band of disciples sat at the feet of the philosopher. Both were born teachers. Each had his idiosyncracies in dress—Socrates' same-weight winter-and-summer robe and bare feet, Wittgenstein's light flannel trousers and open-necked tieless shirt. Socrates often dreamed of composing music, with a voice in the dreams commanding, "Socrates, make music!" Wittgenstein played a clarinet, which he carried around wrapped in an old sock, and he could whistle forty Schubert songs and all of Brahms's St. Anthony variations. Both philosophers did creditable military service as soldiers. In the First World War, Wittgenstein fought with distinction as a lieutenant on the Russian and Italian fronts, winning two medals for bravery. Socrates saw action at Delium and at Potidaea, where he passed up a decoration for valor. Both men lived their lives in terms of a total commitment to their discipline; and at the end, both faced death bravely.

At the same time, no one can fail to be struck by the differences between the two men as human beings and as philosophers. Socrates was almost always relaxed and good-humored; Wittgenstein was tense, irritable, and had a strong capacity to wound. Socrates was gregarious, was married, and had three children; Wittgenstein was a loner and never married. The Socrates we know through Plato and Xenophon was a moral philosopher. Wittgenstein left no major writing on ethics. "If a man could write a book on ethics," he said, "this book would, with an explosion, destroy all the other books in the world." (When Fania Pascal, who gave him Russian lessons, told him of her election to the Cambridge Committee of the Soviet Union, Wittgenstein failed to congratulate her, saying instead, "What you should do is to be kind to others. Nothing else.")

*

Let's look at the background of this extraordinary man, who captured the imagination not only of philosophers but of artists, sculptors, musicians, and novelists as well. He was the eighth and youngest child of Karl Wittgenstein and Leopoldine Kalmus. Karl Wittgenstein amassed great wealth in the Austrian steel industry. Of Jewish ancestry, Karl became a Protestant, while his wife, also of Jewish extraction, was baptized a Roman Catholic, the religion in which young Ludwig was brought up. Of Ludwig's four brothers, three committed suicide: Kurt shot himself in the last year of the First World War when the troops under his command refused to obey orders; Hans drowned himself in Chesapeake Bay; and Rudolf took cyanide in a Berlin pub.

The other brother, Paul, gained fame as a concert pianist who performed piano works for the left hand only. His right arm had been shot off in the First World War, and because of the wealth of the Wittgenstein family he was able to commission prominent composers to write piano concertos for the left hand. Those who composed works for him included Sergei Prokoviev, Richard Strauss, and Eric Korngold. These pieces are rarely heard today, except for one that does stand out—the *Concerto for the Left Hand*, by that adorable genius Maurice Ravel.

Ludwig Wittgenstein grew to manhood in the rich, variegated setting of pre-1914 Vienna. The dual monarchy of Austria-Hungary was entering her final years, but her capital Vienna glowed more brightly than ever, lighting up the European sky with the phosphorescent brilliance that so often flares up in the last years of a dying culture. "Vienna 1900" radiated an authentic greatness.

In the natural sciences the great name was Ernst Mach, professor of physics at the University of Vienna, whom we remember as Lenin's enemy because he taught that sensations alone are real, that all the rest is metaphysics, which is idle. In psychiatry and psychology the dominant figure was Sigmund Freud. With him (though not only with him), the concept of sex moved to the absolute center of the image of humanity now entertained by so much of the West. Less well known to us is the psychologist Otto Weininger, a suicide at twenty-three and author of the notorious *Sex and Character*, in which he promoted in "scientific" language the old idea that the feminine is the source of evil; it is as if women have no souls. (Wittgenstein read Weininger's book attentively and never forgot it. What remained with him was not so much the misogyny, but the emphasis on the absolute duty of finding and developing one's genius.)

In literature, there were brilliant writers who took the Vienna scene for their subject. Arthur Schnitzler, a medical doctor, found the material for his bright, cynical tales by sitting in Viennese cafes, drinking his coffee, watching the couples coming and going, noting and translating the little signs of infidelity and deception, the recriminations of lovers and their reconciliations, down to the final betrayal.

Robert Musil's novel *The Man without Qualities* runs to three volumes, and even then it is unfinished. This long chronicle of the lives of some of Vienna's "beautiful people" is done with sly irreverence. It is set entirely in the year 1913, and it provides a compelling picture of that febrile, feverish, sex-obsessed, sex-repressed society.

In music, there were wonders. Richard Strauss was a Bavarian, but he spent much of his time in Vienna. The composer of *Der Rosenkavalier* relied on the Austrian dramatist Hugo von Hofmannsthal for many of his librettos, and he tirelessly travelled the Vienna-Munich railroad axis. Vienna's cultural establishment discovered, Austrian fashion, that it had a great composer in Gustav Mahler only when he died in 1911. Thomas Mann's Aschenbach, the central character of *Death in Venice*, was modeled in part on Mahler; and the film version of the novella uses the *adagietto* of the composer's Fifth Symphony on the sound track. The most revolutionary son of musical Vienna, Arnold Schoenberg, attempted to rescue music from sterility by inventing a new method of composition, the serial tone row. Teacher as well as composer, Schoenberg numbered among his pupils Alban Berg and Anton Webern.

Three remarkable painters emerged from Vienna's "Secessionist" group—Gustav Klimt, Egon Schiele, and Oskar Kokoschka. Klimt made gorgeous silver- and gold-papered portraits of wealthy Viennese ladies, Wittgenstein's sister Margarete among them. His work exudes the "aesthetische-erotische" atmosphere of the time and place.

Wittgenstein, who had expert architectural talent, was strongly influenced by the ideas of Adolf Loos—the simplification of building structures along straight, geometrical lines, all ornamentation stripped away. He was also intensely interested in cultural criticism, particularly that provided by Karl Kraus, editor of the journal *Die Fackel* (The Torch). Typical of Kraus' corrosive wit was his definition of psychoanalysis as the disease of which it holds itself to be the cure. Wittengstein took to heart a thesis held by Kraus and by Fritz Mauthner: language has the power to corrupt culture.

The products of "Vienna 1900" were not without military-political relevance. Adolf Hitler was born in Austria in April 1889, six days apart from his compatriot, Ludwig Wittgenstein. It was not the sight of some old Jew in Vienna that drove the iron into Hitler's soul, though he makes out in *Mein Kampf* that it was. The door of the Vienna art establishment was shut in his face not once but twice. His paintings and drawings were rejected by the Vienna art academy; and though he was told that his drawings showed architectural talent, the school of architecture refused him admittance because he had not completed the required school studies. And indeed then the iron did enter his soul, and the resolve, "Someday I'll come back." In 1913 he left Vienna for Munich and served in the First World War as a corporal, displaying almost suicidal courage as a dispatch runner in the trenches. He declined promotion to sergeant because sergeants were not permitted to serve as dispatchers, whose average survival rate was six or seven days. He was decorated with the Iron Cross, First Class, an unusual award for a soldier of such low rank. The rest of the story is well known. In the spring of 1938 Hitler returned to Vienna, standing upright in a six-wheeled Mercedes-Benz, acknowledging the frantic cheers of the crowd, as Austria was incorporated into the Third Reich. That return in triumph to the Vienna that had rejected him was the fulfillment of a dream, a passionate desire close to his strange and terrible heart. For like Nero, Hitler believed himself to be an artist.

Needless to say, Ludwig Wittgenstein's early career was quite different from that of the future dictator. As a youth Wittgenstein was at home with objects, handled tools naturally, and could take intricate mechanisms apart and put them back together correctly. His first ambition was to be an engineer. After studying at the Technische Hochschule in Berlin, he travelled to England to do research on jet propulsion and propeller design. The mathematical problems involved in the latter led him to wonder about the foundations of mathematics. To this end he consulted Gottlob Frege of the University of Jena, a pioneer in mathematical logic. Frege recommended study with Bertrand Russell, who at this time was working with his mathematics tutor, Alfred North Whitehead, on their joint work *Principia Mathematica*, the first volume of which appeared in 1910. Russell and Whitehead accepted Frege's "logicist thesis," that the first principles of mathematics derive from the postulates and rules of formal deductive logic.

Wittgenstein received a friendly welcome from Russell and from G.E. Moore, both prominent figures in philosophy at

Cambridge. There, at Trinity College, Wittgenstein began to work out the plan of his logico-philosophical work, now known by the title Moore suggested: *Tractatus Logico-Philosophicus*, the only book Wittgenstein published during his lifetime. He worked on it through the war years, and when he was captured on the Italian front in 1918 he had it in his knapsack. He was eventually permitted to send the manuscript out of the prison camp and on to Russell, and it was finally published in 1922 in the form Wittgenstein wanted—bilingual: German on the left page, English on the right.

*

Wittgenstein's *Tractatus* is one of the most extraordinary books ever written, and it is still brooded over intensely by expert readers. Wittgenstein himself thought—though he later revised his opinion—that this book put an end to philosophy by furnishing an instrument capable of solving all problems of philosophy, provided they are real problems and not just disguised nonsense. He took much of the technical apparatus and symbolism from Whitehead and Russell's *Principia*, including that part which sets out truth-functional logic. You are probably familiar with this kind of symbolism, taught in most elementary courses in formal logic. The small letters of the second part of the alphabet—p, q, r, and so on—stand for sentences. They are variables, that is, blank spaces in which we may write any statement we choose, such as "It is raining" or "Gases when heated expand." These may be combined with certain basic logical concept-forms or constants, such as negation ("not-p"), alternation ("or"), implication ("if...then"), or conjunction ("and"). So we can write "$\sim p$" for, say, "New Haven is not the capital of Connecticut," or "$p \lor q$" for, say, "It is raining or it is snowing," and so on.

According to *Tractatus*, these logical forms will yield matrices of all possible statements, and these statements have two basic characteristics. First, statements of logic and mathematics are tautologies, that is to say, such statements are always true, true no matter what; and second, *all* statements are logical pictures of facts (*facts* being, in Wittgenstein's words, "whatever is the case").

Since Wittgenstein believed at the time that the main business of language is to make statements about facts, he considered propositions of ethics, of metaphysics, of aesthetics, of religious matters to be neither true nor false, but meaningless. He does not deny the importance of the genuine concerns that underly such propositions, but he insists that these propositions cannot be expressed in such a way as to make logical sense. They must be *shown*. Hence the famous closing statement of *Tractatus*: "Wovon man nicht sprechen kann, darüber muss man schweigen" ("Whereof one cannot speak, thereof one must be silent").

To illustrate Wittgenstein's doctrine, consider a football field, lighted at night. The lighted area contains the meaningful sentences, true or false. But out beyond the lighted field dwell the things we cannot talk about; out there are ethics, art, aesthetics, religion, metaphysics. To use an Augustinian-Lutheran distinction, it is as if the sentences which are meaningful belong to the order of necessity. The rest belong to the order of grace; they refer to matters that cannot be spoken about, only shown.

At the end of *Tractatus*, the author tells us that the book itself is nonsense (*unsinnig*). It is, however, useful nonsense. It's like a ladder: if you want to climb up to a certain height, you use it to get you up there; but then you can kick it away, you don't need it anymore. So, after you have read and understood *Tractatus*, this takes care of philosophy, and that's the end of it.

*

After the First World War Wittgenstein entered upon a moratorium in which he taught elementary schoolchildren in small villages in lower Austria. He had a class in calculus for eleven-year-olds. This pedagogic tour was brought to an end by an unfortunate incident. In a fit of temper he hit a boy and knocked him out. This was not the first time that Wittgenstein had lost control of himself in class, and a formal complaint was lodged against him. Resigning his teaching post, Wittgenstein went to work as a gardener's assistant at a monastery. This may have been his way of doing penance for his actions. (Later he confessed to some friends that there were two things he was bitterly ashamed of having done. One was physically abusing his students, and the other concerned his misrepresenting the number of his Jewish forebears.)

Wittgenstein returned to philosophy during a sojourn in Vienna. His sister Margarete—subject of the Klimt portrait—asked him to return to the city to act as consultant to the architect of the new house she was building. Wittgenstein threw himself into the task with enthusiasm, demanding constant attention to details. (Another sister, Hermine, overheard a locksmith working on a keyhole appealing to her brother, "Tell me, Herr Ingenieur, does a millimeter here or there really matter so much to you?" Wittgenstein responded with a shouted "YES!" that almost blew the locksmith out of his skin.) A group of logical positivists (the "Vienna Circle") found him out and pressed him to attend some of their meetings. Wittgenstein declined but agreed to discuss philosophy with selected members. These hot-eyed mathematical logicians had been using some of the material in *Tractatus* to confirm their doctrine, which held that there are only two kinds of propositions which can be meaningful: those of formal logic which are analytic, that is to say, tautologies true by definition (like "A bachelor is an unmarried man"), and those testable by the methods of the empirical sciences to see whether they are true or false. All other propositions, such as those of metaphysics, are unverifiable and therefore meaningless, insignificant, nonsensical, and are of no importance when compared to the propositions of logic and science. The message of the logical positivists read, "Metaphysicians, shut your traps!" To which Rudolf Carnap added, "Metaphysicians are musicians without musical talent."

As a young man, the British philosopher A. J. Ayer shuttled back and forth between Oxford and Vienna. It was Ayer who introduced to the Anglo-American world the message of the Vienna Circle. Joining Humean skepticism with logical positivism, in 1938 Ayer brought out his *Language, Truth and Logic*, a small book that crashed like a brick through the dusty panes of American academic philosophy. To sample this book, we might open it to the pages on metaphysical and theological propositions. Consider the theist who believes that the proposition "God exists" is true. His proposition is not true, but neither is it false; it is meaningless. Now take the atheist. He believes that "God exists" is false, but his mistake lies in his belief that the proposition is significant, meaningful. The agnostic sits in the same leaky boat, for he believes that the proposition "God exists" is meaningful, but we just don't know whether it is true or false. Thus, theist, atheist, and agnostic are all wrong, because they treat the proposition "God exists" as if it were significant, but it is not. Such propositions have no real significance; they are just as meaningless as the statement, "The sky is in the key of B flat."

Wittgenstein never accepted the dogmas of the Vienna Circle. Although he agreed that concerns about metaphysics, ethics, and aesthetics could not be put in the form of meaningful statements, he continued to believe that these realms are important. To Wittgenstein the world of poetry, for example, ranked high, in some cases higher than philosophy. One day someone told him that a certain professor had just published a book on the poet William Blake. "Blake!" exclaimed Wittgenstein. "Why, that fellow [the professor] doesn't even understand *philosophy!*"

*

In January 1929 Wittgenstein returned to Cambridge and applied for a money grant, a favor the authorities were reluctant to approve because they knew that he came from a wealthy family. (What they did not know was that he had transferred his inheritance to his brothers and sisters and was therefore poor.) Moore and Russell believed it would help if Wittgenstein had a Ph.D., so they hurriedly arranged for a *pro forma* examination. The *Tractataus* was accepted as a dissertation and Moore attempted to get a discussion going, a procedure Wittgenstein brought to an end by clapping his examiners on the shoulders and saying, "Don't worry. I know you'll never understand me." The degree was conferred, and a money grant approved for two terms. In 1930 Wittgenstein was awarded a fellowship at Trinity

College. He lectured there throughout the thirties, except for trips to Norway, Austria, and the Soviet Union (where, he said, he "felt like a private"). Wittgenstein was elected professor of philosophy at Cambridge in February of 1939 and in June received his British passport.

In his memoir of his teacher, Norman Malcolm describes the setting and atmosphere of Wittgenstein's classes in the late 1930s—the devoted band of students sitting on orange crates brought into the master's room, the long silences which one dared not break for fear of making a Mistake. Sometimes Wittgenstein forbade his students to take notes lest his teaching be misconstrued by those outside the circle. (In this respect he resembled the third-century Alexandrian philosopher Ammonius Saccas, teacher of Plotinus, who ordered his students on pain of expulsion to keep his teachings secret.) At other times Wittgenstein dictated notes which his students would circulate among themselves in mimeographed form.

Wittgenstein was very touchy about admitting to his class persons he did not know. Ernest Nagel, professor of philosophy at Columbia University, told me that he had a Guggenheim Fellowship that took him to Cambridge when Wittgenstein was teaching at Trinity College. Nagel introduced himself to G.E. Moore, who welcomed him warmly and encouraged him to attend any lectures or classes he wished: "One exception though. If you wish to attend Wittgenstein's lectures, you must get his permission to do so." So Nagel, already noted for his work in the philosophy of science, stood respectfully before Wittgenstein, cited his status as a visiting American scholar, and asked if he could attend the lectures. Wittgenstein stared at him coldly and said, in that Teutonic accent which he never quite lost, "I don't take tourists." Nagel, a gentle soul, thought he would make one more try, and the next day he told Wittgenstein of his own work in philosophy, which was already well known. This time Wittgenstein's tone was softer: "Mr. Nagel, when I teach, I suffer. And when I see a strange face in my class, I suffer more. Now you wouldn't want me to suffer, would you?" Nagel gave it up.

*

Hermetically speaking, there came out of Wittgenstein's well-guarded crystal retort at Cambridge a series of writings finally published in part after his death under the title *Philosophical Investigations*. The book was edited by Elizabeth Anscombe with the assistance of colleagues who also knew Wittgenstein's work and had taken down notes dictated by him. The format of *Investigations* resembles that of *Tractatus*, with German and English on facing pages. Wittgenstein had long since decided that *Tractatus* had been too narrowly positivist (though never to the extreme of the Vienna Circle). He now believed that good language is not restricted to statements of the hard sciences and deductive logic, that the business of language is not just to state facts. Think, he said, of the numerous ways in which we use language in everyday life—presenting a hypothesis and testing it, making jokes, solving an arithmetic problem, translating from one language to another, asking, thanking, cursing, greeting, praying. Think of exclamations alone, with their completely different functions:

> Water!
> Away!
> Ow!
> Help!
> Fine!
> No!

We do all this in ordinary language. People think that philosophy needs an ideal language, but "ordinary language is all right."

When Wittgenstein studied the usage of ordinary language and found how very subtle and versatile it is, and how resistant to analysis, he concluded that the future problems of philosophy would be in the province of the philosophy of language. And today in our country, courses in the philosophy of language are standard offerings in nearly every philosophy department. Wittgenstein may not have mentioned it, but he never forgot the work of Karl Kraus and Fritz Mauthner. Their criticism emphasized the power of language to corrupt culture; Wittgenstein stressed the power of language to *confuse*. The task of philosophy, he said, is to rescue intelligence from the bewitchment of language; not to build a house, but to tidy its rooms.

Sometimes his illustrations resemble those of Zen:

- What is the aim of philosophy?
- To show the fly the way out of the fly-bottle.
- Look! It's out!

Philosophical confusion resembles the state of mind of a man who finds himself in a room from which he wants to get out. He tries the window, but it is too high; he tries the chimney, but it is too narrow. If he would only turn around he would see that the door has been open all the time.

In Augustine's *Confessions* (a book Wittgenstein admired), the saint tells of how he learned language by pointing to an object and saying its name. This shows us, says Wittgenstein, that language is a game, the language game. The language game starts by naming things but there is much more to come, since language does not confine itself to naming objects and there are philosophical prejudices to be overcome.

Consider definitions, for example. Socrates believed that the method of philosophy should be to try for an exact definition of what is under discussion. He asks Theaetetus, "What is knowledge?" And Theaetetus replies, "Well, Socrates, there is the knowledge of the geometers like myself, and the knowledge of the carpenters, and the knowledge of the cobblers—" "No, no!" says Socrates. "You are just giving me a list of various kinds of knowledge. I want to know what knowledge *is*. What do all these kinds of knowledge have *in common*, so that we can define knowledge?"

Wittgenstein believed that this search for a common element leads to philosophical confusion. We might offer an example from Clausewitz's *On War*. Clausewitz begins his inquiry by considering the various kinds of wars and endeavoring to pin down their common element. No, Wittgenstein would say, that's the wrong move in the language game. Wars may resemble one another, but there is no "essence" of war.

Take the term *game* itself. Is there something common to all games? Football, chess, bridge, war games, ring-around-the-rosy? No, says Wittgenstein, there is no common element; but there is a family relationship, such as that we perceive when looking at a photograph of a family. There is a family resemblance, but no identical quality that is part of each member of the group.

Wittgenstein views the problem as follows:

> Think of the tools in a tool-box: there is a hammer, pliers, a saw, a screw-driver, a rule, a glue-pot, nails and screws. The functions of words are as diverse as the functions of these objects. (And in both cases there are similarities.)

Suppose somebody says that *all* tools serve to modify something. Wittgenstein replies, What does the glue-pot modify? Or the ruler?

Language is far more than learning the names of objects. The meaning of *wrench*, for example, does not consist simply in the object it names, but in the way it is *used* in language. When I say "wrench" while fixing a pipe, you hand me a wrench; and when I say "tape," you hand me tape. Hence Wittgenstein's maxim, which became his disciples' slogan: *"Don't ask for the meaning, ask for the use."*

From *Philosophical Investigations* we learn that all sorts of questions raise difficulties: "Can a machine think?"; "Can a machine feel pain?"; "Can I know, really know, that another is in pain?" There are many ways of talking, each with its own peculiar interest and value. There are jokes, scientific descriptions, discourses about God ("God-talk"). There is a whole gallimaufry of statements that cannot be "verified" by the standard procedures recommended by the logical empiricists. One should treat these statements not so much as nonsense, but as pieces in a language game. If we clarify the rules and make the game more understandable, we may succeed in containing the bewitchment of language.

During the Second World War, Wittgenstein left Cambridge to work as a porter in a London hospital and later as a laboratory assistant in Newcastle. After the war he gave his last lectures at

Cambridge, then went to live for a while in a cottage on the west coast of Ireland. He made a brief visit to the United States, staying in Ithaca, New York, with Norman Malcolm and his wife, but did not feel well enough to lecture at Malcolm's university, Cornell. He was already afflicted with the cancer that would kill him. He returned to England, where his doctor told him that his case was hopeless. Wittgenstein had just one favor to ask: he did not want to die in a hospital. So the doctor's wife asked him to come into their house and stay with them, and he died there in April 1951. Before he slipped into a coma he said to the doctor's wife, "Tell them I've had a wonderful life."

*

What can we say about this strange man? Nietzsche's words about his teacher Schopenhauer come to mind: "What he taught, we may put aside. What he lived, that will abide. Behold a man. Subject was he to none."

Wittgenstein lived a life of complete commitment to philosophy. That is why he said to his students, "Don't go into philosophy," and "Don't marry a lady philosopher." The latter imperative came not so much from misogyny—although that cannot be entirely ruled out—but from his conviction that philosophy is a full-time job. It is not just teaching a class as a comfortable professor. Wittgenstein's rule was, Give all you have to your work. That was his commitment. We find it as well in certain artists, priests, and in the military profession. Malcolm remembers Wittgenstein reading Brigadier Desmond Young's life of Rommel and saying, "Such a decent man."

But the commitment must be there. In his own war service, Wittgenstein chafed at being assigned to duty behind the lines. He wanted to go to the front, and once he got there he chose to place himself at an artillery post, a most dangerous position. His superiors commented on his complete commitment to duty, and his soldiers gave him high marks for it. When he was awarded his second decoration for valor, the citation noted that "his exceptionally courageous behavior, calmness and heroism won the total admiration of the troops."

Wittgenstein said that he measured a man's work by what it cost him. Perhaps he was thinking of Beethoven, one of his heroes. While the composer was working on his *Missa Solemnis*, despairing of ever getting it finished in the time promised, he labored on it for two days and nights without taking food or drink. When he found the maids fallen asleep and the meal on the fire burned to a crisp, he roared, "Could you not watch one hour with me?" Terrified, the servants fled the house, leaving him alone and unfed. Later two worried friends banged on his door. Finally the door was flung open and Beethoven stood there distraught, unseeing, clothes awry, shouting that he had been deserted. He had eaten nothing. The friends quickly sent out for food, set his clothing to rights, and soothed him until his bellowing died away.

Remember the counsels of perfection in the New Testament. Jesus said, "Be ye perfect." This is a hard saying; the very thought makes us uncomfortable. Yet Fania Pascal once asked Wittgenstein, "Do you want to be perfect?"; and he replied, "*Of course* I want to be perfect."

The counsels of perfection can only be fulfilled through the order of grace, not the order of necessity. It may be that the order of necessity compels so much of our attention that only a few, if any, can attain to the order of grace. Yet the imperative "Be ye perfect" was addressed not to the few, but to all. Could this help to explain Wittgenstein's intolerance of human weakness—including his own?

Wittgenstein had a prophetic, priestly side to him, and on more than one occasion he thought of becoming a monk. Although not religious in any sectarian sense, he knew sudden moments when he "felt safe," suffused by the conviction that nothing could harm him; and the notion that God is the meaning of the world did not seem strange to him ("not *how* the world is, but *that* it is, is the mystical"). To Wittgenstein Christianity was not a set of beliefs, but the way one lives one's life. At his burial service in St. Giles, Cambridge, a Roman Catholic priest said prayers; but Wittgenstein's biographer, Ray Monk, says,

The reconciliation with God that Wittgenstein sought was not that of being accepted back into the arms of the Catholic Church; it was a state of ethical seriousness and integrity that would survive the scrutiny of even that most stern of judges, his own conscience, "the God who in my bosom dwells."

Wittgenstein was not afraid to take the word *God* into his mouth, though this only rarely. Once, while teaching school in lower Austria, he took his young charges to Vienna to see paintings and hear music. They returned by a train which let them off a mile from their village, and they had to walk in the dark across the fields. A little girl started to cry, and Wittgenstein knelt beside her and said, "What is it? Are you frightened? Then you must think of God."

*

To the ethic of commitment Wittgenstein joined the ethic of silence ("whereof one cannot speak, thereof one must be silent"). He hated what he called "gassing"—meaningless talk, the witless passion for communication. He knew the passage from Matthew, "I say unto you that for every idle word men shall speak, they shall give account thereof on the day of judgment. For by thy words thou shalt be justified and by thy words thou shalt be condemned."

Silence. . . . Silence is a military virtue. Just think: the order understood and obeyed without question; the silence of the soldier on guard at his post; the silence of the midwatch at sea.

And think of the apostles of silence. Remember Dostoyevsky's story of "The Grand Inquisitor" from *The Brothers Karamazov*, in which the old cardinal does all the talking while Jesus stands before him in silence, as once he stood before Pilate. (Jesus' trial was very different from that of Socrates. The Athenian philosopher had a great deal to say for himself, Jesus little or nothing.)

The eccentric Danish theologue Søren Kierkegaard (whom Wittgenstein greatly admired) had a division of three kinds of silence: *Stilhed*, the tranquil quiet of a natural scene; *Taushed*, the inward silence that prepares us to receive grace; and *Huile*, the complete repose which is in God.

We are told in the Chinese classics that one day the teacher Confucius sat with his pupils and said nothing. They waited a long time, but the silence continued. Finally one pupil spoke up: "Master, we your students sit here to listen to your words of wisdom, and you are silent." And Confucius replied, "Look at the heavens. The stars revolve in their orderly courses, and does heaven say anything?" (Wittgenstein's students often spoke of the long silences, intent and expectant, that prevailed at his lectures.)

The silence of the heavens bothered Blaise Pascal. Looking up at night at the mysterious blurs of light coming from galaxies scattered in an abyss of darkness, the geometer remarked, "The silence of those infinite spaces frightens me."

The silence of the heavens made a deep impression on young Albert Camus. Once in Algiers he happened to be at the scene of an accident. A little Arab boy had been run over by a car, and from the Moslem crowd a wailing arose. Pointing his finger to the sky, Camus turned to his companion and said, "You see? *He* doesn't say anything."

There is a novel titled *Silence* by the Japanese writer Shusaka Endo. It is based on a historical fact: the ordeal of a Christian missionary, Father Rodriguez, during that period of the shogunate when Christians were cruelly persecuted. A Christian could escape torture and death by apostasizing, and the gesture of apostasy was trampling on a crucifix or on a brass plate engraved with a likeness of Christ. The inquisitor, Inouye, anxious to secure the apostasy of Father Rodriguez, tries to get him to step on the Christian image. A mere formality, says the shogun's officer: these things don't really matter; you can believe what you like; just step on it. When Father Rodriguez refused, Inouye led him over to the pit where the ordeal of the hold-out Christians was taking place. The pit was filled with boiling excrement, and the victim was hung upside down above it, his forehead lightly slashed with a sword so he would bleed slowly and not die too quickly. The left arm was kept free so that the victim could make the gesture of apostasy. Inouye showed the missionary the frightful agony of a recalcitrant Christian, who was calling upon Jesus for mercy. "You see," said Inouye to Rodriguez, "your God, your *Deus*, does not answer. He is silent." Father Rodriguez in turn was trussed up and hung over the infernal pit. After a while he could stand the torment no longer, and he made the gesture of apostasy. . . .

Finally, three admirals and silence. In describing his experience in "Alcatraz," the North Vietnamese prison reserved for American incorrigibles, Jim Stockdale could not forget the silence in which he and his fellow POWs struggled to survive:

> This support, this girder of our unity and integrity, was unwittingly strengthened by our captors, who kept most of us in enforced silence in solitary confinement. Except for our tapping on the walls, which we did stealthily and of necessity sparingly, each one of us lived in a silent world.

A naval officer, once aide to the U.S. Navy's top admiral, the chief of naval operations, told this story. In his quarters the admiral was confronted by his grown-up daughter. Distraught, angry, in tears, she upbraided her father for some fancied neglect. The admiral said nothing, but quietly drew a comb from his pocket and silently combed his daughter's hair until she regained her composure.

The third admiral was Japanese. Standing on the bridge of the *Akagi* at the battle of Midway, Ryunosuke Kusaka watched as a shot-up American plane screamed past him and cartwheeled into the sea. He silently said a prayer for the dead pilot's soul, and then turned back to defend his carriers. He turned, as must we all, from the order of grace to the order of necessity.

*

Not to end on too somber a note, consider a story about Woody Hayes, famed coach of Ohio State University's mighty football team. Sometime after his retirement from coaching, Woody read about the course Admiral Jim Stockdale was teaching at the Naval War College. So he crossed the country to attend the last meeting of "Foundations of Moral Obligation" for that year of 1978-79. Woody listened attentively then gave a little talk to the officers present in the crowded lecture room. He praised the former heroism and current ethical enterprise of the admiral-president, and added that he was pleased to learn that the philosopher Wittgenstein had said much the same thing he used to tell his players between the halves of their hard-fought games:

Was kommt leicht hat keinen Wert.

Or, in Woody's words,

If it comes easy, it ain't worth a damn!

Epilogue

A story is told of an old French savant who was taken to the Jardin des Plantes for his first view of a rhinoceros. Gazing intently at the formidable beast, he asked his companion, "But what is the point of it?" A similar tale is told of the astronomer Laplace. On hearing for the first time Beethoven's Ninth Symphony, he asked, "But what does it prove?" Our own tour of moral philosophy and related matters has none of the grandeur of the Ninth or the majesty of the rhinoceros, but to the question "What does all this add up to?" we can answer only that, like the symphony and the rhino, moral philosophy has no bottom line, no demonstrable conclusion as to what is, after all, the right and the good.

We have looked a little into some inquiries made, doctrines taught, and lives lived by human beings of flesh and bone who in their own way have tried to throw some light on problems concerning the good and the right. Nearly all of them have implicitly agreed that no ethical philosophy of any depth can be constructed apart from some related concern, whether this be a theory of knowledge, a philosophy of mind, a religious belief, or an investigation of the basic conditions of human existence. Aristotle held that moral philosophy is a practical study, concerned with acting as well as knowing: if such an enterprise is worth anything at all, it should make us better; but we should not expect exactness of it.

Someone has said that philosophy is what a man does with his solitude. We began our inquiry with Jim Stockdale, a prisoner of war in a small Hanoi prison cell. His confinement was solitary, interrupted by relentless interrogation and frequent punishment "in the ropes." Stripped of all the high-tech weapons that a powerful industrial nation could provide, only his will remained his own. His belief in the power of that will, fortified by his memory of some lines of the Stoic Epictetus, helped him through the long night of courage that Plato's General Laches calls "endurance of soul." In the crucible of closed space, the downed navy pilot discovered powers of transcendence within himself that he had not suspected were there. In this way he joined a long line of prisoners—Socrates in his death cell, Cervantes in the dungeon of the Bey, Dostoyevsky in the House of the Dead, Solzhenitsyn in his gulag—all of whom have experienced the paradox of the discovery of freedom in captivity.

Whether Job, self-confined on his ash-heap, is enlightened by his meeting with God in the whirlwind or simply silenced (but not defeated) must be left to those of us who still wonder why bad things happen to good people, why a human who has done his best finds human ethical standards apparently incommensurable with the ways of the almighty and the infinite. Both believers and nonbelievers have written of their love for the Book of Job, of their feeling for the tormented man from Uz. To the believer, the story of Job is a book about faith; the nonbeliever finds in it a compelling chronicle of a fellow human who is beaten but fights back anyway. The devout Pascal says that we humans may know that the universe will crush us, but at least we *know*; the universe knows nothing of that. Therein, he claims, lies the greatness of the human, this thinking reed supreme in its frailty over the mindless indifference of the cosmos.

To Socrates in his prison-cave, death itself would come as a physical and spiritual liberation. His pupil Plato used that cave as a symbol of a prisoner's struggle through the shadows of darkness and ignorance toward the light of unfettered knowledge. Through Plato's dramatizing of the thoughts and events of his teacher's life, we confront Socrates' questions about the just and the unjust, the problem of duty to self and country: Can moral values be taught? Should we obey an unjust law? Should we stick by the principle of life in the face of death? Or, confronted with that hard choice, should we go over to the other side? Should we take the emergency exit of suicide, or should we say with Socrates that our lives are given to us by God and it is better to wait for the hour when we are summoned by him?

Plato's great pupil Aristotle brings us back to earth with his *Nichomachean Ethics*, the first textbook of moral philosophy. Right actions are what we expect of a good man. Aristotle's model of excellence, the great-souled man, is not a warm, caring person but an imperturbable leader who values honor more than pleasure or riches. To Aristotle, moral excellence is a disposition of character, a mean between two extremes, the mean determined by reason. So courage represents the mean between cowardice and rashness. Bravery in combat is the highest form of courage, for on the battlefield the citizen-soldier willingly faces death, the greatest of evils. Yet there are circumstances in which a man should die rather than do an act which would be a shame before God and man. The highest good is happiness, and that is activity in accord with virtue or excellence, "and if there be many of these with that which is best." At the conclusion of the *Nichomachean Ethics*, "that which is best" takes us into the rarified Platonic realm of contemplative happiness, a happiness which has its source in the contemplation of the divine, the immutable.

Two thousand years have passed, and we are in a small German city on the Baltic. Kant's ethic, preceded by a formidable analysis of the limits of human knowledge, rests on the concept of duty—duty as an end in itself, done because it is our duty and not out of hope for reward. Although his social ideal was perpetual peace among united nations, Kant preferred soldierly duty instead of the struggle for profit as the rule of life. His categorical imperative based itself on the unconditioned ought (thou oughtst because thou oughtst): in a situation of moral choice, can we honestly say to ourselves that everyone should act as we propose to act, or are we making an exception in favor of ourselves? Possessing moral sovereignty, capable of acting out of good will, we must regard all persons in the same way, always treating them as ends in themselves and never as means only. Reason presents us with the moral law, but only will can act upon it. Act, not knowledge, defines us morally. We know with only part of ourselves, but we act with all of ourselves. Kant would not like Dostoyevsky's Underground Man, but he would understand why he says, "You see, gentlemen, reason is an excellent thing, there's no disputing that, but reason is nothing but reason, and satisfies only the rational side of man's nature, while will is a manifestation of the whole life, that is, of the whole human life including reason and all the impulses."

Results, not motive, form the test of an act of moral worth, says John Stuart Mill, in this way providing a striking contrast to Kant's analysis. Mill's utilitarianism required him to state that beneficial consequences to all concerned are what count in determining the moral worth of an act. Yet Mill, like Kant, proclaims the autonomy of the self, leading him to a radical liberalism based on the principle that over his own body and mind an individual person is sovereign, and may not be forced by others or by law to do or not to do something for his own good—so long as the exercise of that sovereignty does not interfere with the liberty of others.

The lightning-charged atmosphere of the Second World War and its aftermath in Europe lent dramatic power to the doctrine of "irrational freedom" proclaimed in Sartre's existentialism. The existential choice is, in a sense, pre-ethical, for in ultimate situations of moral choice reason can give us arguments just as compelling for one alternative as for another. It is the act itself that counts. Our choices, and therefore our acts, make us what we are. Existentialists agreed with the Spanish philosopher Unamuno that we are not born with a soul, but we die with one we have manufactured. Albert Camus' more traditional humanism held as its moral hero the man who knows he is beaten but fights back anyway—a type present in world literature from the Book of Job to Hemingway's *Old Man and the Sea*. To Camus' Dr. Rieux, moral heroism means no more than common decency, in his case doing his job as a physician in a town overwhelmed by the plague, even though he knows he can't do much good.

In contrast to the radical ethical individualism of wartime existentialism, the ideology of Marx and Lenin preached the stern ideal of absolute duty to the collective, the revolution, the party, as well as the acknowledgement of the leadership of the Soviet Union in the struggle for a social order that would liberate humanity from the chains of greed and oppression. Lenin's *What Is To Be Done?* is a classic treatise in the ideology and technique of securing a social end, judged supremely good, by ruthless means. How quickly this doctrine led to the years of Stalinist terror is all too well known. But the sense of the value of the individual human dies hard, as Arthur Koestler's parable *Darkness at Noon* testifies through the character of the old Bolshevik Rubashov, who learns too late that the "I" cannot long be suppressed, even by an all-powerful "We."

By the late 1960s the tide of party omnipotence had begun to lose some of its force, and a ripple of humanism, of openness to Western thought, appeared. By the 1980s the influence of dialectical materialism, the official philosophy of the Soviet Union, had faded. Soviet scholars discovered humanism, and Soviet utilitarianism weighed the economic results of seventy years of government control and found them wanting. The party, once supreme in authority, found itself deserted by those who had once been its most loyal adherents, thus recalling the lamentation of the prophet Jeremiah: "How doth the city sit solitary that was full of people!" The Soviet Union disintegrated, and the world cautiously proclaimed an end to the Cold War.

No study of moral philosophy would be complete if it ignored the presence of science and its effects in our world, or over-looked the role of technology in our lives. What is the relation between science and ethical values? What difference would it make to our lives, thoughts, and acts if humans were not created fully formed by God but instead evolved from nonhuman ances-tors? Would the truth of such a theory of human evolution mean that there was no God, no almighty and caring Creator who in some way presides over our destinies, compelling them or leaving them up to us? And if so, what difference would that make in our ethical values, our moral attitudes, our sense of responsibility toward ourselves and others?

Jacques Monod, whose work on the DNA molecule brought a Nobel Prize, writes in his book *Chance and Necessity* that there is no truth in the belief that there exists a transcendent entity. Stating his own belief that there is only one ethic, the ethic of knowledge, Monod declares that when the truth of scientific materialism dawns on a world still not ready for it, a profound shock awaits those masses of humans who have deluded them-selves with false hopes of salvation from one or another "animism," whether this be dialectical materialism or Christianity.

In *My Early Life* Winston Churchill takes a more cheerful tack, completely unbothered by the apparent conflict between reason and faith: "Certainly nothing could be more repulsive both to our minds and feelings than the spectacle of thousands of millions of universes—for that is what they say it comes to now—all knocking about together forever without any rational or good purpose behind them. I therefore adopted quite early in life a system of believing whatever I wanted to believe, while at the same time leaving reason to pursue unfettered whatever paths she was capable of treading."

Despite his earlier reservations, Ludwig Wittgenstein hoped one day to write a book about ethics, but death took him before he could turn to it. Of one truth he was convinced: ethical realities cannot be stated; they must be shown. This may have been his way of saying what Socrates said long ago: that philosophy is not just doctrine taught but the truth and beauty of a life well lived. To the prisoner escaped from the cave or released at last from the prison cell, the right and the good cannot be taught by precepts mounted with fine words like *values*, *integrity*, *morality*, or even *leadership*. Instead, the right and the good must be demonstrated every day in the choices that we make, the actions we take, the example we set.

*

We U.S. Americans number few great names in philosophy, though many in literature and the arts. Some say that this is because we are a practical people, impatient with what appear to us as abstractions. We are a results-oriented folk, and our major tradition in philosophy is pragmatism, its best known sons William James and John Dewey. A belief is true if it works, said James; truth is "the expedient—in the long run and on the whole, of course." And Dewey taught that ideas are instruments of action rather than objects of contemplation. "Moral insight," says Dewey, "and therefore moral theory consist simply in the everyday workings of the same ordinary intelligence that measures dry-goods, drives nails, sells wheat, and invents the telephone."

But philosophy is not the only carrier of ideas that have awesome power to create. The stern Calvinist theology of the Puritans who settled Massachusetts was supplemented by their conviction that they had a covenant with God, after the manner of Abraham. On the deck of *Arbella*, flagship of the little Puritan armada, governor-elect John Winthrop recalled the words of Matthew's gospel and proclaimed that this new Puritan community would be as that City on a Hill whose light could not be hid, that would shine before all men.

The Puritans of the Great Migration did not come to found the United States of America but to purify a religion that had strayed from Jehovah's iron path. But our nation grew out of Puritan soil, as well as from the seeds of the European Enlightenment later blown westward. And the conviction planted by the Puritans that we are indeed that City on the Hill took deep root, from which our nation to this day draws sustenance, even though we style ourselves—and with truth—as a mix of all newer emigrants in search of freedom and opportunity, a melting pot or mosaic of all races, creeds, traditions.

It is this unconscious awareness of ourselves as spiritual descendants of an ancient covenant which holds us back from rejecting the criticisms, often bitter, of our nation's faults. These reproaches come because more is expected of us than any other nation. In 1843 Herman Melville returned from a three-year wandering that began with his voyage on the whaler *Acushnet*, sailing from Fairhaven, across the river from New Bedford, Massachusetts. For passage home he enlisted as a common seaman in the American frigate significantly named *United States*. Aboard that navy ship he witnessed the punishment of flogging, the whips laid on young sailors' backs until the blood ran down in streams. In his novel *White Jacket* Melville described that voyage, including a chapter on what to him was the abomination of flogging, a brutal practice unworthy of the nation after which the ship was named. From his condemnation of this barbarous practice he passed imperceptibly to recall the tradition in which this nation had its roots, his language that of covenant theology:

"Escaped from the house of bondage Israel did not return to the ways of the Egyptians. To her was given a special dispensation, to her were given new things under the sun. And we Americans are a chosen people, the Israel of our time. We bear the ark of the liberties of the world."

It is now thirty years since I attended a memorable dinner at New York's Waldorf Astoria, a dinner commemorating the fiftieth anniversary of the founding of that city's French Institute. Vice President Lyndon Johnson presided on that May evening of 1962, and the guest of honor was André Malraux, De Gaulle's minister of culture. The author of *Man's Fate*, a novel set against the bloody background of Chiang Kai-shek's repression of the Chinese Communists in Shanghai in 1927, Malraux had espoused the Communist cause, had helped edit the revolutionary paper *L'Indochine* in French Indochina, had helped organize the Loyalist air force in the Spanish Civil War, and for years had been the spokesman of the literary Left in France. He had often criticized U.S. foreign policy, and already the first U.S. support troops had arrived in Vietnam and the U.S. Military Assistance Command had been formed. When Lyndon Johnson rose to his feet to make a toast to France, I wondered what Malraux, nervous, face twitching, could possibly say in response to the courteous gesture of the vice president of the nation he had often criticized. This is what he said, with passionate intensity, in incandescent French: "I raise my glass to the only nation that has made war without loving it, achieved the greatest power in the world without seeking it, and held in its hands the most terrible weapon of death without longing to use it."

*

Looking back over the pages of this book, I can see that much of the high fun of the course is diminished by the inevitable evaporation of the spirit of the "lectures," if that is the word, and I don't think it is. Our own philosopher Emerson was nearly always right, but the day he said that the lecture hall would replace the church was not one of his good days. Maybe that's why, in a bit of Socratic irony, we in the course agreed to call the talks "sermons."

In Plato's dialogue *Phaedrus,* Socrates tells a promising student that the trouble with books is that you can't ask questions of them and expect to get a helpful answer. He adds that the rhetorical lectures of the sophists are no better, for the sophists positively do not want to answer questions. True teaching, he says, is not simply holding forth on serious matters; it is not simply a display from the outside, but rather a clarifying, a drawing out from the mind of the student the knowledge that is already there.

In another dialogue, *Euthydemus,* Socrates follows this up with a bit of advice to his friend Crito, whose son has some interest in studying philosophy. Crito is uneasy because he has heard that some of the professors (sophists) of moral philosophy are dubious characters, primarily interested in taking money for tuition and showing off their learning. Socrates admits that there are such types, but let us hope, he says, that clear-eyed youth can see through these pretenders and beyond them to the pursuit of real knowledge and the love of wisdom itself. "Be reasonable then, Crito," concludes Socrates, "and do not mind whether the teachers of philosophy are good or bad, but think only of philosophy herself. Try to examine her well and truly, and if she isn't any good then try to turn everybody away from her, and not just your sons; but if she is what I believe she is, then follow her and serve her, you and your house, as the saying is, and be of good cheer."

*

The *Phaedrus* ends with a pagan prayer, rather moving. Socrates gets up from the grassy slope on the banks of the Ilissus, where he and his student Phaedrus have been resting, enjoying the warmth of the summer sun, the fragrance of the trees, the river water cool to their feet. "Shouldn't we offer a prayer to the divinities here?" asks Socrates of his pupil.

"Why not?" says Phaedrus.

"Well then," says Socrates, "how about this?"

Beloved Pan and all you other gods that haunt this place, grant that I may become good and fair within, and that such outward things as I may possess may not conflict with what I have of true spirit within me. May I call that man rich who is wise, and, as for gold, may I have just so much of it as a temperate man might bear and carry with him.

"Anything more we can ask for, Phaedrus?"

And Phaedrus replies, "Make it a prayer for me, Socrates, since friends have all things in common."

"Right," says Socrates. "Let's go."

Appendix

Reading List for "Foundations of Moral Obligation"

The material is listed in the order of reading assignment. For complete citation of the material, see the Bibliography.

Stockdale, James B. "The World of Epictetus."

Koestler, Arthur. *Darkness at Noon.*

Walzer, Michael. "Prisoners of War: Does the Fight Continue after the Battle?"

The Book of Job (Old Testament).

Solzhenitsyn, Alexander. *One Day in the Life of Ivan Denisovich,* and *A World Split Apart.*

Plato. *Euthyphro, Apology, Crito,* and *Phaedo.*

Aristotle. *Nichomachean Ethics* (Books 1-7; 10).

Conrad, Joseph. *Typhoon.*

Kant, Immanuel. *Foundations of the Metaphysics of Morals.*

Hart, H. L. A. "Laws and Morals."

Mill, John Stuart. *Utilitarianism.*

Dostoyevsky, Fyodor. *Notes from Underground* I.

Emerson, Ralph Waldo. "Self-Reliance."

Sartre, Jean-Paul. "Existentialism Is a Humanism."

Camus, Albert. *The Plague.*

Marx, Karl, and Engels, Friedrich. *The Communist Manifesto.*

Lenin, Vladimir I. "What Is To Be Done?"

Dostoyevsky, Fyodor. "The Grand Inquisitor."

Gabriel, R. A. "The Nature of Military Ethics."

Monod, Jacques. *Chance and Necessity.*

Smith, Homer. *Kamongo.*

Epictetus. *Enchiridion.*

Malcolm, Norman. *Ludwig Wittgenstein: A Memoir.*

Wittgenstein, Ludwig. *Tractatus* (selections).

Stockdale, James B. "Heroes and Heroism."

Notes

For complete citation of the sources abbreviated below, see the Bibilography that follows these notes.

1. "Prison and the Hermetic"

p. 1   Sadat on the prison cell: Sadat, *In Search of Identity*, 73.

1   Kerouac, "prison is where": Jack Kerouac, *On the Road* (New York: The Viking Press, 1953), 132.

2   Stockdale, "it was in prison": Letter to author.

2   Solzhenitsyn, "as I lay there on the rotting straw": Alexander Solzhenitsyn, *The Gulag Archipelago*, edited and abridged by E. E. Ericson, Jr. (New York: Harper & Row, 1985), 321-322.

2   Havel, "not to be surprised at anything": *The New York Times*, 12 January 1989, p. A14.

2   hermetic: Our discussion of the hermetic owes much to Thomas Mann's novel *The Magic Mountain*. In the section titled "A Soldier and Brave," the Jesuit Naptha's discourse on the hermetic tradition encourages Hans Castorp, the tubercular hero of the novel, to apply the idea of hermetic transformation to his experience at an Alpine sanatorium.

4   Moses when he was a baby: Exodus 2:5-9.

4   Jesus driving out "them that sold doves": Mark 11:15.

5   "sealing the stone": Matthew 27:66.

6   DNA molecule: James D. Watson and Francis Crick shared the Nobel Prize for their discovery of the structure of the DNA molecule. Watson tells the story in *The Double Helix* (New York: New American Library, Mentor Books, 1968).

6   François Jacob, "the dream of every cell": cited by Monod in *Chance and Necessity*, 20.

6   Johan Huizinga, *Homo Ludens* (Boston: Beacon Press, 1950).

7   Ray Floyd penalized himself one stroke: Wayne Tryhuk, "A Shocking Sports Story," *The New York Times*, 24 August 1986 (Tryhuk's subhead: "Moral losers may be victors, but they're also the ultimate spoilsports").

8   "on a destroyer off the coast of Vietnam": conversation with Commander Douglas Quelch, USN (Ret.)

8   the submarine and the hermetic: "The 165 man crew volunteers for submarine duty and must pass rigorous academic, physical and psychological exams . . . it is an almost hermetically sealed world maintained by a group of men who want to keep it that way." (From Eric Schmitt, "Run Silent, Run Deep, Beat Foes, (Where?)," *The New York Times*, 30 January 1992.)

8   Saint-Exupéry on flying: Antoine de Saint-Exupéry, *Night Flight* (New York: Century, 1932) and *Wind, Sand and Stars* (New York: Reynal & Hitchcock, 1939).

8   "An Irish Airman Foresees His Death": W. B. Yeats, *Collected Poems* (New York: Macmillan, 1954), 133.

8   "it was alchemy, the heating of the still": Nicholas Freeling, *Strike Out Where Not Applicable* (New York: Harper and Row, 1967), 177.

9   Umberto Eco, *The Name of the Rose*, translated by William Weaver (New York: Harcourt Brace Jovanovich, 1983).

9   "to the person in the bell jar": Sylvia Plath, *The Bell Jar* (New York: Harper and Row, Bantam Edition, 1972), 216.

10   the body as the prison-house of the spirit: Plato, *Phaedo* 82e ff. (Passages in the dialogues of Plato are customarily identified by marginal (Stephens) numbers common to all editions and translations. A similar system is used for citing passages from Aristotle's works.)

11   "and they laid him in a manger": Luke 2:7.

11   he heard a great voice crying "Read!": *The Holy Qur'an*, translated with commentary by A. Yusuf Ali (American Trust Publications for the Muslim Students Association, U.S. & Canada, 2d ed., 1977), Introduction, C. 30.

12   Many centuries after Boethius' death, Arab philosophers, including Avicenna and Averroes (Ibn Rashd 1126-1188), translated and wrote learned commentaries on Aristotle's scientific, metaphysical and ethical treatises. In this way Islamic scholars lent medieval Jewish and Christian theologians a strong Aristotelian foundation to their philosophies. The greatest Jewish philosopher of the Middle Ages, Moses Maimonides (1135-1204, wrote his commentary on the Mishna, a monumental code of Jewish law, in Arabic. For many years in Córdoba, Spain, Arab and Jewish philosophers lived in peace and harmony.

12   Lady Philosophy, "Don't you realize that Dame Fortune is a very fickle
      lady?": Boethius, *The Consolation of Philosophy*, 21. (Boethius's book opens
      with Lady Philosophy's appearance and closes with her departure.)

13   Socrates, "no evil can befall a good man": Plato, *Apology* 41d.

14   "Lepanto": G. K. Chesterton, *Poems* (London: Burns & Oates, Ltd.
      1915).

14   Cervantes captured by Algerian corsairs: Cervantes tells the story
      of his captivity, lightly fictionalized, in *Don Quixote* I, 39-41.

15   The Myth of the Cave: Plato, *Republic*, book 7, chapter 25, 514a-
      521b.

16   The Divided Line: Plato, *Republic*, book 6, chapter 24, 509d-511b.

18   "for every upgoing": See John Senior, *The Way Down and Out*
      (Ithaca, N.Y.: Cornell University Press, 1959).

18   Saint Bonaventure, "let us die": See Saint Bonaventure, *The Mind's
      Road to God*, translated by G. Boas (New York, 1953). According to
      the Franciscan Bonaventure (1217-1274), the spiritual journey
      begins with purgation ("darkness of the mind") then mounts
      through Grace to the illuminative stage and finally the unitive
      (union with God).

19   "Get him up and begone as one shaped awry": More Thomas Hardy
      (*In Tenebris* II) than Plato, but it fits well here.

19   Plato, "if they could lay their hands on the man": *Republic*, book 7,
      chapter 25, 517a.

2.   "Job and the Problem of Evil"

21   Job, "Oh, that I might find Him": Job 23: 3, 8-9. One of the
      "wisdom" (*hokma*) books of the Bible, the Book of Job stands
      eighteenth in the order of books in the Old Testament. Its ap-
      proximate date places it as contemporary with the Greek pre-
      Socratics. The identity of the author is not known, nor is the
      location of the "land of Uz," from which Job came. As set forth in
      the Old Testament, Job's story appears to be the work of more than
      one hand.

21   Fray Luis de Leon's meditations on Job: Fray Luis de Leon, *El libro
      de Job* (Madrid: Ediciones la Idea, 1987).

22 Wiesel in Auschwitz: "Some talked of God, of his mysterious ways, of the sins of the Jewish people, and of their future deliverance. But I had creased to pray. How I sympathized with Job!" (*Night*, 42)

22 Wiesel, *The Trial of God: A Play in Three Acts* (New York: Random House, 1979): The play was staged in San Minato on August 29, 1983. Before the performance Wiesel said to the largely Christian audience, "I say this although it may hurt you. The cross that for you symbolizes charity and love, for me as a Jew rooted in tradition, it symbolizes fear. But you see me before you, and I shall be with you. And I offer you my memories to share." ("A Drama about God Opens to Bravos in Italy," *The New York Times*, 11 September 1983, p. 6)

23 the story of the *zayda* [grandfather]: Leo Rosten, *The Joys of Yiddish* (New York: McGraw-Hill, 1968), 5.

23 God's *retorquendo* to Job: Job 38:4.

24 Nietzsche, "he who has a why to live by": Nietzsche, *The Genealogy of Morals* III, 28.

24 Rubashov awaiting execution: Koestler, *Darkness at Noon*, 206.

24 Zophar, "canst thou by searching": Job 11:7.

24 Kierkegaard on the incommensurability between God's ways and our ways: Kierkegaard, "Fear and Trembling," in *A Kierkegaard Anthology*, 131-134. Kierkegaard says that the story of Abraham, ready to sacrifice his son at God's command, contains a "teleological suspension of the ethical." Although from a human point of view God's order was anti-ethical, Abraham takes it as a test of faith. Compare Isaiah 55:8-9: "For My thoughts are not your thoughts, neither are your ways My ways. . . . For as the heavens are higher than the earth so are My ways higher than your ways, and My thoughts than your thoughts."

24 Stockdale on "why me?": Letter to author dated 24 November 1975 (see Preface, page xix).

26 Oedipus [486-406 B.C.]: The central character in Sophocles's drama *Oedipus Tyrannos*. Oedipus slew a man (Laius) he did not know was his father and married a woman (Jocasta) he did not know was his mother. On discovering their true identities, Oedipus destroyed his eyes and Jocasta hanged herself. Sigmund Freud took this Greek play as a paradigm of the suppression that may lead to the so-called Oedipus complex, the disorder in a human male that arises from the suppressed desire to kill his father and possess his mother.

26   body versus soul: The classical locus of Plato's body-soul, spirit-matter dualism may be found in *Phaedo* 81. The cosmological factor of Necessity, over which God does not have complete power, is obscurely present in the creation-myth of the *Timaeus* 28a-30c. The doctrine of a "third kind of being," the matrix or space in which the created universe is lodged, is discussed in *Timaeus* 52b-d. Its nature can be grasped only by a faculty inferior to reason.

28   Gnosticism: The Gnostics had their own scriptures. See Elaine Pagel's *The Gnostic Gospels* (New York: Random House, 1979).

28   early Christians and military service: C. John Cadoux, *The Early Christian Attitude toward War* (New York: The Seabrook Press, 1982), 16.

28   Jesus striking the sword from Peter's hand: Matthew 26:52 ("put up again thy sword into its place; for they that take the sword will perish with the sword").

28   Jesus, "render to Ceasar": Mark 12:17.

29   Manichaeism: The best short account of medieval dualism is Runciman's *The Medieval Manichee*, to which I am much indebted.

31   Runciman, "confident of the truth of their cause": Runciman, *The Medieval Manichee*, 180.

31   Augustine: Augustine's *Confessions* offers a first-person account of his search for religious truth, from Manichaeism and Neo-Platonism to Christian conversion.

31   Plotinus [205-270 A.D.]: The last of the great pagan philosophers, Plotinus was the dominant figure in the Neo-Platonic school of Alexandria. He studied philosophy with Ammonius Saccus, the Wittgenstein of his day, and in turn taught Porphyry, who wrote Plotinus's biography and collected his lectures and writings under the title of the *Enneads*. Plotinus's theory of creation by emanation had considerable influence on certain medievals, particularly the Arab philosophers.

32   Augustine on evil: Augustine, *Enchiridion: On Faith, Hope and Love*, in *The Basic Writings of Saint Augustine*, 2 vols., edited by Whitney J. Oates (New York: Random House, 1948), 1:482 ff ("He [God] can bring good out of evil. For what is that which we call evil but absence of good?")

32   Lactantius [240-320 A.D.]: A North African father of the Christian church, and late in life the tutor of the Emperor Constantine's oldest son. Lactantius is noted more for his eloquent writing, particularly in defense of Christian belief, than for advancing the

development of Church doctrine. He had much sympathy for
pagan philosophers and for the Judaic prophets of the Old Testament, and he even had a good word for the semi-legendary hermetists of older generations. Though he modeled his writing on
Cicero's, Lactantius criticized the Roman orator for affecting a Stoic
indifference to the death of his beloved daughter in accordance
with the Stoic teaching that evil does not exist.

33   Augustine, "O felix culpa!": An interesting variation of the "happy
      fault" comes from the pen of Sor Juana Inez de la Cruz, a learned
      Mexican nun of the seventeenth century. Her concept of God's
      "negative benefaction" or abstinence from giving would have it that
      God could have made things better for us but held back "the sea
      of his infinite love" because of the danger of our likely ingratitude
      for such blessing. By holding back in some degree the full tide of
      his creative love, God allowed us more room for doing good to one
      another. (Sor Juana, letter, "Carta Atenagorika," discussed in
      Octavio Paz, *Sor Juana or The Traps of Faith*, translated by Margaret
      Syers Peden (Cambridge: Harvard University Press, 1988). "Nega-
      tive benefaction" is mentioned in the preface to Alan Trueblood's
      translation of Sor Juana's poems, *A Sor Juana Anthology*
      (Cambridge: Harvard University Press, 1988).

33   Solzhenitsyn on suffering: Solzhenitsyn, *A World Split Apart*, 35.

34   "a key to the enigma exists": The spirit if not the letter of François
      Mauriac, *What I Believe*, translated by Wallace Fowke (New York:
      Farrar, Strauss & Co., 1963), 97.

34   the old Jews at the execution of one of their number: In Lion
      Feuchtwanger's novel *Power* ("Jew Süss") (New York: Viking,
      1948), there is near the end a powerful scene describing the
      execution of the eighteenth-century Württemberg financier
      Joseph Süss Oppenheimer. As the "court Jew" is hanged "higher
      than Hamann" in an iron cage, the small circle of watching Jews
      intones the *Schma*, the last sound to be heard by the dying man.

34   Bahtrahari, "in the forest, in battle, amid javelins": Bahtrahari is the
      name of a semi-mythical poet who wrote in Sanskrit. The historical
      Bahtrahari may have lived in the seventh century, dying about 650
      A. D., but later poets produced a rich poetic augmentation in his name.
      Barbara Stoler Miller has translated a number of these poems in
      Bahtrahari: Poems (New York: Columbia University Press, 1967).

34   Siddhartha Gautama (Buddha) and his tutor: I have taken some
      liberty in simplifying this story. Most of the myriad variations of it posit
      a fourth "encounter" with a saint who has renounced desire, self,
      the world, and thus found peace. The doctrine of "tat twam asi"

("this thou art") is older than Buddha and his teaching; it comes down from the Vedic religion of ancient India, formulated in the Upanishads.

35   "Song of Myself" is included in the first edition of Walt Whitman's *Leaves of Grass* (1855), and "Crossing Brooklyn Ferry" appears in the second edition (1856). (Walt himself was the editor, publisher, and supplier to bookshops.)

3. "Love: From Eros to Agapē"

37   Hesiod and Homer: The early Greek philosophers had no books of revelation comparable to the Old and New Testaments or the Holy Koran. What theology they possessed they took from older poets, particularly Homer and Hesiod. The latter's *Theogony* offers a creation story in terms of primordial Chaos, a far-reaching Earth (personified by the earth-goddess Gaia-Tellus), and Love (Eros), a cosmic power that joins things together.

    The *Iliad* is a long epic poem, its subject the war ignited by Paris, son of the king of Troy, running off with the beautiful Helen, wife of Menelaus of Sparta, whose brother, King Agammemnon, then launched the famed expeditionary force of Achaeans (Greeks) against Troy. The identity of the author (or authors) of the *Iliad* has long been the subject of scholarly dispute, giving rise to a well-known Irish bull. "Did ye know," asks a Dubliner, "that the *Iliad* was not written by Homer?" "No!" his friend exclaims. "By who, then?" The reply: "'Twas written by another Greek of the same name!"

38   Stockdales, *In Love and War*: Themes of love and war are interwoven throughout the book, an effect achieved in part by alternating chapters written by each of the two authors.

38   Empedocles: Born in Agrigentum, Sicily, about 455 B.C., Empedocles is best known for his doctrine of the four basic elements—earth, air, fire, and water—combined and separated in cyclical order by the cosmic forces of love (*eros*) and strife (*neikos*). In humans, Mind is an illuminative process that darts in and out among the elements. Legend says that the philosopher committed suicide by jumping into Mount Etna's Crater.

39   "in moments like these": Gray, *The Warriors*, 45.

39   Aristotle on true friendship: *Nichomachean Ethics*, book 8, chapter 3, 1156b.25; chapter 6, 1156a.11-12.

40   Weil, "in a perfect friendship": *The Simone Weil Reader*, 370.

40   *84 Charlie Mopic*: "War's Face Seen through Lens Intimately," *The New York Times*, 19 March 1989, pp. 15, 23.

40   *Agapē*: Rhymes with "do right away." Some translate it "loving-kind-ness."

40   Jesus described as writing something: John 8:3-11.

41   Socrates on teaching by writing: Plato, *Phaedrus* 275.

41   Socrates trying to prove a favorite thesis: Plato, *Meno* 82a-85d. The thesis is that knowledge is recollection—remembering what we once knew and have forgotten. Compare Wordsworth: "Our birth is but a sleep and a forgetting. . ." ("Intimations of Immortality," in *Recollections of Early Childhood*).

43   Socrates and the book by Anaxagoras: Plato, *Phaedo* 98b-98c.

44   Michael Levin, *The Socratic Method* (New York: Simon and Schuster, 1987).

45   Jesus, "a certain man went down from Jericho": Luke 10: 30-37.

45   Jesus, "therefore I speak to them in parables": Matthew 13: 10-13, 34-35.

45   Nietzsche on a married philosopher: *Genealogy of Morals*, III. Nietzsche asks, "Up to the present [1887] what great philosophers have been married? Heracleitus, Plato, Descartes, Spinoza, Leibniz, Kant, Schopenhauer—they were not married and, further, one cannot *imagine* them as married. A married philosopher belongs to *comedy*. As for that exception of Socrates—the married Socrates married himself *ironically* just to prove this very rule."

45   Xanthippe saying farewell to Socrates: Plato, *Phaedo* 60.

45   Socrates talking to one of his sons: Xenophon, *Memorabilia*, II, ii, 7-9.

46   Jesus, "think not that I am come to send peace": Matthew 10: 34.

46   Jesus, "let the dead bury the dead": Matthew 8:22 and Luke 11:60.

46   Jesus at the marriage feast at Cana: John 2:1-11.

47   "three kraters only do I mix for the temperate": Quoted by Oswyn Murray in "The Greek Symposium in History," *London Times Literary Supplement*, 6 November 1981. Murray cites Eubulus in *Athenaeus* 2.35.

48   Socrates on his inner voice: Plato, *Apology* 31d.

48   Alcestis and Antigone: In Greek mythology, Alcestis is the model of wifely virtue. When her husband, Admetis, was condemned to death by the Fates, unless someone should take his place and die, Alcestis sacrificed herself so that her husband might live.

        Antigone, the heroine of Sophocles's play of that name, defies the tyrannical order of Creon that her dead brother should be left unburied. Though defiance of the order means death, Antigone scatters ritual burial earth over her brother's body.

49   "then, sly arch-lover that he was": Thomas Mann, *Death in Venice*, in *Stories of Three Decades*, translated by H. T. Lowe Porter (New York: Alfred A. Knopf, 1937), 378.

49   "if music be the food of love": Shakespeare, *Twelfth Night*, opening lines (Act I, Scene 1).

50   hymn to Love the Navigator: Plato, *Symposium* 197d-e. Michael Joyce's translation in *The Collected Dialogues of Plato*.

51   "The love the young have"; Thomas Mann, letter to author, December 12, 1948.

52   Jesus on the Holy Spirit: John 14:15-18.

54   Paul, "though I speak with the tongues of men and angels": 1 Corinthians 13. Benjamin Jowett, eminent nineteenth-century translator of Plato and master of Balliol College, Oxford, considered Diotima's allocution on love to be the pagan anticipation of Paul's thirteenth letter to the Corinthians.

55   the writings of Saint John of the Cross: See *The Poems of Saint John of the Cross*, translated by Willis Barnstone (Bloomington, Ind.: Indiana University Press, 1968; New York: New Directions, 1972).

56   Schopenhauer on art: Schopenhauer, *The World as Will and Idea*, volume 1, book 3.

56   Freud on civilization: Sigmund Freud, *Civilization and Its Discontents*, translated by James Strachey (New York: W. W. Norton, 1961).

56   Artistotle on Aphrodite: Aristotle quoting Homer in *Nichomachean Ethics*, book 7, chapter 6, 1149b. 25-26.

56   Artistotle on the creative power in the cosmos: *Metaphysics*, book 12, chapter 7, 1072a. 26-27 ("and the object of desire and the object of thought move in this way: they move without being moved").

56   Dante, "c'est l'Amor che muove": *The Divine Comedy*, Paradiso, Canto 33.

4. "Aristotle: The Ethics of Happiness"

57   Alexander the Great: Peter Green, *Alexander of Macedon: A Historical Biography* (Berkeley, Calif.: University of California Press, 1991). Alexander's military conquests led to the spread of Hellenistic culture to the south and east, thus clearing the way for the eastward expansion of the Roman Empire and later the Christian religion.

58   Aristotle mentioned in a Supreme Court case: Edwards vs. Aguillard, 1986 (see chapter 9, page 162).

58   Judaic account of creation: Genesis 1: 1-4.

58   Time in *Timaeus*: Plato, *Timaeus* 28b, 38b. In the dialogue named for him, the Pythagorean astronomer Timaeus says, "Time and the heavens came into being at the same instant." This is part of his answer to his earlier question, Was the world always in existence or was it created? Timaeus supports the latter position, Aristotle the former.

58   Stephen Hawking, *A Brief History of Time* (New York: Random House, 1988).

59   Plato's name for God: Plato, *Timaeus* 27c. Plato uses the word *poites* (maker), which the Greeks often used in the sense of artistic production. To the Plato of the *Timaeus*, God is the "poet" (maker) of the world.

59   Aristotle's metaphysics or First Philosophy: In book 12 of his *Metaphysics*, Artistotle deals concisely with the ideas of substance, matter, form, potentiality, and actuality, and with the idea of the world moving toward its cause. "It is necessary," he says, "that there should be an eternal unmovable. . . .the object of desire and the objects of thought move without being moved. . . .The final cause, then, produces motion as being loved." (chapter 6, 1071b.5; chapter 7, 1072a. 26-27, 1072b.5)

63   Aristotle's argument for the existence of a Prime Mover: Aristotle, *Metaphysics*, book 12, chapter 7.

64   Aquinas's proofs for the existence of God: Aquinas, *Summa Theologica* I, Q2, art 3. The first three of these proofs derive from Aristotle's proof from motion: the first reasons to a prime mover, the second to a first cause, and the third to a necessary (as opposed to a merely possible) being.

64   Leibniz and "sufficient reason": In his *Theodicy* (1710), Leibniz accepts as a first principle that nothing exists or happens unless

there is a *sufficient reason* for it. Therefore, there must be a reason for the existence of the universe; and this reason is God.

64 Whitehead and the existence of God: Whitehead, *Science and the Modern World*, 178. Whitehead advances an argument for a much modified Prime Mover: "A metaphysical factor is needed to explain why the world is the way it is and not some other. Some particular *how* is necessary and some particularization in the *what* of matter of fact is necessary. . . .There is a metaphysical need for a principle of limitation."

64 Why should there be something rather than nothing? Why should there be anything at all?: In chapter 4 of *Creative Evolution*, the French philosopher Henri Bergson declares that the first of these two questions is bogus, that it does not "prove" anything, including the existence of God. As for the second question, Bergson says that it derives from our inability to conceive of "nothing" other than as an emptiness from which "something" has been withdrawn.

64 Wittgenstein, "not *how* the world is, but *that* it is, is the mystical": Wittgenstein, *Tractatus*, 6:44. Unlike Whitehead, Wittgenstein is struck not by the "how" or the "what" of the world, but that there *is* a world at all.

65 Aristotle, "for we always choose happiness": Aristotle, *Nichomachean Ethics*, book 1, chapter 7, 1097b. 1-6.

65 Aristotle, "the good of the human": Aristotle, *Nichomachean Ethics*, book 1, chapter 7, 98a. (Repeated in expanded form in book 10, chapter 7, 1177a.)

67 "the noble Brutus": Shakespeare, *Julius Caesar*, Act 3, Scene 2.

67 Clausewitz on seeking honor and renown: Clausewitz, *On War*, 105.

67 Aristotle, "virtue or excellence": Aristotle, *Nichomachean Ethics*, book 2, chapter 6, 1106b. 38-1107.

68 Artistotle and the ship captain: *Nichomachean Ethics*, book 3, chapter 1, 1110a. 8-11.

68 Aristotle, "for example, when a man acts improperly": Aristotle, *Nichomachean Ethics*, book 3, chapter 1, 1110a.24-29. Admiral Stockdale was particularly interested in Aristotle's discussion of voluntary versus involuntary acts. With his Vietnam experience in mind, Stockdale noted Aristotle's observation that a human act can be extorted under pressure, but a residue of choice remains.

68 Aristotle, "if happiness is activity": Aristotle, *Nichomachean Ethics*, book 10, chapter 7, 1177a.12-17.

69   Aristotle and the term *soul*: Aristotle, *De Anima*, book 2, chapter 2, 413a.20-24. Aristotle writes that ". . .what has soul in it different from what has not is that the former displays life." (The Greek title of *De Anima* is *Peri Psyche* (On the Soul)).

70   Aristotle, "with the mind it is different": Aristotle, *De Anima*, book 1, chapter 4, 408b.19-20, 24-25.

70   Aristotle, "we have no evidence": Aristotle, *De Anima*, book 2, chapter 5, 429a.20-25.

70   Alexander of Aphrodisias: An early commentator on Aristotle who taught in Athens about 200 A.D. Alexander held that the active intellect is an element in us which partakes of the divine nature.

71   Aristotle, "perfect happiness" and "this activity": Aristotle, *Nichomachean Ethics*, book 10, chapter 7, 1177a.12 ff., and chapter 8, 1179b.23 ff. In these and related passages, Aristotle makes clear his conviction that the happiest life is one ruled by intelligence, and that the highest ethic is the ethic of knowledge—knowledge pursued for its own sake and not primarily for immediate practical benefit. "So life guided by intelligence," he says, "is the best and most pleasant for the human since intelligence is the primary distinguishing human quality. Consequently, this kind of life is the best." (*Nichomachean Ethics*, book 10, chapter 7, 1178a.6-8)

73   Spinoza, "he who truly loves God": Spinoza, *Ethics*, Fifth Part, Proposition 19.

73   Aristotle, Pythias, and Herpyllis: Aristotle's respect for Pythias and Herpyllis coexisted with his assured belief in the inferiority of women to men. This belief, rooted in the cultural values of his time, was supported to Aristotle's satisfaction by his biological research, particularly in the field of embryology, in which he was a pioneer investigator.

    Aristotle believed that the female's contribution to the conception of new life was to provide the matter on which the male acted, and that the female sex was the result of something not completed in the process of conception. Hence the female, as it were, was an imperfect male. (This was, however, a "happy fault," for if it had not occurred there would be no way of perpetuating the species.)

    Aristotle observed that depression is more common in women than in men, and that women are more compassionate but also "more jealous, more quarrelsome, more void of shame or self-respect, more false of speech, more apt to scold."

    Such views, considered definitive by the ancients, helped to fix in the medieval and even the modern mind the concept of woman as "the weaker vessel." (See Aristotle's *Generation of Animals* in *The Complete Works of Aristotle*, vol. 2.)

5. "Kant and the Metaphysics of Morals"

74 Thomas Mann, *Buddenbrooks* (1901), translated by H. T. Lowe Porter (New York: Alfred Knopf, 1936). (The present writer pays tribute to the novel and its author in "*Buddenbrooks* and After," *The American Scholar*, Washington D.C., Winter 1993.)

75 Descartes, "cogito ergo sum": Descartes, *Discourse on Method*, Part IV, 32. Descartes writes, "Since this truth, I think therefore I am, was so firm and assured . . . I judged that I could safely accept it as the first principle of the philosophy I was seeking."

75 Kant and the Enlightenment: Kant wrote a brief essay titled "What Is Enlightenment?" in which he equates enlightenment with self-reliance, that is, "thinking for oneself." This essay appears in the edition of *Foundations of the Metaphysics of Morals* cited in the bibliography.

77 Kant at the university library: Henry R. Meisels, "Immanuel Kant and the Royal Castle Library in Königsberg," *Journal of Library History*, Austin, Texas, Summer 1981.

77 Kant as a teacher: John Ladd gathers some testimony together in his "Kant as Teacher," in *Teaching Philosophy*, Philosophy Documentation Center, Bowling Green State University, Bowling Green, Ohio, January 1982.

78 Locke on the primacy of experience: Locke, *An Essay concerning Human Understanding*, volume 1, 121-123.

79 Berkeley on our perception of objects: Berkeley, *Three Dialogues*, in *A New Theory of Vision and Other Writings* (New York: Dutton, 1934), 287. A cherry, Berkeley says, is no more than the sum of our sensations of it.

80 Hume on "mind": Hume, *A Treatise on Human Nature*, 636.

81 Isaac Newton, *Principia* (1687), translated by Florian Cajori (Berkeley, Calif.: University of California Press, 1934).

81 Kant, "it was the warning voice": Immanuel Kant, *Prolegomena to Any Future Metaphysics* (La Salle, Ill.: Open Court, 1902), 6.

83 Kant's three great questions: Kant, *Critique of Pure Reason*, 833.

83   the ideas of pure reason: Kant, *Critique of Pure Reason*, 325. In a
      note added to the second edition of this critique, Kant writes,
      "Metaphysics has as the proper object of its enquiries three ideas
      only: God, freedom and immortality."

84   Paley, "in crossing a heath": Paley, *Natural Theology*, 9.

84   Hume's response to a similar argument: David Hume, *Dialogues
      concerning Natural Religion* (New York: Hafner, 1943), 94. Hume
      does not altogether dismiss the teleological argument, but he says
      that the very most that argument can support is the inference that
      "the cause or causes of order in the universe probably bear some
      remote analogy to human intelligence."

85   the dialectical character of the ideas of pure Reason: Kant, *Critique
      of Pure Reason*, 549. Strictly speaking, Kant says that the ideas of
      pure Reason are not dialectical in themselves, but in the use to
      which they are put.

86   Kant, *Critique of Practical Reason* (1788), translated by Lewis White
      Beck (New York: Liberal Arts Press, 1956).

87   Kant, "the good will is": Kant, *Foundations of the Metaphysics of
      Morals*, 10.

88   "thou oughtst because thou oughtst": Kant uses the word *duty* more
      frequently than *ought* (i.e., "I should do this because it is my duty"
      rather than "I ought to do this because I ought").

89   Princess Marie de Cröys: Rowland Ryder, *Edith Cavell* (New York:
      Stein & Day, 1975), 128. Unlike Nurse Cavell, the princess escaped
      the death sentence, partly because she had also aided a wounded
      German officer of influential family. The princess's sentence was
      ten years.

90   Kant, "there is one imperative": Kant, *Foundations of the Metaphysics
      of Morals*, 33.

90   Kant, "thou shalt not make a false promise": Kant, *Foundations of
      the Metaphysics of Morals*, 420.

91   Kant, "act only according to that maxim": Kant, *Foundations of the
      Metaphysics of Morals*, 39.

91   Kant, "now I say man": Kant, *Foundations of the Metaphysics of Morals*,
      46.

92   Aristotle on slaves: Aristotle, *Nichomachean Ethics*, book 5, 1134b.
      10. To Aristotle, wife, child, and slave are property, but not in the
      same way. As a "living tool," the slave's natural function is to serve
      his master; he has no choice. A wife, however, can deliberate, and

shares certain powers with her husband—managing the household, for example. Aristotle had some qualms about the status of slaves who were Hellenes: how could they lose their status as humans by the accident or fortunes of war? (For more on the slave as property and instrument, see Aristotle, *Politics*, book 1, chapter 4.)

93   Kingdom of Ends: Kant, *Foundations of the Metaphysics of Morals*, 51-52. *Realm* would be a better word than *kingdom* for Kant's "systematic union of different rational beings through common laws."

93   Thoreau's anarchy: In his essay "On the Duty of Civil Disobedience" (1848), Thoreau agreed with the proposition that "that government is best which governs least," and looked forward to the day when "that government is best which governs not at all." Thoreau believed that democracy was the best form of government, but his democracy was "participative" rather than "representative," with each person free, according to his conscience, to obey or disobey a law imposed by a government through its representatives.

93   Luther, "we must divide all the children": Luther, *Treatise on Secular Authority*, in *Martin Luther*, edited by Dillenberger, 365-402.

94   Hobbes: Thomas Hobbes (1588-1679), author of *Leviathan*, believed that the natural state of humanity is conflict, with each man a wolf to the next (*homo homini lupus*). Life, therefore, would be "nasty, brutish, and short" were it not for the fact that for their own good, men have surrendered some of their autonomy to the ruling authority of the State. The State's prime purpose is to keep men from killing each other, to maintain a modicum of order in which humans can enjoy at least some moments free from the fear of death or injury at the hand of their fellows.

94   Kant's model for peace: Kant, *Perpetual Peace*, second Definitive Article. Kant writes that "the law of nations shall be founded on a federation of free states."

94   Kant, "war . . . has something sublime about it": Kant, *Critique of Judgment* (1790), book 2, paragraph 28. In calling war "sublime," Kant is referring not to any moral quality but to the awe that war inspires. Kant believed that war is a violation of the human right to live in peace. I am indebted to Professor John Ladd for locating this passage and commenting on it.

94   the sixth Dalai Lama, "the demons and serpentiform gods": Fosco Maraini, *Secret Tibet* (New York: Viking, 1952), 178 (plate 35).

94   the story of Prince Arjuna: *The Bhagavad Gita*, chapter 1, 32; chapter 2, 31, 47; chapter 18, 73.

6. "Utilitarianism: John Stuart Mill"

In writing this chapter, I am much indebted to Michael St. John Packe's biography *The Life of John Stuart Mill.*

96   Rodó's essay: José Enrique Rodó, *Ariel* (Montevideo: Imprenta de Dornaleche y Rey, 1900).

97   Mill, "the creed which accepts": Mill, *Utilitarianism*, 10.

99   Mill's two basic rules for a just society: For Mill's principle of maximum individual liberty, see the passage from *On Liberty* cited on page 111 of this chapter. Mill's principle of equality is implied though not explicitly stated in chapter 5 of *Utilitarianism*, where he discusses the rewarding of individuals for their contributions to society.

99   Rawls's "Two Principles of Justice": Rawls, *A Theory of Justice*, 60.

99   Socrates, "the unexamined life is not worth living": Plato, *Apology* 38a. Much has been made of this axiom, but I once knew a good man who seemed to enjoy every moment of his life, never paused to examine it, and went happily drunk to his own funeral.

100   Jeremy Bentham: The best biography of Bentham is in Leslie Stephens, *The English Utilitarians* (1900) (New York: A. M. Kellen, 1968), vol. 1.

103   Malthus's essay: Thomas Robert Malthus, *An Essay on the Principle of Population as It Affects the Future Improvement of Society* (1798). See John Maynard Keynes, "Robert Malthus: The First of the Cambridge Economists," in *Essays in Biography* (New York: Harcourt, Brace & Co., 1933).

104   Grote's books: Grote's *History of Greece* was published in twelve volumes between 1846 and 1856. His *Plato* was reviewed by John Stuart Mill for the *Edinburgh Review* in 1865.

104   Mill reading the memoirs of Marmontel: In her introduction to Mill's *On Liberty*, Gertrude Himmelfarb finds Freudian significance in Mill's account of this episode in his *Autobiography*, and she expresses surprise at Mill's innocence "in so blandly recounting it." A rereading of this section of the *Autobiography* has not helped this writer to grasp its Freudian significance.

105   Harriet Taylor: This description of Harriet and of Mill's passion for her is cited from contemporary sources in Packe, *The Life of John Stuart Mill*, 110-111.

108   Carlyle's books: Thomas Carlyle's major works include *Sartor Resartus* (1836), *The French Revolution* (1837), and *On Heroes, Hero-Worship, and the Heroic in History* (1841).

109   Packe, "night and day now made no difference": Packe, *The Life of John Stuart Mill*, 394.

111   Mill, "the object of this essay": Mill, *On Liberty*, 14-15.

112   Socrates, "a man should wait": Plato, *Phaedo* 62c.

113   Alexis De Tocqueville, *Democracy in America*, edited by J. P. Mayer and translated by George Lawrence (Garden City, N.Y.: Doubleday, 1969).

114   Mill, "at the election of the President": Mill, *On Representative Government*, 351.

115   Mill, "we have put away the natural weapon": Packe, *The Life of John Stuart Mill*, 456 (source given as Hansard, *Parliamentary Debates*, volume 189, 5 August 1867).

115   Mill, "war is an ugly thing": Mill, "The Contest in America," in *Fraser's Magazine*, February 1862, 269. I am grateful to Gertrude Himmelfarb for supplying this information.

115   Mill, "there are assuredly cases": Mill, "A Few Words on Non-Intervention," in Mill, *Dissertations and Discussions* (Boston: Spencer, 1865), 3:251.

117   "the soul of Harriet Mill had gone": Paraphrase of Marcel Proust, *Remembrance of Things Past: The Past Recaptured*, translated by Fredrick A. Blosson (New York: Modern Library, 1932), 383.

117   Mill, "in the very first rank": Mill, *Three Essays on Religion*, 254-255.

117   Mill, "that the world was made": Packe, *The Life of John Stuart Mill*, 443 (source given as letter to A. W. Greene, Mill-Taylor Collection in the British Library of Political and Economic Science, London).

118   Clement of Alexandria: A third-century Church father and leader of the early Christian Alexandrian school of theology, Clement was sympathetic to Greek philosophy (particularly Plato) and to the Judaic prophets of the Old Testament, whom he believed had a valuable, if partial, insight into the truth. Clement was curious about all the natural wonders of the world. His disapproval of the habits of the female hyena probably stemmed from the belief, widely held in his time, that the hyena was a hermaphrodite (a belief refuted by Aristotle in his *Generation of Animals*). Robin Fox's *Pagans and Christians* (New York: Alfred Knopf, 1987) provides

interesting information on Clement, including this remark about the hyena.

7. "Existentialism: Sartre and Camus"

123   Apollinaire, "sur la côte du Texas": Apollinaire, *Oeuvres Poètiques* (Paris: Bibliothèque de la Pléiade, Editions Gallimard, 1959), 65.

123   Dostoyevsky's Underground Man: Dostoyevsky, *Notes from Underground*.

124   Thoreau, "quiet desperation": Henry David Thoreau, *Walden* (1854) (New York: Collier Books, 1978), 18 ("the mass of men lead lives of quiet desperation").

124   "I did that": Nietzsche, *Beyond Good and Evil*, IV, 68.

125   Merleau-Ponty, "[phenomenology] tries to give": Maurice Merleau-Ponty, *Phenomenology of Perception*, translated by Colin Smith (New York: Humanities Press, 1962), vii.

126   the lycée professor of philosophy: An example is the famous Alain (Emile Chartier), professor of philosophy at Simone Weil's lycée. Gabriella Fiori writes that "he [Alain] was the sole polarizing model of her [Weil's] education, the Socrates of her thought and style" (*Simone Weil: An Intellectual Biography*, 28).

127   Jean-Paul Sartre, *The Transcendence of the Ego: An Existentialist Theory of Consciousness* (1938), translated by Forrest Williams and Robert Kirkpatrick (New York: Farrar, Straus, 1957).

128   the German authorities and French writers: This subject is examined in Herbert R. Lottman, *The Left Bank* (Boston: Houghton-Mifflin, 1981). Mavis Gallant's review of this book is worth reading (*The New York Times Book Review*, 4 April 1982).

128   "yes, a very good tale you have there": Conversation between publisher Gaston Gallimard and novelist Louis Aragon. Gerhardt Heller had a kind of gentleman's agreement with major French book publishers: if they exercised a mild self-censorship, their writers would not be interfered with.

129   Miguel de Unamuno, *The Tragic Sense of Life*, translated by J. S. Crawford Flitch (London: Macmillan, 1926) (New York: Dover, 1954).

130   encounter between Beauvoir and Weil: Beauvoir, *Memoirs of a Dutiful Daughter*, 252. The biographers of Weil and Beauvoir use this source for their description of this confrontation.

130 Sartre, "the important thing": Marius Perrin, *Avec Sartre Au Stalag 12D* (Paris: Delage, 1980).

131 Joseph Conrad, *Lord Jim: A Tale* (1900) (New York: Oxford University Press, 1983).

132 Camus's early life: Much of the information presented here derives from the biographies of Camus by Lottman and McCarthy.

134 Joseph K., "like a dog!": Kafka, *The Trial*, 340.

135 Nicholson, "the actor is": *The New York Times Magazine*, 13 July 1986.

135 Søren Kierkegaard, *Either-Or: A Fragment of Life*, in *A Kierkegaard Anthology*, Bretall (ed.), 19-108.

137 Camus, "I have always condemned": Quoted in *Le Monde*, 13 December 1956, and in other sources, including McCarthy, *Camus*, 294.

138 Sartre, "insofar as Camus's humanism": *France-Observateur*, 7 January 1960; *Le Monde*, 8 January 1960.

138 Sartre, *Critique of Dialectical Reason*: Published in two volumes by Verso, the first volume in 1976 and the second (unfinished) in 1991.

139 Sartre's preface to Genet's plays: Published separately as *St. Genet, Actor and Martyr*, translated by Bernard Frechtman (New York: Pantheon, 1983).

139 "Sartre and Mme de Beauvoir have long been regarded": Bair, *Simone de Beauvoir*, 527-528 (source given as A. M. Sheridan-Smith, "Obsessions," *London Magazine*, April 1969, 99).

139 Sartre, "I am not Shakespeare": Cited by Joseph McClellan in his obituary notice on Sartre in *The Washington Post*, 18 April 1980 (source given as Interview, *Le Nouvel Observateur*, March 1980).

140 *Bariona:* I have used the description of *Bariona* provided by Douglas Johnson in his review of Marius Perrin's *Avec Sartre au Stalag 12D* (*Times Literary Supplement*, 27 February 1981, 224).

8. "Lenin and Soviet Philosophy"

In writing this chapter, I am indebted to the work of Loren Graham, particularly *Science and Philosophy in the Soviet Union* and *Science, Philosophy, and Human Behavior in the Soviet Union*.

141 Siiak, "it was done with respect": Henry Kamm, *The New York Times*, 24 August 1991, p. 1.

141   Lenin, "it is impossible to understand": *The Lenin Anthology*, Tucker (ed.), 639.

142   "Overboard with philosophy!": Positivist opposition to philosophy and Lenin's defense of the discipline are described in Gustav Wetter, *Dialectical Materialism* (New York: Praeger, 1958).

143   Zhdanov's speech: Zhdanov made it clear that the work of intellectual merit envisioned was to be done under strict ideological control. And it was: the intellectual reign of terror that followed came to be known as "Zhdanovchina."

143   *Voprosy filosofii*: although Loren Graham tells me that he had not seen an issue of *Voprosy filosofii* for almost a year (1991), a representative of Victor Kamkin's Russian Language Bookstore said that it was still being published in Moscow. This was later confirmed by Professor Graham who has recently received vols. 1 and 2 of 1992.

143   Stalin's *Letters on Linguistics*: Published in New York in 1951 under the titles *Marxism and Linguistics* (Progress Publishers) and *Letters on Marxism and Linguistics* (International Publishers). The two publishers were probably one and the same.

143   Nikolai Yakovlovich Marr: The quixotic adventures of Marr on linguistics, including Stalin's reaction, are told in Wetter's *Dialectical Materialism*.

144   Vygotsky and Luria: Graham, *Science, Philosophy, and Human Behavior in the Soviet Union*, 168ff, 184ff. Vygotsky's *Thought and Language* is available in English (Cambridge, Mass.: M.I.T. Press, 1962).

145   "the tasks of this chapter": *A Soviet History of Philosophy*, translated by William Edgerton (Washington, D.C.: Public Affairs Press, 1950).

146   "among the problems": Review of Brennan, *The Meaning of Philosophy*, 2d ed., from *Voprosy filosofii* (Problems of Philosophy) (published by the Institute of Philosophy of the Soviet Academy of Sciences), number 11, 1968, 169. Review translated by Loren Graham.

148   Descartes, "machine designed by the hand of God": Descartes, *Discourse on Method*, IV, 371.

149   Marx, "extract the rational kernel of dialectic": Karl Marx, *Capital*, vol. 1, "Afterword to the Second German Edition," third paragraph from the end. (This is reprinted in all editions after 1873.) Thanks to Stanley Moore for this note and the one that follows.

150   Lenin, "nobody can understand": *V. I. Lenin: Collected Works* (Moscow: Progress Publishers, 1965), 32:94. Plekhanov, the father of Russian Marxism, was treated with great respect by Lenin until the older man expressed reservations about the 1905 revolution and later defended Russia's entry into the First World War. Lenin saw Russia's participation in the war as the further exploitation of the people and denied that true revolutionaries had the right to support it. Hence his later contemptuous references to Plekhanov.

152   the Lysenko controversy: Graham, *Science and Philosophy in the Soviet Union*, chapter 4 ("Genetics").

153   Niels Bohr: For an interesting portrait of Bohr's world, see Abraham Pais, "Niels Bohr's Times," in *Physics, Philosophy, and Polity* (New York: Oxford University Press, 1992).

153   Zhdanov, "the Kantian vagaries": Graham, *Science and Philosophy in the Soviet Union*, 325.

155   Lenin, "I don't know anything greater": Robert Payne, *Lenin* (New York: Simon and Schuster, 1964), 249.

157   Graham, "I was in Moscow a month ago": Graham, letter to author, 14 October 1989.

158   atheism and the Soviet bureaucracy: L. N. Nitrokhin, "Philosophy and Religion," in *Voprosy filosofii*, number 9, 1989.

158   Gorbachev-Yeltsin telecast: *The New York Times*, 7 September 1991.

9. "Evolution and Ethics"

160   Jefferson, "moral philosophy": *The Portable Thomas Jefferson*, edited by Merrill D. Peterson (New York: Viking Press, 1975), 423-425.

161   Arkansas's definition of creation science: *The New York Times*, 6 June 1982, p. B8. This article includes excerpts from the U. S. Supreme Court decision that overturned the Arkansas law on the teaching of creation science.

163   Richard Leakey on Lucy: See Leakey, *The Making of Mankind*.

163   Wilson and Savich: The comparatively recent date ascribed by Wilson's co-workers to the "mother of us all" shows that they regarded her as a *homo sapiens*, a human more or less like us, rather than a proto-human like *australopithecus*. As the reader knows, substantial changes in hominid and pre-hominid dating by paleontologists and molecular biologists may be expected to occur

frequently. For further information on the debate over mitochondrial evidence of human origins, see the *The New York Times*, 1 October 1991, pp. C1, C6.

164 "most of those old bones": Nicholas Wade, "How Old Is Man?" *The New York Times*, 4 October 1982, The Editorial Notebook.

164 Alvarez, "I don't like to say bad things": Malcolm W. Brown, "The Debate over Dinosaur Extinction Takes an Unusually Rancorous Turn," *The New York Times*, 19 January 1988, p. C4.

167 Darwin, "the reckless, degraded and often vicious members of society": Darwin, *The Descent of Man*, 2d ed., 141.

169 Darwin, "the main conclusion of the whole work": Darwin, *The Descent of Man*, 1st ed., concluding paragraph. In the second edition of the book, Darwin deleted the phrase "the mark of the beast."

170 Kipling, "The Mark of the Beast": In Rudyard Kipling, *Life's Handicaps* (Garden City, N.Y. : Doubleday Page & Co., 1921), 294-310.

170 Darwin, "for my own part": Darwin, *The Descent of Man*, 2d ed., 684.

170 Barnard, "if organic evolution were true": Cited in Loren Eisely, *Darwin's Century* (Garden City, N.Y.: Doubleday, 1958), 194-195.

173 Arthur Conan Doyle, *The Lost World* (New York: Hodder & Stoughton, 1912).

173 Gould, "to rub English noses": Gould, "Piltdown Revisited," in *The Panda's Thumb*, 108-124.

175 Samuel Alexander, *Space, Time, and Deity*, 2 vol. (London: Macmillan, 1934).

176 "a rocket rising": Teilhard de Chardin, *The Phenomenon of Man*, 52.

176 Teilhard de Chardin, "to a Martian": Teilhard, *The Phenomenon of Man*, 183.

177 Teilhard de Chardin, "after all, is there any other way": Teilhard, *The Phenomenon of Man*, 268.

177 Monod, "thanks to an engaging style": Monod, *Chance and Necessity*, 26.

177 Monod, "for my part I am most struck": Monod, *Chance and Necessity*, 32.

177 Monod, "the traditional concepts": Monod, "On Values in the Age of Science," in *The Place of Value in a World of Facts*, 18.

178 Confederate soldiers and evolution: Douglas Southall Freeman, "Lee as a Leader," in *Douglas Southall Freeman on Leadership*, Smith (ed.), 167.

179   Joel, "your life has no more purpose": Smith, *Kamongo*, 166.

179   "Joel watched the priest": Smith, *Kamongo*, 166-167.

180   "and the Lord God made man": Genesis 2:7.

180   Monod, "thus the appearance of life itself": Monod, "On Values in the Age of Science," in *The Place of Value in a World of Facts*, 22.

181   Williams, "we are the gooks and geeks": Tennessee Williams, "Carrousel Tune," in Tennessee Williams, *In the Winter of Cities* (New York: New Directions, 1956), 91.

10. "Wittgenstein and the Ethic of Silence"

In writing this chapter, I am indebted to Ray Monk's *Ludwig Wittgenstein: The Duty of Genius*, a recent full-length biography of the philosopher; to Norman Malcolm's *Ludwig Wittgenstein: A Memoir*, which remains the most memorable recollection of Wittgenstein as a personality and as a teacher at Cambridge; and to Rush Rhees's *Recollections of Wittgenstein*.

182   "Socrates, make music!": Plato, *Phaedo* 61a. Most scholars agree that Socrates used the term *musike* in the broad sense, meaning all the arts, including philosophy.

182   Brahms's St. Anthony variations: Also known as *Variations on a Theme by Haydn*.

182   Wittgenstein's military service: *Ludwig Wittgenstein: Geheime Tagebucher* [Secret Diaries] *1914-1916*, edited by Wilhelm Baum (Vienna: Turia and Kant, 1991).

182   Wittgenstein, "Wittgensteins Kriegsdienst im Ersten Weltkrieg," 127-144 and Franz Parak, "Wittgenstein in Monte Cassino," 145-158, in Baum (ed.), *Ludwig Wittgenstein: Geheime Tagebucher 1914-1916*.

183   Wittgenstein, "if a man could write a book on ethics": M. O'C. Drury, "Some Notes on Conversations with Wittgenstein," in Rhees (ed.), *Recollections of Wittgenstein*, 82.

183   Wittgenstein, "what you should do": Fania Pascal, "Wittgenstein: A Personal Memoir," in Rhees (ed.), *Recollections of Wittgenstein*, 22.

184   Weininger on women: Otto Weininger, *Sex and Character* (authorized translation from the sixth German edition) (New York: G. P. Putnam's Sons, name of translator and date of publication

not given), 186. Weininger believed that both men and women possess elements of the opposite sex in varying degrees. If a woman has only a small element of masculinity in her nature, she represents a point on a continuum moving toward the polar extreme of the Absolute Woman. "In such a being as the absolute female," writes Weininger, "there are no logical or ethical phenomena and therefore the ground for the assumption of a soul is absent." One need not be a Marxist to see that such a belief represents a reflection, albeit a distorted one, of the social and economic conditions of women in the particular society that the author knew.

188   Wittgenstein, "wovon man nicht sprechen Kann": Wittgenstein, *Tractatus*, 6.54.

190   "the sky is in the key of B flat": My example, not Ayer's.

190   Wittgenstein, "Blake!": M. O'C. Drury, "Conversations with Wittgenstein," in Rhees (ed.), *Recollections of Wittgenstein*, 150-151. Blake was one of Wittgenstein's favorite poets, and the philosopher could quote long passages of Blake from memory.

190   Wittgenstein, "don't worry": Monk, *Ludwig Wittgenstein*, 271-272.

191   Wittgenstein, "[I] felt like a private": Monk, *Ludwig Wittgenstein*, 271.

192   "water! away! ow!": Wittgenstein, *Philosophical Investigations*, I, 27.

193   "what is the aim of philosophy?": Wittgenstein, *Philosophical Investigations*, I, 309.

193   Wittgenstein on the language game: Wittgenstein, *Philosophical Investigations*, I, 7 ff, 67.

194   Wittgenstein, "think of the tools in a tool-box": Wittgenstein, *Philosophical Investigations* I, 11.

195   Wittgenstein, "tell them I've had a wonderful life": Malcolm, *Ludwig Wittgenstein*, 100.

195   Nietzsche, "what he taught": Thomas Mann, "Schopenhauer," in Thomas Mann, *Essays of Three Decades*, translated by H. T. Lowe-Porter (New York: Alfred Knopf, 1947), 377.

195   Wittgenstein, "such a decent man": Malcolm, *Ludwig Wittgenstein*, 99. According to Malcolm, Wittgenstein was referring not necessarily to Brigadier Young himself but to "the thoroughly *decent* way in which his biography of Rommel was written." Wittgenstein's highest praise was awarded to anyone he thought "decent" or "a real *human being*" (Malcolm, 64). Of William James, Wittgenstein

said, "That is what makes him a good philosopher; he was a real human being" (Monk, 478).

195   "his exceptionally courageous behavior": Monk, *Ludwig Wittgenstein*, 154.

196   Beethoven and *Missa Solemnis*: According to Ray Monk, Wittgenstein told Bertrand Russell this story about Beethoven and said, "That's the sort of man to be." (Monk, *Ludwig Wittgenstein*, 45).

     The version of the Beethoven story that I have used is taken from Kretschmar's lecture in Thomas Mann, *Doctor Faustus* (translated by H. T. Lowe-Porter (New York: Alfred Knopf, 1948), 58).

     The story has its origins in Anton Schindler's reminiscences of Beethoven (1819). Schindler knew Beethoven, helped him with certain tasks, and had "Friend of Beethoven" engraved on his calling card. Musicologist Jo-Ann Reif tells me that many scholars today believe that Schindler made the whole thing up. Dr. Reif notes that Schindler's portrait of Beethoven is included in O. G. Senneck, ed., *Beethoven: Impressions by His Contemporaries* (1926) (New York: Dover Publications, 1967).

196   Jesus, "be ye perfect": Matthew 5:48.

196   Wittgenstein, "of course I want to be perfect": Fania Pascal, "Wittgenstein: A Personal Memoir," in Rhees, *Recollections of Wittgenstein*, 37.

196   Wittgenstein "felt safe": Malcolm, *Ludwig Wittgenstein*, 70.

197   Monk, "the reconciliation with God": Monk, *Ludwig Wittgenstein*, 580. Wittgenstein was not a Catholic in either belief or practice, but most of those who knew him at the end thought it appropriate that a Catholic priest say the usual prayers at the grave.

197   "I say unto you that for every idle word": Jesus in Matthew 12:36-37. M. O'C. Drury recalls Wittgenstein saying that Matthew was his favorite gospel: "Matthew seems to me to contain everything." (Drury, "Some Notes on Conversations with Wittgenstein," in Rush (ed.,), *Recollections of Wittgenstein*, 164)

198   Confucius and his pupils: Confucius, *The Analects of Confucius*, translated and annotated by Waley, 214. Waley translates this passage as follows: "The Master said, 'Heaven does not speak; yet the four seasons run their course thereby, the hundred creatures, each after its kind, are born thereby. Heaven does no speaking!'"

198   Pascal, "the silence of those infinite spaces": Pascal, *Pensées*, 313.

198   Shusaka Endo, *Silence* (Chinmoku) (English translation published by Sofia University, Tokyo, in cooperation with C. E. Tuttle Company, Rutland, Vermont, 1969).

199   Stockdale, "this support, this girder of our unity": Commencement address, John Carroll University, Cleveland Ohio, 24 May 1981.

Epilogue

201   "endurance of soul": Plato, *Laches* 192c, in *The Collected Dialogues of Plato.*

202   Pascal on the greatness of the human: Pascal, *Pascal's Pensées*, Stewart (ed.), 160.

203   "you see, gentlemen": Dostoyevsky, *Notes from Underground* I, in *Existentialism from Dostoyevsky to Sartre*, Kaufmann (ed.), 73.

205   Jeremiah, "how doth the city": The Lamentations of Jeremiah 1:1.

206   Churchill, "certainly nothing could be more repulsive": Winston Churchill, *My Early Life: A Roving Commission* (New York: Charles Scribner's Sons, 1930), 117.

206   James, truth is "the expedient": William James, *Pragmatism and four essays from The Meaning of Truth* (New York: World Publishing Company, 1970), 145.

206   Dewey, "moral insight": John Dewey, "Moral Theory and Practice," in *The Philosophy of John Dewey*, edited by J. Ratner (New York: Holt, Rhinehart and Winston, 1928), 310.

207   John Winthrop and the City on a Hill: Cited in *The American Puritans*, edited by Perry Miller (New York: Doubleday, 1956), 83.

208   Melville, "escaped from the house of bondage": Herman Melville, *White Jacket* (1850) (Evanston, Ill.: Northwestern University Press, 1970), 150-151.

208   Malraux's toast: I need not have worried. On the same U. S. visit Malraux and his wife Madeline were the guests of President and Mrs. Kennedy at a White House dinner, during which Malraux declared, "There is no American Empire. There is, however, the United States. For the first time a country has become the world's leader without achieving this through conquest." Eight months later Malraux opened the Washington exhibit of the Louvre-loaned *Mona Lisa* by stating that the loan of Leonardo's masterpiece was

little "compared to the risk American soldiers had faced in France in two World Wars." (Axel Madson, *Malraux: A Biography* (New York: William Morrow, 1976), 310, 313)

208   Emerson and the lecture hall: *Journals and Miscellaneous Notebooks of Ralph Waldo Emerson*, 14 vols., edited by William H. Gilman et al. (Cambridge, Mass.: Harvard University Press, 1960), 7:277.

209   Socrates on true teaching: Plato, *Phaedrus* 275d, 276a.

209   Socrates and Crito: Plato, *Euthydemus* 306d, 307b-c.

209   Socrates and Phaedrus: Plato, *Phaedrus* 279b-c.

Bibliography

Aquinas, Thomas. "The Existence of God" (*Summa theologica*, Q2, art 3). In *Basic Writings of Thomas Aquinas*, vol. 1, edited by A. C. Pegis. New York: Random House, 1945.

Aristotle. *The Complete Works of Artistotle* (Revised Oxford Translation). 2 vols. Edited by Jonathan Barnes. Princeton, N. J.: Princeton University Press, 1984.

————. *The Nichomachean Ethics*. Translated by H. Rackham. Cambridge: Harvard University Press, Loeb Classical Library, 1934. Includes Greek text.

————. *The Nichomachean Ethics*. Translated by Martin Oswald. Indianapolis: Bobbs-Merrill, The Library of Liberal Arts, 1962.

Aristophanes. *The Clouds*. In *Fifteen Great Plays*, translated by Gilbert Murray et al. New York: Oxford University Press, 1943.

Augustine (Aurelius Augustinius). *The Confessions of Saint Augustine*. Translated with introduction and notes by E. B. Pusey. New York: Dutton, 1951.

Ayer, Alfred Jules. *Language, Truth and Logic* (1937). 2d rev. ed. London: Gollancz, 1946. New York: Dover, 1952.

Bair, Deirdre. *Simone de Beauvoir: A Biography*. New York: Summit Books, 1990.

Beauvoir, Simone de. *Memoirs of a Dutiful Daughter* (Memoirs d'une jeune fille rangée) (1958). Translated by James Kirkup. Cleveland and New York: World Publishing Co., 1959.

Bergson, Henri. *Creative Evolution* (1907). Translated by Arthur Mitchell. New York: Holt, Rhinehart & Winston, 1911.

Berkeley, George. *A Treatise Concerning the Principles of Human Knowledge*. La Salle, Ill.: Open Court, 1903.

Bhagavad Gita, The. Translated and interpreted by Franklin Edgerton. New York: Harper & Row, Harper Torchbooks, 1964.

Boethius (Anicus Manlius Severenus). *The Consolation of Philosophy*. Translated with introduction and notes by Richard Green. Indianapolis: Bobbs-Merrill, The Library of Liberal Arts, 1962.

Brennan, Joseph Gerard. *The Meaning of Philosophy*. 2d ed. New York: Harper & Row, 1967.

——. "Retort and Bell Jar: Closed Space and Hermetic Transformation of Modernist and Postmodernist Novels." In *Space and Boundaries* (vol. 2 of Proceedings of the XIIth Congress of the International Comparative Literature Association, 1988). Munich: Judicum Verlag, 1990.

Camus, Albert. *The Stranger* (L'Etranger) (1942). Translated by Stuart Gilbert. New York: Alfred Knopf, 1946. Translated by Matthew Ward. New York: Vintage Books, International Edition, 1989.

——. *The Myth of Sisyphus* (Le Myth de Sisyphe) (1942). New York: Alfred Knopf, Vintage Books, 1955.

——. *The Plague* (La Peste) (1947). Translated by Stuart Gilbert. New York: Alfred Knopf, 1948.

——. *The Rebel* (L'Homme revolte) (1951). Translated by Anthony Brown. New York: Alfred Knopf, 1956.

——. *The Fall* (La Chute) (1956). Translated by Justin O'Brien. New York: Alfred Knopf, 1957.

Cervantes, Miguel de. *Don Quixote* (1605, 1615). Translated by Samuel Putnam. New York: Viking Press, 1949.

Churchill, Winston. *My Early Life: A Roving Commission*. New York: Charles Scribner's Sons, 1930.

Clark, Ronald W. *Lenin: The Man behind the Mask*. New York: Harper & Row, 1988.

Clausewitz, Carl von. *On War* (1832). Edited and translated by Michael Howard and Peter Paret. Princeton, N. J.: Princeton Univeristy Press, 1976.

Cohen-Solal, Annie. *Sartre: A Life*. Translated by Anna Cancogn. New York: Pantheon Books, 1987.

Confucius. *The Analects of Confucius*. Translated and annotated by Arthur Waley. New York: Vintage, 1938.

Conrad, Joseph. *Typhoon* (1914). In *Typhoon and Other Tales*. New York: New American Library, Signet Classic, 1962.

Darwin, Charles. *The Descent of Man* (1871). New York: Appleton & Co., 1925.

——. *The Origin of Species* (1859). New York: Hunt & Co., 1890.

Descartes, René. *Discourse on Method* and *Meditations*. Translated by Laurence J. Lafleur. Indianapolis: Bobbs-Merrill, Library of Liberal Arts, 1960.

Dickens, Charles. *Hard Times* (1854). New York: W. W. Norton & Co., 1966.

Dostoyevsky, Fyodor. *The Brothers Karamazov* (1880). Translated by Constance Garnett. New York: Random House, Modern Library, n. d.

—————. "The Grand Inquisitor" (from *The Brothers Karamazov*). Introduction of Anne Fremantle; translated by Constance Garnett. New York: Frederick Ungar Publishing Co., 1956.

—————. *Notes from Underground*. Translated by Mura Ginsburg. New York: Bantam Books, 1974.

—————. *Notes from Underground* I. In *Existentialism from Dostoyevsky to Sartre*, edited by Walter Kaufmann. New York: New American Library, 1975.

—————. *The Possessed* (*The Demons*, 1872). Translated by Constance Garnett. New York: Random House, Modern Library, 1936.

Emerson, Ralph Waldo. "Self-Reliance" (1841). In *The Complete Essays and Other Writings of Ralph Waldo Emerson*, edited by Brooks Atkinson. New York: Random House, Modern Library, 1940.

Epictetus. *The Enchiridion*. Introduction by Albert Salomon; translated by Thomas W. Higginson. 2d ed. Indianapolis: Bobbs-Merrill, Library of Liberal Arts, 1979.

Fiori, Gabriella. *Simone Weil: An Intellectual Biography*. Translated by Joseph R. Berrigan. Athens, Ga.: Univeristy of Georgia Press, 1989.

Fischer, Louis. *The Life of Lenin*. New York: Harper & Row, 1964.

Freeman, Douglas Southall. "Lee as a Leader" (lecture at Army War College of 2 February 1939). In *Douglas Southall Freeman on Leadership*, edited by Stuart W. Smith. Newport, R. I.: Naval War College Press, 1990.

Gabriel, Richard A. "The Nature of Military Ethics." In *To Serve with Honor: A Treatise on Military Ethics and the Way of a Soldier*. Foreword by James Bond Stockdale. Westport, Conn.: Greenwood Press, 1980.

Gould, Stephen Jay. "Piltdown Revisited." In *The Panda's Thumb and Other Essays*. New York: Norton, 1980.

Graham, Loren R. *Science and Philosophy in the Soviet Union*. New York: Alfred Knopf, 1972.

—————. *Science, Philosophy, and Human Behavior in the Soviet Union*. New York: Columbia University Press, 1987.

Gray, J. Glenn. *The Warriors: Reflections on Men in Battle*. Introduction by Hannah Arendt. New York: Harper & Row, 1967.

Hart, H. L. A. "Laws and Morals." In *The Concept of Law*. New York: Oxford University Press, 1961, 1976.

Heidegger, Martin. *Being and Time* (Zein und Zeit) (1927). Translated by Edward Robinson. New York: Harper & Row, 1962.

—————. "What Is Metaphysics"? Translated by Walter Kaufmann. In *Existentialism from Dostoyevsky to Sartre*, edited by Walter Kaufmann. New York: New American Library, 1975.

Hume, David. *A Treatise on Human Nature*. Oxford, 1896.

Huxley, Thomas. *Evolution and Ethics and Other Essays*. New York: D. Appleton & Co., 1899.

Job. The Book of Job (Old Testament).

Johanson, Donald C. and Edey, Maitland A. *Lucy: The Beginnings of Humankind*. New York: Simon and Schuster, 1981.

Jones, J. Sydney. *Hitler in Vienna (1907-1913)* (translation of *Hitlers Weg begann in Wien*). New York: Stein & Day, 1988.

Kafka, Franz. *The Trial* (Der Prozess) (1925). Translated by Willa and Edwin Muir. New York: Alfred Knopf, 1965.

Kant, Immanuel. *Critique of Pure Reason* (Kritik der reinen Vernunft) (1787). Translated by Norman Kemp Smith. New York: St. Martin's Press, 1965.

—————. *Foundations of the Metaphysics of Morals* (Grundlegung zur Metaphysik der Sitten) (1785) and "What Is Enlightenment?" Translated with introduction by Lewis White Beck. Indianapolis: Bobbs-Merrill, Library of Liberal Arts, 1959.

—————. *Perpetual Peace*. Translated with introduciton by Lewis White Beck. New York: Liberal Arts Press, 1948.

Kierkegaard, Søren. *A Kierkegaard Anthology*. Edited by Robert Bretall. New York: Random House, Modern Library, 1946.

Koestler, Arthur. *Darkness at Noon*. New York: Macmillan Co., 1941.

Lawrence, J. and Lee, R. E. *Inherit the Wind* (drama). New York: Random House, 1955.

Leakey, Richard E. *The Making of Mankind*. New York: Dutton, 1981.

Lenin, V. I. *The Lenin Anthology*. Selected, edited, and introduced by Robert C. Tucker. New York: W. W. Norton & Co., 1975.

—————. *Materialism and Empirio-Criticism*. In *Selected Works*, vol. 11. New York: International Publishers, 1943.

—————. *What Is to Be Done?* (1902). In *The Lenin Anthology*, edited by Robert C. Tucker. New York: W. W. Norton & Co., 1975.

Lloyd Morgan, C. *Emergent Evolution*. New York: Holt, Rhinehart & Winston, 1927.

Locke, John. *An Essay concerning Human Understanding* (1689). London: Oxford University Press, 1894.

Lottman, Herbert R. *Albert Camus: A Biography*. Garden City, N. Y.: Doubleday, 1979.

Luther, Martin. *Treatise on Secular Authority* (1523). In *Martin Luther*, edited by John Dillenberger. Garden City, N. Y.: Doubleday, Anchor Books, 1961.

McCarthy, Patrick. *Camus*. New York: Random House, 1982.

Malcolm, Norman. *Ludwig Wittgenstein: A Memoir*. New York: Oxford University Press, 1958, 1977. Includes a biographical sketch by Georg Henrik von Wright.

Mann, Thomas. *The Magic Mountain* (Der Zauberberg) (1924). Translated by H. T. Lowe Porter. New York: Alfred Knopf, 1968.

Marx, Karl, and Engels, Friedrich. *The Communist Manifesto* (1848). Translated by Samuel Moore with an introduction by A. J. P. Taylor. New York: Penguin Books, 1967.

Mill, John Stuart. *Autobiography* (1873). Edited by Jack Stillinger. New York: Houghton Mifflin Co., 1969.

————. *On Liberty* (1859). Introduction by Gertrude Himmelfarb. New York: Penguin, 1981.

————. *Utilitarianism* (1863). New York: Bobbs-Merrill, Liberal Arts Press, 1957.

Monk, Ray. *Ludwig Wittgenstein: The Duty of Genius*. New York: Macmillan, Free Press, 1990.

Monod, Jacques. *Chance and Necessity* (Le Hasard et la Necéssité) (1970). Translated by Austryn Wainhouse. New York: Random House, Vintage, 1971.

————. "On Values in the Age of Science." In *The Place of Value in a World of Facts* (14th Nobel Symposium, Stockholm, 1969). New York: Wiley, 1970.

Moore, G. E. *Principia Ethica* (1902). London: Cambridge University Press, 1951.

Mure, G. R. G. *Aristotle*. New York: Oxford University Press, 1964.

Musil, Robert. *The Man without Qualities* (Der Mann ohne Eigenschaften) (1930, 1932). Translated by Eithne Wilkins and Ernst Kaiser. New York: Coward-McCann, 1953.

Nietzsche, Friedrich. *Beyond Good and Evil* and *The Genealogy of Morals*. In *Basic Writings of Nietzsche*, translated and edited by Walter Kaufmann. New York: Random House, Modern Library, 1968.

Packe, Michael St. John. *The Life of John Stuart Mill.* New York: Macmillan Co., 1954.

Paley, William. *Natural Theology.* London: Baldwyn & Co., 1821.

Pascal, Blaise. *Pascal's Pensées.* Translated by H. F. Stewart, D. D. New York: Pantheon Books, 1950.

Pétrement, Simone. *Simone Weil: A Life.* Translated by Raymond Rosenthal. New York: Random House, 1976.

Plato. *The Collected Dialogues of Plato.* Edited by Edith Hamilton and Huntington Cairns; translated by Lane Cooper et al. New York: Random House, Pantheon Books, 1967. There are convenient editions of the Socratic dialogues—*Euthyphro, Apology, Cirto, Phaedo*—in the Bobbs-Merrill Liberal Art series.

Plato. *The Republic.* Translated with introduction and notes by Francis MacDonald Cornford. New York: Oxford University Press, 1941, 1977.

Rawls, John. *A Theory of Justice.* Cambridge: Harvard University Press, Belknap Press, 1971.

Rhees, Rush, ed. *Recollectons of Wittgenstein.* New York: Oxford University Press, 1984.

Runciman, Steven. *The Medieval Manichee: A Study of the Christian Dualist Heresy.* New York: Viking Press, 1961.

Sadat, Anwar el-. *In Search of Identity: An Autobiography.* New York: Harper & Row, 1977.

Sartre, Jean-Paul. *Being and Nothingness* (L'Etre et le Néant) (1943). Translated by Hazel Barnes. New York: Philosophical Library, 1956, and Washington Square Press, 1966.

————. "Existentialism Is a Humanism" (1946). In *Existentialism from Dostoyevsky to Sartre*, edited by Walter Kaufmann. New York: New American Library, 1975.

————. *The Flies* (Les Mouches) (1943) and No Exit (Huis clos) (1944). Both in *No Exit and The Flies*, translated by Stuart Gilbert. New York: Alfred Knopf, 1948.

————. *Nausea* (La Nausée) (1938). Translated by Lloyd Alexander. New York: New Directions, 1948, 1964.

_____. *The Words* (Les Mots) (1963). Translated by Bernard Frechtman. New York: George Braziller, 1964, and Vintage Books, 1981.

Schnitzler, Arthur. *Vienna 1900: Games with Love and Death.* New York: Penguin Books, 1975.

Schopenhauer, Arthur. *The World as Will and Idea* (1819). 3 vols. Translated by R. B. Haldane and J. Kemp. London: Routledge & Kegan Paul, 1948.

Schrödinger, Erwin. *What Is Life?* New York: Macmillan Co., 1945.

Smith, Homer. *Kamongo.* New York: Viking Press, 1932.

Solzhenitsyn, Alexander I. *One Day in the Life of Ivan Denisovich.* New York: Praeger Publishers, 1963.

_____. *A World Split Apart* (Commencement Address at Harvard University, 8 June 1978). Translated by Irina Ilovayskaya Alberti. New York: Harper & Row, 1978.

Spinoza, Benedict. *Ethics* (1677). New York: E. P. Dutton, 1938.

Stalin, V. J. *Letters on Marxism and Linguistics.* New York: International Publishers, 1951.

Stockdale, James B. "Heroes and Heroism" (Address at the John M. Olin Center for Inquiry into the Theory and Practice of Democracy, University of Chicago, 18 April 1990).

_____. "The World of Epictetus." *The Atlantic Monthly,* April 1978.

Stockdale, Jim and Sybil. *In Love and War: The Story of a Family's Ordeal and Sacrifice during the Vietnam Years.* New York: Harper and Row, 1984.

Teilhard de Chardin, Pierre. *The Phenomenon of Man.* New York: Harper & Row, 1956.

Vlastos, Gregory. *Socrates: Ironist and Moral Philosopher.* New York: Cambridge Univesity Press, 1991.

Walzer, Michael. "Prisoners of War: Does the Fight Continue after the Battle?" In *The American Political Science Review,* September 1969.

Watson, James D. *The Double Helix.* New York: Athenaeum, 1968.

Weil, Simone. *The Simone Weil Reader.* Edited by George A. Panichas. New York: David McKay Co., 1977.

Weiner, J. S. *The Piltdown Forgery.* New York: Dover, 1980.

Whitehead, Alfred North. *Science and the Modern World* (The Lowell Lectures, 1925). New York: Macmillan Co., 1931.

Whitman, Walt. *The Complete Poetry and Selected Prose and Letters of Walt Whitman.* Edited by Emory Holloway. London: Nonesuch Press, 1967.

Wiesel, Elie. *Night.* Translated by Stella Rodway. New York: Hill & Wang, 1960. Foreword by Francois Mauriac.

Wittgenstein, Ludwig. *Philosophical Investigations.* Translated by G. E. M. Anscombe. New York: Macmillian Co., 1953.

————. *Tractatus Logico-Philosophicus.* New York: Harcourt, Brace & Co., 1922. Introduction by Bertrand Russell.

Wolfson, Harry Austryn. *The Philosophy of Spinoza.* 2 vols. Cambridge, Mass.: Harvard University Press, 1934.

Xenophon. *Memorabilia and Oeconomicus.* Translated by E. C. Marchand. New York: G. P. Putnam's Sons, Loeb Classical Library, 1923. Includes Greek text.

Index

Absolute Spirit (Hegel), 62, 149

Achilles, 38

Active intellect (*nous energeaia*), 70-71

Actuality versus potentiality, 60-61, 69-70

Adler, Mortimer, 44

Agammemnon (king of Greece), 38

Agapē, 37, 40, 54-55

Agathon, 47, 50-51

Agrégation, 125

Alcestis, 48

Alchemy and the hermetic, 3, 8-9

Alcibiades, 53-54

Alciphron (Berkeley), 79

Alexander of Aphrodisias, 70

Alexander, Samuel (author of *Space, Time, and Deity*), 175-176

Alexander the Great, 47, 57-58, 62

Alvarez, Luis, 164, 165

Amberly, Lord and Lady, 118

Ambition as the "Nameless virtue," 67

Ambrose (bishop of Milan), 32

Anabasis (Xenophon), 42

Analysis of Sensations (Mach), 151

Anaxagoras, 43

Anscombe, Elizabeth, 192

Antigone, 48

Apassionata Sonata (opus 57) (Beethoven), 155

Aphrodite, 49, 56

Apollinaire, Guillaume, 122-123

Apology (Plato), 44

Aquinas, Thomas, 30, 56, 59, 64, 70

Arendt, Hannah, 38

"Ariel" (Rodó), 96

Aristophanes, 43, 49, 50

Aristotle: his definition of humans as rational animals, 7; his treatises on logic translated by Boethius, 12; his definition of true friendship, 39-40; and eros, 56; his definition of happiness, 57, 65, 68-69, 71; and Alexander the Great, 57-58; and Plato, 57, 65, 202, 203; and organic evolution, 58; his theory of creation, 58, 59, 62-64; his metaphysics, 59-64; and mutable versus immutable being, 59-61; and matter versus form, 60-61, 69-70; and potentiality versus actuality, 60-61, 69-70; and the nature of God, 61-64; his ethics, 64-71, 201, 202-203; and the virtues (intellectual and moral), 66-69, 71, 203; and the act of moral worth, 68; and the nature and capabilities of organic life, 69-71; and the active intellect, 70-71; on contemplative versus practical knowledge, 71, 203; and the Stoics, 71-72; and Spinoza, 72-73; his family and the last years of his life, 73; and Kant, 87; and slaves, 92; and business friendships, 92; and J. S. Mill, 98, 106-107, 113, 116; and Sartre, 129; and Hegel, 149

Arjuna, Prince, 94-95

Atheneus (author of *Banquet of the Wise* (Dneipnosophistae)), 47

Atlantic Monthly, 138

Augustine, Saint: his relics, 11; on the conditions of a just war, 29; and the problem of evil, 31-33; and the notion of love not wanting anything for itself (*agapē*), 55; and Rousseau, 75; and Luther, 75, 188; and Camus, 133; and Wittgenstein, 193

Aurelius, Marcus, 72

Austin, John, 104

Autobiography (Mill), 99, 106, 109, 117

Ayer, A. J. (author of *Language, Truth and Logic*), 189-190

Bahtrahari, 34

Banquet of the Wise (Dneipnosophistae) (Atheneus), 47

Bariona (Sartre), 140

Barnard, Frederick, 170

Beauvoir, Simone de, 120, 125, 126, 127, 128, 130, 139-140

Beckett, Samuel (author of *Endgame*), 120

Beethoven, Ludwig van, 155, 196, 201

Being and Nothingness (L'Etre et le Néant) (Sartre), 121, 128-131, 138-139

Being and Time (Heidegger), 125-126

Bell Jar, The (Plath), 9

Benatar, Pat, 1

Bentham, Jeremy, 98, 99, 100-102

Bentham, Samuel, 102, 103

Berg, Alban, 185

Bergson, Henri (author of *Creative Evolution*), 174-175, 177

Berkeley, George, 79-80, 97, 149, 151, 154

Bernard-Levi, Henri, 154

Bhagavad Gita, 94-95

Blake, William, 190

Body and its relation to soul, 9-11, 26-27, 28, 69-70

Boethius, 11-13, 20

Bogdanov, A. (author of *Materialism and Empirio-Monism*), 151

Bogomils, 30

Bohr, Niels, 153-154

Bonaventure, Saint, 18

Bradlaugh, Charles, 116

Brezhnev, Leonid, 156

Brief History of Time, A (Hawking), 58-59

Briseis, 38

Broglie, Maurice de, 153

Brothers Karamazov, The (Dostoyevsky), 197

Bryan, William Jennings, 162

Buddenbrooks (Mann), 74

Buddha (Siddartha Gautama), 34-35

Bunim, Rabbi, 180

Caesar, Sid, 126

Cain, James (author of *The Postman Always Rings Twice*), 124

Camus, Albert: and evil, 25, 133; and Sartre, 120-121, 123-124, 131-132, 136, 137, 138, 204; his early life, 131-133; and *The Myth of Sisyphus*, 133, 135-136; and *The Stranger* (L'Etranger) 133-135, 137; and *The Plague* (La Peste), 136, 137, 204; and *The Rebel* (L'Homme révolté), 136-137; and *The Fall (La Chute)*, 137-138; his death, 138; and Monod, 178; and the silence of the heavens, 198

Carlyle, Jane, 104, 109

Carlyle, Thomas, 104, 108-109

Carnap, Rudolf, 189

Carter, Jimmy, 24

Castorp, Hans, 1

Castries, General Christian de, 43

Categorical Imperative (Kant), 88-94, 203

Cathars, 30-31

Catherine the Great, 103

Cavell, Edith, 89, 90

Celestial Mechanics (Mécanique céleste) (Laplace), 148

Cervantes, Miguel de, 13-15, 202

Chance and Necessity (Monod), 177, 205-206

Chandler, Raymond, 124

Chesterton, Gilbert K., 14, 15

Children of Paradise (Les Enfants du Paradis), 128

Churchill, Winston, 66, 115, 206

Clausewitz, Carl von (author of *On War*), 67, 74, 193

Clement of Alexandria, 118

Clouds, The (Aristophanes), 43

Cohen-Solal, Annie, 121

Communist Manifesto (Marx and Engels), 107-108

Comte, Auguste, 103, 113, 142

Concerto for the Left Hand (Ravel), 183-184

Confessions (Rousseau), 75

Confessions (Saint Augustine), 32-33, 133, 193

Confucius, 198

Conrad, Joseph, 99, 131

Consolation of Philosophy, The (Boethius), 12

Constantine, 29

Contemplative versus practical knowledge, 71

Courage as a moral virtue, 66, 201, 203

Covenant theology, 207-208

"Creationism," 58, 160, 161-162

Creative Evolution (Bergson), 174, 177

Crick, Francis, 148

Critique of Dialectical Reason (Sartre), 138-139

Critique of Practical Reason, The (Kant), 74, 86-94

Critique of Pure Reason, The (Kant), 77, 81-86

"Crossing Brooklyn Ferry" (Whitman), 35

Cröys, Princess Marie de, 74, 89-90

Dada, 122, 158

Dalai Lama (the sixth), 94

Dante (author of *Paradiso*), 56

Darkness at Noon (Koestler), 24, 136, 205

Darrow, Clarence, 162

Dart and Broome, 163

Darwin, Charles: and his theory of evolution, 58, 161-162, 166-171, 179; and *The Origin of Species*, 110, 162, 166, 169, 178; and *The Descent of Man*, 148, 166-167, 169-170

Darwin, Erasmus (author of *Zoonomia*), 166

Das Capital (Marx), 141-142

Dawson, Charles, 172-174

De Anima (Aristotle), 69-71

Dean, James, 134

Death in Venice (Mann), 48-49, 185

Deborin, A.M., 142

Demiurge, 27, 28, 30

Democracy in America (de Tocqueville), 113-114

Democritus, 147

Demosthenes, 119

Der Rosenkavalier (Strauss), 185

Descartes, René, 72, 74-75, 77-78, 147-148

Descent of Man, The (Darwin), 148, 166-167, 169-170

Dewey, John, 129, 206-207

Dialectical materialism, 150, 153-154, 156, 157, 205

Dickens, Charles (author of *Hard Times*), 96

Diotima of Mantinea, 51-53

Disraeli, Benjamin, 109

Don Quixote (Cervantes), 14-15

Dostoyevsky, Fyodor, 123, 132, 136, 159, 197, 202, 203-204

Doxographers, 45

Doyle, Sir Arthur Conan, 173

Dualism, 27, 28-31

Dubois, Eugene, 171

Duchamp, Marcel (painter of *Nude Descending a Staircase*), 122

Duncan, Patrick (writer and director of *84 Charlie Mopic*), 40

Eco, Umberto (author of *The Name of the Rose*), 9

Edey, Maitland (coauthor of *Lucy: The Beginnings of Humankind*), 163

84 Charlie Mopic (Duncan), 40

Einstein, Albert, 153

Either-Or (Kierkegaard), 135

Elkäim, Arlette, 139

Emergent Evolution (Lloyd Morgan), 174, 175-176

Emerson, Ralph Waldo, 58, 121, 208

Empedocles, 38-39, 147

Enchiridion (Epictetus), 72

Endgame (Beckett), 120

Endo, Shusaka (author of *Silence*), 198

Engels, Friedrich, 107-108, 150

Enlightenment, 75, 161, 207

Epictetus, 1, 22, 24, 72, 201

Epicureans, 98

Erixymachus, 49

Eros, 37-40, 48-53, 55, 56

Essay on Human Understanding (Locke), 78-79, 148-149

Essay on Population (Malthus), 103-104, 166

Ethics (or moral philosophy): the two ways of approaching (Aristotle versus Kant), 87; as a sovereign kingdom, 90; as a discipline, 160, 201, 206

Ethics (Spinoza), 72-73

Euthydemus (Plato), 209

Evil: and Boethius, 11-13, 20; and Socrates, 13, 20; and Job, 20-24; and Wiesel, 22-23; and Nietzsche, 24; and Rubashov, 24; and Kierkegaard, 24; and Stockdale, 24; and Western religion, 24-34; and Sartre and Camus, 25; and the ancient Greeks (including Plato), 26-27; and the early Christians (including the Gnostics, Manichaeans, and Cathars), 27-31; and Saint Augustine, 31-33; and everyday experience, 33-34; and the old Jews, 34; and the holy men of ancient India (including Bahtrahari), 34; and Siddartha Gautama (Buddha), 34-35; and Walt Whitman, 35-36

Evolution: and religion, 58, 160, 161-162, 170-171, 177-180, 205-206; and Teilhard de Chardin, 160, 172, 173-177; and Charles Darwin, 161-162, 166-171; recent findings, 162-164, 171-174; development of the scientific doctrine, 164-171; and Bergson, 174

Existentialism, 120-122, 139, 204

Experience as the test of truth, 78-83, 149

Eyre, Governor Edward, 116

Fabre, Henri, 117-118

Fall, The (La Chute) (Camus), 137-138

Faulkner, William, 124, 132, 136

Faustus (teacher of Saint Augustine), 31

Fénelon, François de, 133
Fichte, Johann, 97, 149
Flaubert, Gustave, 139
Flies, The (Les Mouches) (Sartre), 128
Floyd, Ray, 7
Fock, V.I., 154
Forms, the divine, 10, 16-17, 27, 51, 52-53, 59
Form versus matter, 60-61, 69-70
Foundations of the Metaphysics of Morals (Kant), 86
Fox, W.J., 105
Fray Luis de Leon, 21-22
Frederick the Great, 77
Freeling, Nicholas, 8-9
Freeman, Douglas, 178
Freemasonry and the hermetic, 3
Frege, Gottlob, 186
Freud, Sigmund, 56, 184
Frolov, I.T., 145

Galileo, 61, 77-78
Gallimard, Gaston, 133, 138
Gaulle, Charles de, 139, 208
Gautama, Siddartha (Buddha), 34-35
Generosity as a moral virtue, 66
Genet, Jean, 139
Gladstone, William, 116
Gnostics, 28-29, 30
Gorbachev, Mikhail, 156, 157, 158
Gorky, Maksim, 150, 155
Gould, Stephen Jay (author of "Piltdown Revisited"), 173
Graham, Loren, 155, 157-158
"Grand Inquisitor, The" (from *The Brothers Karamazov*) (Dostoyevsky), 197
Gray, J. Glenn (author of *The Warriors*), 38-40
Gray, Ursula, 39
Grote, George, 104

Hammett, Dashiell, 124

Happiness: as defined by Aristotle, 57, 65, 68-69, 71, 98, 113, 203; and utilitarianism, 97-98, 113

Hard Times (Dickens), 96

Harding, Warren G., 114

Havel, Vaclav, 2

Hawking, Stephen (author of *A Brief History of Time*), 58-59

Hayes, Woody, 199-200

Hegel, Friedrich: and evil, 25; and his concept of Absolute Spirit, 62, 149; and *The Phenomenology of the Spirit*, 72; and Heine, 77; and Kant, 97, 149; and Lenin, 141-142, 150; and idealism, 149; and dialectical materialism, 150

Heiddeger, Martin, 38, 125-126, 128

Heine, Heinrich, 77

Heisenberg, Werner, 153-154

Helen of Troy, 37

Heller, Gerhardt, 128

Hemingway, Ernest (author of *The Old Man and the Sea*), 204

Hermetic: meaning of the word, 1-2; and the military, 1, 2, 7-8; and the prison experience, 1-2, 9-19; and alchemy, 3, 8-9; and Freemasonry, 3; and religion, 4-5; and science, 5-6; and sports, 6-7; and the garden, 8; and the library, 9; and the bell jar, 9

Hermias (tyrant of Assos), 73

Herpyllis, 73

Hesiod, 37, 48

History of Greece (Grote), 104

Hitler, Adolf, 185-186

Hobbes, Thomas, 94

Hofmannsthal, Hugo von, 185

Homer, 37-38, 56

Hudson, Airman David, 89

Hughes, Chris, 1

Huizinga, Johan (author of *Man the Player* (Homo Ludens)), 6-7

Hume, David, 80-81, 83, 84-85, 97, 127, 129-130, 189

Husserl, Edmund, 125

Huxley, Thomas H., 148, 169, 170

Idealism versus materialism, 147-152, 153-154

Inherit the Wind, 162

In Love and War (Stockdales), 38
Innocent III (pope), 30
"Irish Airman Foresees His Death, An" (Yeats), 8
Isaiah, 20

Jacob, François, 6
James, William, 206
Java Ape-Man, 171-172
Jean, Raymond, 154
Jefferson, Thomas, 129-130, 160-161
Jeremiah, 205
Jesus: driving the money changers out of the temple, 4; and the Resurrection, 5; and his birth in a stable, 11; and the Gnostics, 28; on military service, 28-29; and the three wise men, 29; and the Cathars, 30; as compared to Socrates, 40-46, 197; and his doctrine of love (agapē), 40, 54-55; and his method of teaching, 40, 44-45; and his literacy (the stoning of the adultress), 40-41; and the sources on his life, 41-42; and his social status, 45; and his view of family, 45, 46; telling his disciples of the Holy Spirit, 52; and the Golden Rule as the spirit of utilitarianism, 96; and the counsels of perfection, 196; on idle speech, 197; in "The Grand Inquisitor," 197; at his trial, 197
Job, the story of, 20-24, 34, 202, 204
Johanson, Donald, 163, 170
John of Austria, 13, 14, 15
John of the Cross, Saint 55
John Paul II (pope), 22
John, Saint, the Gospel of, 40-41, 52
Johnson, Lyndon, 208
Joys of Yiddish, The (Rosten), 23
Juan, Don, 135

Kafka, Franz, 123-124, 132, 134
Kamongo (Smith), 178-180
Kant, Immanuel: versus Aristotle, 65, 87; and *The Critique of Practical Reason*, 74, 86-94; and the military, 74, 94; and Descartes, 74-75, 77-78; and Rousseau, 75; and Luther, 75-76, 93; his life, 76-77; and *The Critique of Pure Reason*, 77, 81-86; and Berkeley, 80; and Hume, 81-83; his theory of knowledge, 81-86, 203; his moral theory, 86-94, 203; on knowledge versus

will, 86, 203-204; and the categorical imperative, 88-94, 203; his social philosophy, 93-94, 203; on war, 94; and J.S. Mill, 97, 204; and Hegel, 97, 149; and John Rawls, 99; and James Mill, 99-100; and idealism, 149, 153

Kennedy, John F., 8, 66

Kerouac, Jack, 1

Khrushchev, Nikita, 153, 155, 156

Kierkegaard, Soren: on the incommensurability between the Infinite and the finite, 24; and the word *existence*, 123; and Don Juan, 135; and silence, 197-198

Kipling, Rudyard (author of "The Mark of the Beast"), 170

Klimt, Gustav, 185, 189

Knowledge of the external world, 77-83, 147-152

Koestler, Arthur (author of *Darkness at Noon*), 24, 136, 205

Kokoschka, Oskar, 185

Korngold, Eric, 183

Kraus, Karl, 185, 192-193

Krishna, 94-95

Kusaka, Jinichi, 199

Laches, General, 201

Lactantius, 28, 32

Lady Philosophy, 12-13, 20

Laertes, Diogenes, 45-46

Lamarck, Jean-Baptiste, 152-153, 166, 167

La Mettrie, Julien (author of *Man a Machine* (L'Homme machine)), 148

Language, Truth and Logic (Ayer), 189-190

Laplace, Pierre-Simon de (author of *Celestial Mechanics* (Mécanique céleste)), 148, 201

Leakey, Mary, 163

Leakey, Richard, 163

Lee, Robert E., 178

Leibniz, Gottfried, 64, 143

Lendl, Ivan, 7

Lenin, Vladimir I. (Ulyanov): as a revolutionary, 141, 155, 204-205; and philosophy, 141-142, 143, 147-152, 156; a visit to his tomb, 155-156; and Mach, 184

Lepanto, battle of, 13-14

"Lepanto" (Chesterton), 14, 15

Les Belles Images (Beauvoir), 139

Les Mots (Sartre), 140

Letters on Linguistics (Stalin), 143-144

Levin, Michael (author of *The Socratic Method*), 44

Lewis and Clark, 161

Lincoln, Abraham, 115

Lloyd, Morgan C. (author of *Emergent Evolution*), 174, 175-176

Locke, John (author of *Essay on Human Understanding*), 78-79, 97, 148-149

Logic (Hegel), 142, 149

Loos, Adolf, 185

Lord Jim, 131

Lost World, The (Doyle), 173

Lottman, Herbert, 121

Love: as a spirit mediating between the divine and the mortal (eros), 37, 40, 51-53; as that which "seeketh not her own" (*agapē*), 37, 40, 54-55; and the military, 37-38; and the cosmic force of eros, 38-39; and comradeship versus friendship, 39-40; as the oldest of the gods, 48-49; superior versus inferior love, 49; and harmony between body and mind, 49; as the search for our "better half," 50; as the youngest of the gods, 50; as the creative power in the cosmos, 56

Lucy: The Beginnings of Humankind (Johanson and Edey), 163, 170

Ludwig Wittgenstein: A Memoir (Malcolm), 191

Luria, Alexander Romanovich, 144-145

Luther, Martin, 75-76, 93, 188

Lysenko, Trofim, 145, 152-153, 166

McCarthy, Patrick, 121, 136

MacEnroe, John, 7

Mach, Ernst (author of *Analysis of Sensations*), 150-151, 152, 153, 184

Magic Flute, The (Mozart), 3

Magic Mountain, The (Mann), 1

Magnanimous or great-souled man, 66-67, 202-203

Mahabharata, 94

Mahler, Gustav, 185

Maimonides, 59, 72

Malcolm, Norman (author of *Ludwig Wittgenstein: A Memoir*), 191, 195

Malraux, André, 125, 132, 133, 208

Malthus, Thomas (author of *Essay on Population*), 103-104, 166

Man a Machine (L'Homme machine) (La Mettrie), 148

Mani, 29-30

Manichaeism, 29-31, 133

Mann, Thomas, 1, 48-49, 74, 185

Man's Fate (Malraux), 208

Manstein, Field Marshal Erich von, 42-43

Man the Player (Homo Ludens) (Huizinga), 6-7

Man without Qualities, The (Musil), 184

"Mark of the Beast, The" (Kipling), 170

Mark, Saint, the Gospel of, 4

Marmontel, Jean-François, 104

Marr, Nikolai Yakovlovich, 143-144

Marx, Karl, 62, 107-108, 136, 141-142, 147, 149, 150, 152, 204

Masters of Retreat (proposed by Brennan), 42-43

Materialism and Empirio-Criticism (Lenin), 150-152

Materialism and Empirio-Monism (Bogdanov), 151

Materialism versus idealism, 147-152, 153-154, 160, 177-180, 205-206

Matter: as the principle of heaviness, 10; as the root of disorder in the world, 26-27, 28; as earth, air, fire, and water, 38; versus form, 60-61, 69-70

Matthew, Father Theobald, 46

Matthew, Saint, the Gospel of, 5, 197, 207

Mauriac, François, 136

Mauthner, Fritz, 185, 192-193

Meaning of Philosophy, The (Brennan), 146

Mehta, Zubin, 29

Mein Kampf (Hitler), 185

Melville, Herman, 124, 207-208

Memorabilia (Xenophon), 42, 45

Meno (Plato), 41

Merleau-Ponty, Maurice, 125

Metaphysics (Aristotle), 59, 63

Military, the: and the hermetic, 1, 2, 7-8; and Jesus' teachings, 28-29; and early Christians, 28-29; and the topic of love, 37-38; and Kant, 74, 94; and the order of grace versus the order of necessity, 94-95, 199

Mill, James, 99-100, 102, 103, 108

Mill, John Stuart: and *Utilitarianism*, 96, 97, 99, 109, 113; and utilitarianism, 96-99, 113, 204; as a brilliant philosophical amateur, 97; and Kant, 97, 204; and *On Liberty*, 99, 109, 110-113, 204; and his *Autobiography*, 99, 106, 109,

117; his education, 102-103; his career in the East India Company, 103, 109; and birth control, 103-104, 112-113; his friends, 104-105; his nervous breakdown, 104-105; and Harriet Taylor, 105-110, 112, 116-117, 118; and *The Subjection of Women*, 106, 109, 117; and *System of Logic*, 106-107, 117; and *Principles of Political Economy*, 107, 117; and *On Representative Government*, 109, 113-114; and *Three Essays on Religion*, 109, 117; as a member of Parliament, 114-116; in retirement at Avignon, 116-119

Missa Solmnis (Beethoven), 196

Mitchell, Joni, 49

Moby Dick (Melville), 124

Mohammed (the Prophet), 11

Moiseyev, N.M., 141

Monk, Ray, 196-197

Monod, Jacques, 177-178, 179, 180, 205-206

Montfort, Simon de, 30

Moore, G.E., 182, 186-187, 190, 191

Moral philosophy (or ethics): the two ways of approaching (Aristotle versus Kant), 87; as a sovereign kingdom, 90; as a discipline, 160, 201, 206

Moscow (in September 1989), 157-158

Moses, 4, 41

Mozart, Wolfgang Amadeus (composer of *The Magic Flute*), 3

Muni, Paul, 162

Musil, Robert (author of *The Man without Qualities*), 184

My Early Life: A Roving Commission (Churchill), 206

Myth of Sisyphus, The (Camus), 133, 135-136

Myth of the Cave, The (Plato), 15, 17-19, 202

Nagel, Ernest, 191

Name of the Rose, The (Eco), 9

Napoleon, 62, 148

Natural Theology (Paley), 84

Nausea (La Nausée) (Sartre), 127

Neanderthal Man, 171

Necessity (Anagke), 26

Nero, 186

Newman, John Henry, 101

Newton, Isaac, 78, 81, 148

The New York Times, 1, 7, 141

Nicholson, Jack, 135

Nichomachean Ethics (Aristotle), 57, 66-69, 71, 202-203

Nichomachus, 73

Nietzsche, Friedrich: on human suffering, 24; and Zoroaster (Zarathustra), 29; on a married philosopher, 45; and Diogenes Laertes, 45-46; on the human as an animal that seeks to expend itself, 124; on Schopenhauer, 195

Night (Wiesel), 22

No Exit (Huis clos) (Sartre), 128

Normaliens, 125

Nude Descending a Staircase (Duchamp), 122

Oedipus, 26

Old Man and the Sea, The (Hemingway), 204

On Liberty (Mill), 99, 109, 110-113

On Representative Government (Mill), 109, 113-114

On Secular Authority (Luther), 93

"On Values in the Age of Science" (Monod), 177-178

On War (Clausewitz), 67, 193

Order of grace versus order of necessity, 76, 94-95, 188, 196, 199

Origen, 28

Origin of Species, The (Darwin), 110, 162, 166, 169, 178

Orphic, 9, 10

Packe, Michael, 109-110

Paley, Dean William (author of *Natural Theology*), 84

Paradiso (Dante), 56

Parsees, 29

Pascal, Blaise, 177, 198, 202

Pascal, Fania, 183, 196

Patarenes, 30

Paulicians, 30

Paul, Saint, 37, 41, 42, 54

Paulus, Field Marshal Friedrich von, 43

Pausanius, 49

Pavlov, Ivan, 144, 159

Perpetual Peace (Kant), 94

Phaedo (Plato), 9-11, 26, 43, 45, 112

Phaedrus, 47-49, 50, 209-210

Phaedrus (Plato), 41, 209-210

Phenomenology, 125

Phenomenology of the Spirit, The (Hegel), 72

Phenomenon of Man, The (Teilhard de Chardin), 173, 174, 176-177

Philip (king of Macedon), 57-58, 119

Philip (king of Spain), 13

Philosophes, 148

Philosophical Investigations (Wittgenstein), 192-194

Physics (Aristotle), 59, 63

Picabia, Francis, 122

Pietism, 76

Pilate, Pontius, 5, 197

Piltdown Man, 172-174

"Piltdown Revisited" (Gould), 173

Plague, The (La Peste) (Camus), 136

Plath, Sylvia (author of *The Bell Jar*), 9

Plato: and the separation of the soul from the body at death (*Phaedo*), 9-11, 202; and the Myth of the Cave (*The Republic*), 15, 17-19, 202; and democracy (*The Republic*), 15-19; and the nature of knowledge (*The Republic*), 16-19; on God as the cause of good things only (*The Republic*), 20; and the limitations of matter (*Phaedo*), 26; and his theory of creation (*Timaeus*), 27, 58-59, 61; and his theory of love (*Symposium*), 37, 40, 46-53; and Socrates' literacy (*Phaedrus* and *Meno*), 41; as the richest source on Socrates' life, 42, 183, 202; on Socrates and the Greek philosopher-scientists (*Phaedo*), 43; on Socrates and the leaders of the Athenian democracy (*Apology*), 44; on Xanthippe (*Phaedo*), 45; and the cosmic function of eros as compared to that of the Holy Spirit, 51-52; and Saint Augustine, 55; and Schopenhauer, 55; and Aristotle, 57, 65, 202, 203; and poets, 77; and J.S. Mill, 102; and George Grote, 104; on suicide (*Phaedo*), 112; and Heidegger, 126; and Camus, 133; and idealism, 148; and the teaching of ethics, 160; and General Laches, 201; and the teaching and study of philosophy (*Phaedrus* and *Euthydemus*), 209-210

Plekhanov, G.V., 150, 151-152

Plotinus, 31-32, 133, 191

Postman Always Rings Twice, The (Cain), 124

Potentiality versus actuality, 60-61, 69-70

Pragmatism, 206-207

Pride as a moral virtue, 66-67

Principia Mathematica (Russell and Whitehead), 186, 187

Principles of Political Economy (Mill), 107, 117

Prison: its effect on the human, 1-2, 201-202; and Stockdale, 2, 12, 19, 21-22, 24, 38, 40, 62, 68, 72, 131, 199, 201-202; and Socrates, 9-11, 43, 183, 202; and Boethius, 11-13; and Cervantes, 13-14, 202; and Plato's Myth of the Cave, 15-19, 202

Problems of Philosophy (Voprosy filosofii), 141, 143, 145-146, 156

Progress, the idea of, 164-165

Prokoviev, Sergei, 169, 183

Proust, Marcel, 117

Puritans, 207

Pythias (daughter of Aristotle), 73

Pythias (wife of Aristotle), 73

Quantum mechanics, 153-154

Quest for the Historical Jesus, The (Schweitzer), 124

Quietism, 133, 136-137

Ravel, Maurice (composer of *Concerto for the Left Hand*), 183-184

Rawls, John (author of *A Theory of Justice*), 99

Rebel, The (L'Homme révolté) (Camus), 136-137

Rebel without a Cause, 134

Red Star (Bogdanov), 151

Religion: and the hermetic, 4-5; and the problem of evil, 24-36; and evolution, 58, 160, 161-162, 170-171, 177-180, 205-206; in the Soviet Union, 158; and science, 177-180, 205-206

Republic, The (Plato), 15-19, 20

Requiem for a Nun (Faulkner), 124

Ricardo, David, 104, 107

Rodó, José Enrique (author of "Ariel"), 96

Rodriguez, Father, 198-199

Rommel, Erwin, 195

Rosten, Leo (author of *The Joys of Yiddish*), 23

Rousseau, Jean-Jacques (author of *Confessions*), 75, 121

Rubashov, 24, 205

Runciman, Steven, 31

Russell, Bertrand, 118, 182, 186-187, 190

Saccas, Ammonius, 191

Sadat, Anwar, 1

Saint-Exupéry, Antoine, 8

Sartor Resartus (Carlyle), 108

Sartre, Jean-Paul: and evil, 25, 120, 130-131; and Camus, 120-121, 123-124, 131-132, 136, 137, 138; and moral choice, 122, 129-131, 204; his early life, 124-126; and Simone de Beauvoir, 125, 126, 127, 128, 139-140; and *The Transcendence of the Ego*, 127; and *Nausea* (La Nausée), 127; and World War II, 127-128, 130-131, 140; and *Being and Nothingness* (L'Etre et le Néant), 128-131, 138-139; and *Critique of Dialectical Reason*, 138-139; and Genet, 139; and Flaubert, 139; and Arlette Elkäim, 139; his death, 139-140; and *Bariona*, 140; and *Les Mots*, 140.

Savich, Vincent, 163-164

Scalia, Justice Antonin, 58

Scharnhorst, Count Gerhard von, 74

Schelling, Friedrich, 97, 149

Schiele, Egon, 185

Schnitzler, Arthur, 184

Schoenberg, Arnold, 185

Scholastics, 75

Schopenhauer, Arthur (author of *The World as Will and Idea*), 55-56, 195

Schrödinger, Erwin, 153

Schweitzer, Albert, 124

Science: and the hermetic, 5-6; and religion, 58, 160, 161-162, 170-171, 177-180, 205-206; and our knowledge of the external world, 77-83; in the Soviet Union, 142, 143, 145, 150, 152-154; and materialism, 147-148; and idealism, 148-149.

Scopes, John, 162

Self-control as a moral virtue, 66

Sex and Character (Weininger), 184

Shakespeare, William, 49, 67, 96, 105, 139

Sheehan, Dr. George, 33

Siiak, Aino, 141

Silence (Endo), 198-199

Smith, Adam, 107

Smith, Homer (author of *Kamongo*), 178

Smith-Woodward, Arthur, 172-173

Socrates: and the liberation of the soul from the body at death (*Phaedo*), 9-11, 201; on evil and the good man, 13, 20; as compared to Jesus, 40-46, 197;

and his doctrine of love (eros) (*Symposium*), 40, 51-53; and his method of teaching, 40, 43-44, 149; and his literacy (*Phaedrus* and *Meno*), 41; and the sources on his life, 42-43; and Plato, 42, 183, 202; and the Greek philosopher-scientists (*Phaedo*), 43; and the leaders of the Athenian democracy (*Apology*), 44; and his social status, 45; and his domestic life, 45-46; and his inner voice (*Apology*), 48; and his physical appearance, 48; and his courage and self-control, 53-54; and the gods of the city-state, 63; and philosophy as a life lived, 99, 206; and J.S. Mill, 102; on suicide (*Phaedo*), 112; on everyone desiring his own good, 123; and Wittgenstein, 182-183, 193; at his trial, 197; and the teaching and study of philosophy (*Phaedrus* and *Euthydemus*), 209-210.

Socratic Method, The (Levin), 44

Solas, W.J., 173

Solipsism, 80

Solzhenitsyn, Alexander, 2, 33, 202

"Song of Myself" (Whitman), 35, 36

Song of Solomon, The, 55

Soul and its relation to body, 9-11, 26-27, 28, 69-70

Space, Time, and Deity (Alexander), 175-176

Spinoza, Benedict (author of *Ethics*), 72-73

Sports: and the hermetic, 6-7; as a moral teacher, 7.

Stalin, Joseph: and the purge of the late 1930s, 24; and philosophy, 143-145; and science, 143, 152-154; and Khrushchev, 155, 156; and Lenin, 205.

Stirling, John, 104-105

Stockdale, James B.: and "The World of Epictetus," 1; on finding happiness in prison, 2; and his fascination with the situation of Boethius, 12; and "the dream of this course," 19; remembering Epictetus in prison, 21-22, 201-202; and his attitude toward evil, 24; and *In Love and War*, 38; and J. Glenn Gray, 38; on the love that grows out of comradeship, 40; on the Socratic method, 44; and the Marxist philosophy of history, 62; on torture, 68, 131; and the *Enchiridion* (Epictetus), 72; and silence, 199; teaching "Foundations of Moral Obligation," 199-200

Stockdale, Sybil (coauthor of *In Love and War*), 38

Stoics, the: mottoes, 2, 13; and evil, 25; and Aristotle, 71-72; their cosmology, 72, 147; and Spinoza, 72-73.

Stranger, The (L'Etranger) (Camus), 121, 131, 133-135, 137

Strauss, Richard, 29, 183, 185

Stuart, Sir John and Lady, 100

Subjection of Women, The (Mill), 106, 109, 117
Surrealism, 122
Symposium (Plato), 37, 40, 43, 46-54
System of Logic (Mill), 106-107, 117

Taylor, Harriet, 105-110, 112, 116-117, 118
Taylor, Helen, 110, 116-117
Taylor, John, 105-106, 108
Teilhard de Chardin, Pierre, 160, 172, 173-177
Tempest, The (Shakespeare), 96
Tertullian, 28
Theodoric, 11
Theory of Justice, A (Rawls), 99
Thoreau, Henry David, 58, 93, 121, 124
Three Essays on Religion (Mill), 109, 117
Thus Spake Zarathustra (Also Sprach Zarathustra) (Strauss), 29
Timaeus (Plato), 27, 58-59
Tocqueville, Alexis de, 113-114
Tractatus Logico-Philosophicus (Wittgenstein), 64, 182, 187-188, 190, 192
Tracy, Spencer, 162
Tragic Sense of Life, The (Unamuno), 129
Transcendence of the Ego, The (Sartre), 127
Trial of God, The (Wiesel), 22-23
Tristan and Isolde (Wagner), 55-56
Tryhuk, Wayne, 7
Typhoon (Conrad), 99
Tzara, Tristan, 122

Unamuno, Miguel de (author of *The Tragic Sense of Life*), 129, 204
Under the Banner of Marxism, 142
Universalization as a characteristic of ethical rules, 91
Upstairs, Downstairs, 118
Utilitarianism, 96-99, 113, 204
Utilitarianism (Mill), 96, 97, 99, 109, 113

Vico, Giambatista, 143
Victoria, Queen, 109
Vienna Circle, 189-190

"Vienna 1900," 184-186

Virtues (intellectual and moral), 66-69, 71

Visitors of the Evening (Les Visiteurs du soir), 128

Voprosy filosofii (Problems of Philosophy), 141, 143, 145-146, 156

Vygotsky, Lev Semenovich, 144

Wagner, Richard (composer of *Tristan and Isolde*), 55-56

Wallace, Alfred, 166-169

Warriors, The (Gray), 38-40

Washington, George, 42

Watson, James, 148

Watson, John, 144

Webern, Anton, 185

Weil, Simone, 40, 125, 130

Weininger, Otto (author of *Sex and Character*), 184

What Is To Be Done? (Lenin), 204-205

Whitehead, Alfred North, 64, 175, 186, 187

White Jacket (Melville), 207-208

Whitman, Walt, 35-36

Wiesel, Elie, 22-23

Wilberforce, Samuel, 169

Williams, Tennessee, 160, 181

Wilson, Allan, 163-164

Winthrop, John, 207

Wittgenstein, Hans, 183

Wittgenstein, Hermine, 189

Wittgenstein, Karl, 183

Wittgenstein, Kurt, 183

Wittgenstein, Leopoldine Kalmus, 183

Wittgenstein, Ludwig: and *Tractatus*, 64, 182, 187-188, 190, 192; his influence on philosophy, 182; and Socrates, 182-183, 193, 206; his background, 183-187; his moratorium from philosophy, 188-189; and the Vienna Circle, 189-190, 192; as a professor at Cambridge, 190-191, 194-195; and *Philosophical Investigations*, 192-194; and Saint Augustine, 193; his last years, 194-195; and the ethic of commitment, 195-196; and religion, 196-197; and the ethic of silence, 197-199; and Woody Hayes, 200; and ethics, 206

Wittgenstein, Margarete, 185, 189

Wittgenstein, Paul, 183-184
Wittgenstein, Rudolf, 183
Woods, Professor James Haughton, 104
Wordsworth, William, 105
World as Will and Idea, The (Schopenhauer), 55-56
"World of Epictetus, The" (Stockdale), 1

Xanthippe, 45-46
Xenophon, 42-43, 45, 183

Yeats, William (author of "An Irish Airman Foresees His Death"), 8
Yeltsin, Boris, 158-159
Young, Desmond, 195

Zeno of Clitium, 72
Zhdanov, Andrei, 143, 153
Zoonomia (Darwin), 166
Zophar (friend of Job), 24
Zoroaster (Zarathustra), 29
Zoroastrianism, 29

About the Author

Joseph Gerard Brennan is professor emeritus of philosophy, Barnard College, Columbia University. On retirement from Morningside Heights he joined the faculty of the Naval War College and taught there until his retirement. He is the author of six earlier books, including *Ethics and Morals* (1973) and *The Education of a Prejudiced Man* (1977). A navy veteran of World War II, he served in North Africa, Italy, and southern France, retiring from the naval reserve with the rank of commander. He is married to Mary McLeod Brennan, and they have six children and seven grandchildren. Of himself he says, "Thomas Aquinas laid it down that the teacher of moral philosophy must possess two qualities: he must have studied Aristotle's *Ethics* and he must himself be good. I qualify on the first count."